THE NEW
SH~

Designed to make Shakespeare's great plays available to all readers, the New Folger Library edition of Shakespeare's plays provides accurate texts in modern spelling and punctuation, as well as scene-by-scene action summaries, full explanatory notes, many pictures clarifying Shakespeare's language, and notes recording all significant departures from the early printed versions. Each play is prefaced by a brief introduction, by a guide to reading Shakespeare's language, and by accounts of his life and theater. Each play is followed by an annotated list of further readings and by a "Modern Perspective" written by an expert on that particular play.

Barbara A. Mowat is Director of Research *emerita* at the Folger Shakespeare Library, Consulting Editor of *Shakespeare Quarterly*, and author of *The Dramaturgy of Shakespeare's Romances* and of essays on Shakespeare's plays and their editing.

Paul Werstine is Professor of English in the Graduate School and at King's University College at Western University. He is a general editor of the New Variorum Shakespeare and author of *Early Modern Playhouse Manuscripts and the Editing of Shakespeare*, as well as many papers and essays on the printing and editing of Shakespeare's plays.

Folger Shakespeare Library

The Folger Shakespeare Library in Washington, D.C., is a privately funded research library dedicated to Shakespeare and the civilization of early modern Europe. It was founded in 1932 by Henry Clay and Emily Jordan Folger, and incorporated as part of Amherst College in Amherst, Massachusetts, one of the nation's oldest liberal arts colleges, from which Henry Folger had graduated in 1879. In addition to its role as the world's preeminent Shakespeare collection and its emergence as a leading center for Renaissance studies, the Folger Shakespeare Library offers a wide array of cultural and educational programs and services for the general public.

EDITORS

BARBARA A. MOWAT
Director of Research emerita
Folger Shakespeare Library

PAUL WERSTINE
Professor of English
King's University College at the University of
Western Ontario, Canada

Henry VI

Part 2

By

WILLIAM SHAKESPEARE

EDITED BY BARBARA A. MOWAT
AND PAUL WERSTINE

SIMON & SCHUSTER PAPERBACKS
NEW YORK LONDON TORONTO SYDNEY NEW DELHI

Simon & Schuster Paperbacks
A Division of Simon & Schuster, Inc.
1230 Avenue of the Americas
New York, NY 10020

This book is a work of fiction. Any references to historical events, real people, or real places are used fictitiously. Other names, characters, places, and events are products of the author's imagination, and any resemblance to actual events or places or persons, living or dead, is entirely coincidental.

This Simon & Schuster paperback edition February 2014

SIMON & SCHUSTER PAPERBACKS and colophon are registered trademarks of Simon & Schuster, Inc.

For information about special discounts for bulk purchases, please contact Simon & Schuster Special Sales at 1-866-506-1949 or business@simonandschuster.com.

The Simon & Schuster Speakers Bureau can bring authors to your live event. For more information or to book an event contact the Simon & Schuster Speakers Bureau at 1-866-248-3049 or visit our website at www.simonspeakers.com.

Manufactured in the United States of America

10 9 8 7 6 5 4 3

ISBN 978-0-671-72267-8
ISBN 978-1-4516-4449-4 (ebook)

From the Director of the Folger Shakespeare Library

It is hard to imagine a world without Shakespeare. Since their composition four hundred years ago, Shakespeare's plays and poems have traveled the globe, inviting those who see and read his works to make them their own.

Readers of the New Folger Editions are part of this ongoing process of "taking up Shakespeare," finding our own thoughts and feelings in language that strikes us as old or unusual and, for that very reason, new. We still struggle to keep up with a writer who could think a mile a minute, whose words paint pictures that shift like clouds. These expertly edited texts, presented here with accompanying explanatory notes and up-to-date critical essays, are distinctive because of what they do: they allow readers not simply to keep up, but to engage deeply with a writer whose works invite us to think, and think again.

These New Folger Editions of Shakespeare's plays are also special because of where they come from. The Folger Shakespeare Library in Washington, DC, where the Editions are produced, is the single greatest documentary source of Shakespeare's works. An unparalleled collection of early modern books, manuscripts, and artwork connected to Shakespeare, the Folger's holdings have been consulted extensively in the preparation of these texts. The Editions also reflect the expertise gained through the regular performance of Shakespeare's works in the Folger's Elizabethan Theater.

I want to express my deep thanks to editors Barbara Mowat and Paul Werstine for creating these indispensable editions of Shakespeare's works, which incorporate the best of textual scholarship with a richness of commentary that is both inspired and engaging. Readers who want to know more about Shakespeare and his plays can follow the paths these distinguished scholars have tread by visiting the Folger itself, where a range of physical and digital resources (available online) exist to supplement the material in these texts. I commend to you these words, and hope that they inspire.

Michael Witmore
Director, Folger Shakespeare Library

Contents

Contents

Editors' Preface

In recent years, ways of dealing with Shakespeare's texts and with the interpretation of his plays have been undergoing significant change. This edition, while retaining many of the features that have always made the Folger Shakespeare so attractive to the general reader, at the same time reflects these current ways of thinking about Shakespeare. For example, modern readers, actors, and teachers have become interested in the differences between, on the one hand, the early forms in which Shakespeare's plays were first published and, on the other hand, the forms in which editors through the centuries have presented them. In response to this interest, we have based our edition on what we consider the best early printed version of a particular play (explaining our rationale in a section called "An Introduction to This Text") and have marked our changes in the text—unobtrusively, we hope, but in such a way that the curious reader can be aware that a change has been made and can consult the "Textual Notes" to discover what appeared in the early printed version.

Current ways of looking at the plays are reflected in our brief introductions, in many of the commentary notes, in the annotated lists of "Further Reading," and especially in each play's "Modern Perspective," an essay written by an outstanding scholar who brings to the reader his or her fresh assessment of the play in the light of today's interests and concerns.

As in the Folger Library General Readers' Shakespeare, which this edition replaces, we include explanatory notes designed to help make Shakespeare's language clearer to a modern reader, and we place the notes on the page facing the text that they explain. We also follow the earlier edition in including illustrations—of objects, of clothing, of mythological figures—from books and manuscripts in the Folger Library collection. We provide fresh accounts of the life of Shakespeare, of the publishing of his plays, and of the theaters in which his plays were performed, as well as an introduction to the text itself. We also include a section called "Reading Shakespeare's Language," in which we try to help readers learn to "break the code" of Elizabethan poetic language.

For each section of each volume, we are indebted to a host of generous experts and fellow scholars. The "Reading Shakespeare's Language" section, for example, could not have been written had not Arthur King, of Brigham Young University, and Randall Robinson, author of *Unlocking Shakespeare's Language*, led the way in untangling Shakespearean language puzzles and shared their insights and methodologies generously with us. "Shakespeare's Life" profited by the careful reading given it by the late S. Schoenbaum; "Shakespeare's Theater" was read and strengthened by Andrew Gurr, John Astington, and William Ingram; and "The Publication of Shakespeare's Plays" is indebted to the comments of Peter W. M. Blayney. We, as editors, take sole responsibility for any errors in our editions.

We are grateful to the authors of the "Modern Perspectives"; to Leeds Barroll and David Bevington for their generous encouragement; to the Huntington and Newberry Libraries for fellowship support; to King's University College for the grants it has provided to Paul Werstine; to the Social Sciences and Humanities Research Council of Canada, which provided him with a Research Time Stipend for 1990–91; to R. J. Shroyer of the University of Western Ontario for essential computer support; to the Folger Institute's Center for Shakespeare Studies for its sponsorship of a workshop on "Shakespeare's Texts for Students and Teachers" (funded by the National Endowment for the Humanities and led by Richard Knowles of the University of Wisconsin), a workshop from which we learned an enormous amount about what is wanted by college and high school teachers of Shakespeare today; to Alice Falk for her expert copyediting; and especially to Stephen Llano, our production editor at Washington Square Press, whose expertise and attention to detail are essential to this project.

Our biggest debt is to the Folger Shakespeare Library—to Gail Kern Paster, Director of the Library, whose interest and support are unfailing (and whose scholarly expertise is an invaluable resource) and to Werner Gundersheimer, the Library's Director from 1984 to 2002, who made possible our edition; to Deborah Curren-Aquino, who provides extensive editorial and production support; to Jean Miller, the Library's former Art Curator, who combs the Library holdings for illustrations, and to Julie Ainsworth, Head of the Photography Department, who carefully photographs them; to Peggy O'Brien, former Director of Education and now Senior Vice President, Educational Programming and Services at the Corporation for Public Broadcasting, who gave us expert advice about the needs being expressed by Shakespeare teachers and students (and to Martha Christian and other "master teachers" who used our texts in manuscript in their classrooms); to Mary Bloodworth and Michael Poston for their expert computer support; to the staff of the Research Division, especially Karen Rogers (whose help is crucial), Liz Pohland, Mimi Godfrey, Kathleen Lynch, Carol Brobeck, Owen Williams, Sarah Werner, and Caryn Lazzuri; and, finally, to the generously supportive staff of the Library's Reading Room.

Barbara A. Mowat and Paul Werstine

England and France.
Stephen Llano, based on William Shepherd,
Historical Atlas, 8th ed. (1956).

Henry VI, Part 2

Henry VI, Part 2 puts onstage a kind of story that was very popular in the years before Shakespeare began writing, a story of the fall, one after another, of men and women from positions of great power to their untimely deaths. Such a pattern in this play was obvious to the publishers who first put a version of it into print in 1594. They chose not to call the play by the name of its king, as did the First Folio, and as we do. Instead they gave it the title *The First part of the Contention betwixt the two famous Houses of Yorke and Lancaster, with the death of the good Duke Humphrey: And the banishment and death of the Duke of Suffolke, and the Tragicall end of the proud Cardinall of Winchester, with the notable Rebellion of Iacke Cade: and the Duke of Yorkes first claime vnto the Crowne*. This title, typical of the time in its length, indicates a reading of the play as the beginning or "First part" of a succession of catastrophes.

The first of those catastrophes afflicts "the good Duke Humphrey," or the Duke of Gloucester, who at the beginning of the play is Lord Protector of England and therefore the most powerful man in the kingdom—the one on whom King Henry relies absolutely to dispense justice to all his subjects. Gloucester will be murdered, but only after his beloved Duchess has herself fallen, sent into exile through her own ambitions and the conspiracy of their enemies. After Gloucester's murder, as the title goes on to say, comes "the banishment and death of the Duke of Suffolke." Another of the most powerful men in England, Suffolk was the noble who arranged King Henry's marriage to Queen Margaret and who, as the queen's lover, ruled England through

Ancestry of Richard, Duke of York

[Characters in this play appear in bold]

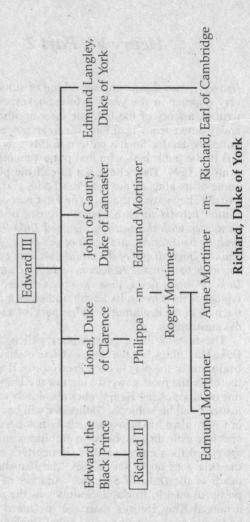

Edward III
┌─────────────┬─────────────┬─────────────┐

Edward, the Black Prince — Lionel, Duke of Clarence — John of Gaunt, Duke of Lancaster — Edmund Langley, Duke of York

Richard II

Philippa -m- Edmund Mortimer

Roger Mortimer

Edmund Mortimer — Anne Mortimer -m- Richard, Earl of Cambridge

Richard, Duke of York

the influence he exerted over the queen, who in turn prevailed over the king. But when Suffolk conspired with the "Cardinall of Winchester" to kill Gloucester, Suffolk was banished and in his newly vulnerable state became the victim of assassination. "The Tragicall end of the proud Cardinall of Winchester" seems almost the result of Gloucester's murder, as the Cardinal dies raving about his guilt and the punishment waiting for him in the next world.

The play shows that the fall of these English nobles and their ability to prey on each other come about through the weakness of their king. Uninterested in politics, King Henry sought a life of spiritual contemplation; almost all of his speeches reveal in their allusions to the Bible his otherworldly interests. Largely absent from deliberations of the affairs of state, King Henry left his royal family and aristocrats free to contend for power. However, as the conclusion of the long title of the 1594 quarto reveals, Henry's own liberty is thereby also put at risk, as first Jack Cade and then the Duke of York openly rise up against him. *Henry VI, Part 2* keeps its audience in suspense about the ultimate fate of the king by ending as it does at the beginning of the Wars of the Roses, which set the white rose of the Duke of York against the red rose of King Henry of the House of Lancaster. The outcome of these wars will be presented in *Henry VI, Part 3*.

After you have read the play, we invite you to turn to the essay printed after it, *"Henry VI, Part 2:* A Modern Perspective," by Nina Levine of the University of South Carolina.

England's Claim to France

[Characters in this play appear in bold]

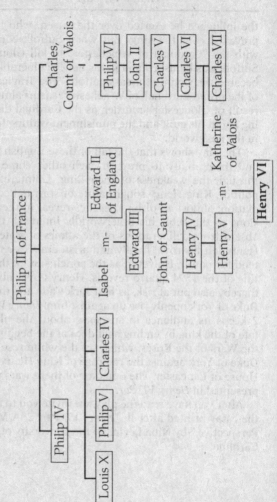

Philip III of France

Philip IV — Charles, Count of Valois

Louis X — Philip V — Charles IV — Isabel — Edward II of England

Philip VI
John II
Charles V
Charles VI — Katherine of Valois

Edward III — John of Gaunt

Henry IV — Henry V — Katherine of Valois

Charles VII

Henry VI

Reading Shakespeare's Language: *Henry VI, Part 2*

For many people today, reading Shakespeare's language can be a problem—but it is a problem that can be solved.* Those who have studied Latin (or even French or German or Spanish), and those who are used to reading poetry, will have little difficulty understanding the language of poetic drama. Others, though, need to develop the skills of untangling unusual sentence structures and of recognizing and understanding poetic compressions, omissions, and wordplay. And even those skilled in reading unusual sentence structures may have occasional trouble with Shakespeare's words. Four hundred years of "static" intervene between his speaking and our hearing. Most of his vocabulary is still in use, but a few of his words are no longer used and many of his words now have meanings quite different from those they had in the sixteenth century. In the theater, most of these difficulties are solved for us by actors who study the language and articulate it for us so that the essential meaning is heard—or, when combined with stage action, is at least *felt*. When we are reading on our own, we must do what each actor does: go over the lines (often with a dictionary close at hand) until the puzzles are solved and the lines yield up their poetry and the characters speak in words and phrases that are, suddenly, rewarding and wonderfully memorable.

---

* For our use of the name *Shakespeare* in this essay, see our appendix "Authorship of *Henry VI, Part 2*," p. 265.

Shakespeare's Words

As you begin to read the opening scenes of a play from Shakespeare's time, you may notice occasional unfamiliar words. Some are unfamiliar simply because we no longer use them. In the early scenes of *Henry VI, Part 2*, for example, one finds the words *alderliefest* (i.e., "very dear"), *yclad* (i.e., "clothed"), *hoise* (i.e., "remove"), and *Methought* (i.e., "it seemed to me"). Words of this kind are explained in notes to the text and will become familiar the more early plays you read.

In *Henry VI, Part 2*, as in all of Shakespeare's writing, more problematic are the words that are still in use but that now have different meanings. In the opening scenes of *Henry VI, Part 2*, for example, the word *depart* is used where we would say "departure," *conference* where we would say "conversation," *vantage* where we would say "profit," and *starved* where we would say "died." Such words will be explained in the notes to the text, but they too will become familiar as you continue to read Shakespeare's language.

Some words and phrases are strange not because of the "static" introduced by changes in language over the past centuries but because these are expressions that Shakespeare is using to build a dramatic world that has its own space, time, and history. In the opening scene of *Henry VI, Part 2*, for example, the dramatist quickly establishes that the action will be played out by those occupying the most elevated strata of late medieval European political culture. King Henry's "procurator," who now "rules the roast," has just "espoused" the king's bride before "the Kings of France and Sicil, / The Dukes of Orleance, Calaber, Britaigne, and Alanson," a "courtly company," to the "overjoy" and "wond'ring" of the royal couple, whose marriage validates "the articles of contracted peace" between two kingdoms. Such words and the world they create will become increasingly familiar as you get further into the play.

Shakespeare's Sentences

In an English sentence, meaning is quite dependent on the place given each word. "The dog bit the boy" and "The boy bit the dog" mean very different things, even though the individual words are the same. Because English places such importance on the positions of words in sentences, on the way words are arranged, unusual arrangements can puzzle a reader. Shakespeare frequently shifts his sentences away from "normal" English arrangements—often to create the rhythm he seeks, sometimes to use a line's poetic rhythm to emphasize a particular word, sometimes to give a character his or her own speech patterns or to allow the character to speak in a special way. When we attend a good performance of the play, the actors will have worked out the sentence structures and will articulate the sentences so that the meaning is clear. When reading the play, we need to do as the actor does: that is, when puzzled by a character's speech, check to see if words are being presented in an unusual sequence.

Often Shakespeare rearranges subjects and verbs (i.e., instead of "He goes" we find "Goes he"). In *Henry VI, Part 2,* "And so *says York*" provides such a construction (1.1.215), as does Gloucester's "on the pieces of the broken wand / *Were placed the heads*" (1.2.28–29). The "normal" order would be "York says" and "the heads were placed." Shakespeare also frequently places the object before the subject and verb (i.e., instead of "I hit him," we might find "Him I hit"). Warwick provides one example of this inversion when he says "Those *provinces* these *arms* of mine *did conquer*" (1.1.126) and another example when he says "Main *chance*, father, *you meant*" (1.1.221). The "normal" order would be "these arms did conquer those provinces" and "you meant main chance."

Inversions are not the only unusual sentence structures in Shakespeare's language. Often in his sentences words that would normally appear together are separated from each other. Frequently such separation creates a particular rhythm, stresses a particular word, or draws attention to a needed piece of information. Take, for example, Gloucester's "Suffolk, the new-made duke that rules the roast, / Hath given the duchy of Anjou and Maine / Unto the poor King Reignier" (1.1.114–16). Here the subject ("Suffolk") is separated from its verb ("Hath given") by an appositive ("the new-made duke") that includes the adjectival clause "that rules the roast." As Gloucester's purpose is to attack Suffolk's new foreign policy, he, the senior member of the royal family, pauses after naming his opponent in order to ridicule the upstart's rank and power. Or take Queen Margaret's first address to King Henry:

> Great king of England and my gracious lord,
> The mutual *conference* that my mind hath had
> By day, by night, waking and in my dreams,
> In courtly company or at my beads,
> With you, mine alderliefest sovereign,
> *Makes* me the bolder to salute my king.

(1.1.27–32)

In Margaret's greeting, the subject "conference" is separated from its verb "makes" by a long adjectival clause ("that my mind hath had . . . with you, mine alder-liefest sovereign") that swells to include a string of antithetical phrases: "By day, by night," "waking and in my dreams," "In courtly company or at my beads." With these phrases Margaret presents herself, fallaciously as will later appear, as the new bride so devoted to her husband that no matter where she is or what she is doing, she never stops imagining that she is with him.

Often in *Henry VI, Part 2*, rather than separating basic sentence elements, Shakespeare simply holds them back, delaying them until other material to which he wants to give greater emphasis has been presented. He provides Gloucester with this kind of construction in these lines: "Brave peers of England, pillars of the state, / To you *Duke Humphrey must unload* his grief" (1.1.80–81). The delay in the appearance of the subject and verb ("Duke Humphrey must unload") throws the emphasis on Gloucester's complimentary characterization of his auditors—"Brave peers of England, pillars of the state"—which is placed first. Such emphatic compliment is appropriate to Gloucester's purpose, which is to woo the "peers" or "nobles" to follow him and not Suffolk; to that end he assures them first of the high esteem in which he holds them. Suffolk's speech that opens the play holds back its essential elements far longer:

As by your high imperial Majesty
I had in charge at my depart for France,
As procurator to your Excellence,
To marry Princess Margaret for your Grace,
So, in the famous ancient city Tours,
In presence of the Kings of France and Sicil,
The Dukes of Orleance, Calaber, Britaigne, and
   Alanson,

Seven earls, twelve barons, and twenty reverend
    bishops,
I have performed my task and was espoused[.]
                                            (1.1.1–11)

In this case, the subject and verb ("I have performed")
do not appear until the ninth line of the speech. The
preceding eight lines lay the emphasis on Suffolk's
attempt to forestall any objections to a marriage that
was already the subject of controversy in *Henry VI,
Part 1*. Thus he first cites the indisputable royal authority according to which he acted as King Henry's proxy
in marrying Queen Margaret: "As by your high imperial Majesty / I had in charge . . . / To marry Princess
Margaret for your Grace." Then his emphasis falls on
the grandeur of the wedding ceremony itself: "in the
famous ancient city Tours, / In presence of the Kings of
France and Sicil, / The Dukes of Orleance, Calaber,
Britaigne, and Alanson, / Seven earls, twelve barons,
and twenty reverend bishops"—an important consideration, because a chief objection to Margaret as King
Henry's bride is her abject poverty. When Suffolk
finally provides the sentence's essential elements, he
has already defended himself rhetorically against
objections he knows are arrayed against him.

   Finally, in Shakespeare's plays, sentences are sometimes complicated not because of unusual structures
or interruptions but because the dramatist omits
words that English sentences normally require. (In
conversation, we, too, often omit words. We say,
"Heard from him yet?" and our hearer supplies the
missing "Have you.") Shakespeare captures the same
conversational tone in the play's early exchange
between Salisbury and his son Warwick. When Salisbury asks Warwick why he is weeping, "But wherefore
weeps Warwick, my valiant son?" Warwick answers

"For grief that they are past recovery" (1.1.120–21). Had Warwick answered in a full sentence, he might have said "[I weep] for [the] grief [I feel] that they are past recovery." Ellipsis, or the omission of words not strictly necessary to the sense, can appear not just in informal conversational exchanges but also in highly formal speeches, the formality of which it highlights. Take, for example, Gloucester's use of it in "O peers of England, shameful is this league, / Fatal this marriage" (1.1.103–4). Strictly speaking, his second line should read "Fatal [is] this marriage," but the omission of the verb, which the reader can supply from the first line ("Shameful *is* this league"), calls attention to the parallelism between the lines and thereby enhances the speech's formality and seriousness.

Shakespeare's Wordplay

Shakespeare plays with language so often and so variously that entire books are written on the topic. Here we will mention only two kinds of wordplay: similes and puns. A simile is a play on words in which one object or idea is expressed as if it were something else, something with which it is said to share common features. While the same definition applies to metaphor, in a simile the comparison is made explicit through the use of some overt indicator such as "like" or "as" or "so." For instance, when the Duchess of Gloucester asks the Duke "Why droops my lord like over-ripened corn?" she uses a simile that compares the Duke's attitude or bearing to that of stalks of wheat that, having stood in the fields long after the kernels atop them have ripened, are bent over by the weight of the kernels.

When York delivers his long soliloquy at the end of 1.1, disclosing his ambitions to ascend the English throne and mourning the loss of English possessions in France, he is given what can be termed an epic simile. In this figure, commonly found in epic poetry, the simile is so fully developed that it creates its own focus of interest, beyond its immediate context in the larger work. The presence of such a simile in York's speech may be designed to suggest that the struggle for the English throne presented in this play has an importance comparable to the wars presented in Homer's *Iliad* or Virgil's *Aeneid*:

> Pirates may make cheap pennyworths of their
>   pillage,
> And purchase friends, and give to courtesans,
> Still reveling like lords till all be gone;
> Whileas the silly owner of the goods
> Weeps over them, and wrings his hapless hands,
> And shakes his head, and trembling stands aloof,
> While all is shared and all is borne away,
> Ready to starve, and dare not touch his own.
> So York must sit and fret and bite his tongue
> While his own lands are bargained for and sold.
>
>   (1.1.231–41)

York begins by detailing the plight of a hypothetical victim of pirates at such length that he seems to have abandoned any attention to his own present situation. Finally, though, he does come back to his own grief— "So York must sit and fret and bite his tongue"—but not before he has engaged his audience's sympathies for an imaginary victim, "the silly [helpless, pitiable] owner of the goods."

A pun is a play on words that sound approximately the same but that have different meanings, or on a single word that has more than one meaning. The first kind of pun figures prominently in *Henry VI, Part 2.*

When, in 1.4, the conjurers Roger Bolingbroke and John Southwell summon up a spirit to answer questions that the Duchess of Gloucester has supplied, the spirit answers one of the questions with a pun:

> BOLINGBROKE, ⌈*reads*⌉
>   *What fates await the Duke of Suffolk?*
> SPIRIT
>   By water shall he die and take his end.
>
>   (1.4.34–35)

We might therefore expect that Suffolk will drown. However, Suffolk is alert to puns on the word *water*, and is alarmed when he falls into the hands of one Walter Whitmore, whose Christian name, in Elizabethan pronunciation, is indistinguishable from *water*:

> Thy name affrights me, in whose sound is death.
> A cunning man did calculate my birth
> And told me that by water I should die.
>
>   (4.1.34–36)

When Whitmore assassinates Suffolk, the prophecy is fulfilled and the pun made.

The play also offers less dire puns, like York's compliment to Buckingham on the latter's conspiracy to bring down the Duchess of Gloucester: "A pretty plot, well chosen to build upon!" (1.4.60). Here the pun is on "plot," which can mean both a scheme and a piece of ground. In another example, as Salisbury is leaving the stage at the end of the opening scene, in which the English learn that Suffolk has given away Anjou and Maine, Salisbury says "Then let's make haste away and look unto the main" (1.1.217). The word *main* in his speech means "the chief matter in hand, or the main chance"; he alludes to the proverb "Have an eye to the main chance." In responding to Salisbury, Warwick begins to pun elaborately on the word *main,* going so far as to explain the pun in the course of making it:

> Unto the main? O father, Maine is lost!
> That Maine which by main force Warwick did win
> And would have kept so long as breath did last!
> Main chance, father, you meant; but I meant Maine,
> Which I will win from France or else be slain.

> (218–22)

Implied Stage Action

Finally, in reading Shakespeare's plays we should always remember that what we are reading is a performance script. The dialogue is written to be spoken by actors who, at the same time, are moving, gesturing, picking up objects, weeping, shaking their fists. Some stage action is described in what are called "stage directions"; some is signaled within the dialogue itself. We must learn to be alert to such signals as we stage the play in our imaginations.

Often the dialogue offers a clear indication of the action that is to accompany it. For example, at 1.1.67, King Henry orders Suffolk to go down on his knees: "Lord Marquess, kneel down." It seems certain that Suffolk immediately kneels because the king goes on to reward him with a new title: "We here create thee the first Duke of Suffolk" (68). Because such gifts of titles were awarded to kneeling subjects, we feel confident in adding to the play's text the stage direction *"Suffolk kneels,"* putting it in half-square brackets as we do all additions to the First Folio's text. When the king then turns away from Suffolk to address York and then others among his nobles, we also feel confident that Suffolk ought not to remain on his knees; we therefore print another stage direction—*"Suffolk rises"*—at 1.1.69 (again in half-square brackets), so that the newly created duke is in a position to exit, as he does a few lines later.

Occasionally, in *Henry VI, Part 2,* signals to the reader are not quite so clear. For example, at 1.1.46, Gloucester begins to read aloud the peace treaty between France and England, and then stops reading in mid-sentence at line 55. When King Henry asks him what's the matter ("Uncle, how now?"), Gloucester replies "Some sudden qualm hath struck me at the heart / And dimmed mine eyes, that I can read no further" (56, 58–59). Then the king asks the Cardinal to "read on" and the Cardinal obeys (60–66). There is no precise indication in the First Folio text about how the paper which the actor playing Gloucester appears to read passes from his hand to the hand of the actor playing the Cardinal. Does Gloucester, finding himself unable to continue, yield it to Suffolk or to the king, who in turn passes it to the Cardinal? Or does Gloucester just drop it when overcome by his qualm, leaving it on the stage for the Cardinal to retrieve? We have chosen the latter alternative and have printed at line 55 the stage direction *"He drops the paper."* We have also added the stage direction "[the Cardinal] *picks up the paper and reads"* just before the speech in which he finishes reading the treaty. We have chosen this alternative as the more dramatic; it was also the one chosen by those responsible for the very different version of this play printed in 1594. (See "An Introduction to This Text," pages lvii–lviii.) The 1594 version provides the stage direction "Duke *Humphrey* lets it fall" at the point that he stops reading the treaty, although it offers no further stage direction when the Cardinal starts read-

ing it. But since there is no good reason to think that
the First Folio version of the play, which our edition
presents, was necessarily performed in the same way
as the 1594 version, we are much less confident in
adding stage directions for the dropping and picking
up of the treaty than in other cases where we have put
in directions. Here, as in other ambiguous moments,
we as editors can do nothing beyond making the
choice that seems best to us, then printing stage directions and, by putting those directions in square brackets, leaving it to readers, directors, and actors to
interpret the matter as they will.

Practice in reading the language of stage action
repays one many times over when one reaches scenes
heavily dependent on stage business. Act 5 opens with
such a scene. It begins with the entry of the Duke
of York, wearing the white rose and accompanied by
an army of Irish soldiers, attendants, drummers, and
standard bearers. They are met by Buckingham, wearing the red rose. York decides to disguise the real reason for his warlike approach; Buckingham in turn lies
about Somerset's location. York, pretending to be satis-
fied, dismisses his soldiers and walks arm in arm with
Buckingham. The king enters and is reassured by the
friendliness displayed by the two men. Iden then enters
with the head of Jack Cade, kneels, and is made a
knight by the king. When Margaret and Somerset
enter, York seizes on Buckingham's lie and announces
the truth about his own intentions. York sends for his
sons; Buckingham, in turn, exits to fetch Clifford for
the king; York's sons enter followed by Lord Clifford
and his son, Clifford kneels to Henry, and an attendant
exits to bring Salisbury and Warwick to York. When
Salisbury refuses to kneel to Henry, the king realizes
that these nobles have turned against him. By the end
of the scene, the lines have been clearly drawn between

Henry's faction and that of York, with much of the action having taken place in the series of entrances, exits, kneelings, and failures to kneel—actions that the reader of the scene must stage in imagination. Only if our imaginations can hold the players in proper position onstage, as the red roses line up against the white, can we receive the full impact of this decisive moment in the Wars of the Roses.

It is immensely rewarding to work carefully with Shakespeare's language—with the words, the sentences, the wordplay, and the implied stage action—as readers for the past four centuries have discovered. It may be more pleasurable to attend a good performance of a play—though not everyone has thought so. But the joy of being able to stage a Shakespeare play in one's imagination, to return to passages that continue to yield further meanings (or further questions) the more one reads them—these are pleasures that, for many, rival (or at least augment) those of the performed text, and certainly make it worth considerable effort to "break the code" of Elizabethan poetic drama and let free the remarkable language that makes up a Shakespeare text.

CATECHISMVS

paruus pueris primùm Latinè
qui ediscatur, proponendus
in Scholis.

LONDINI
Apud Iohannem Dayum Typo-
graphum. An. 1573.

Cum Priuilegio Regiæ Maiestatis.

Title page of a 1573 Latin and Greek catechism for children.

Shakespeare's Life

Surviving documents that give us glimpses into the life of William Shakespeare show us a playwright, poet, and actor who grew up in the market town of Stratford-upon-Avon, spent his professional life in London, and returned to Stratford a wealthy landowner. He was born in April 1564, died in April 1616, and is buried inside the chancel of Holy Trinity Church in Stratford.

We wish we could know more about the life of the world's greatest dramatist. His plays and poems are testaments to his wide reading—especially to his knowledge of Virgil, Ovid, Plutarch, Holinshed's *Chronicles*, and the Bible—and to his mastery of the English language, but we can only speculate about his education. We know that the King's New School in Stratford-upon-Avon was considered excellent. The school was one of the English "grammar schools" established to educate young men, primarily in Latin grammar and literature. As in other schools of the time, students began their studies at the age of four or five in the attached "petty school," and there learned to read and write in English, studying primarily the catechism from the Book of Common Prayer. After two years in the petty school, students entered the lower form (grade) of the grammar school, where they began the serious study of Latin grammar and Latin texts that would occupy most of the remainder of their school days. (Several Latin texts that Shakespeare used repeatedly in writing his plays and poems were texts that schoolboys memorized and recited.) Latin comedies were introduced early in the lower form; in the upper form, which the boys entered at age ten or eleven, students wrote their own Latin orations and declamations, studied Latin historians and rhetoricians, and began the study of Greek using the Greek New Testament.

Since the records of the Stratford "grammar school" do not survive, we cannot prove that William Shakespeare attended the school; however, every indication (his father's position as an alderman and bailiff of Stratford, the playwright's own knowledge of the Latin classics, scenes in the plays that recall grammar-school experiences—for example, *The Merry Wives of Windsor*, 4.1) suggests that he did. We also lack generally accepted documentation about Shakespeare's life after his schooling ended and his professional life in London began. His marriage in 1582 (at age eighteen) to Anne Hathaway and the subsequent births of his daughter Susanna (1583) and the twins Judith and Hamnet (1585) are recorded, but how he supported himself and where he lived are not known. Nor do we know when and why he left Stratford for the London theatrical world, nor how he rose to be the important figure in that world that he had become by the early 1590s.

We do know that by 1592 he had achieved some prominence in London as both an actor and a playwright. In that year was published a book by the playwright Robert Greene attacking an actor who had the audacity to write blank-verse drama and who was "in his own conceit [i.e., opinion] the only Shake-scene in a country." Since Greene's attack includes a parody of a line from one of Shakespeare's early plays, there is little doubt that it is Shakespeare to whom he refers, a "Shake-scene" who had aroused Greene's fury by successfully competing with university-educated dramatists like Greene himself. It was in 1593 that Shakespeare became a published poet. In that year he published his long narrative poem *Venus and Adonis;*

in 1594, he followed it with *Lucrece*. Both poems were dedicated to the young earl of Southampton (Henry Wriothesley), who may have become Shakespeare's patron.

It seems no coincidence that Shakespeare wrote these narrative poems at a time when the theaters were closed because of the plague, a contagious epidemic disease that devastated the population of London. When the theaters reopened in 1594, Shakespeare apparently resumed his double career of actor and playwright and began his long (and seemingly profitable) service as an acting-company shareholder. Records for December of 1594 show him to be a leading member of the Lord Chamberlain's Men. It was this company of actors, later named the King's Men, for whom he would be a principal actor, dramatist, and shareholder for the rest of his career.

So far as we can tell, that career spanned about twenty years. In the 1590s, he wrote his plays on English history as well as several comedies and at least two tragedies (*Titus Andronicus* and *Romeo and Juliet*). These histories, comedies, and tragedies are the plays credited to him in 1598 in a work, *Palladis Tamia*, that in one chapter compares English writers with "Greek, Latin, and Italian Poets." There the author, Francis Meres, claims that Shakespeare is comparable to the Latin dramatists Seneca for tragedy and Plautus for comedy, and calls him "the most excellent in both kinds for the stage." He also names him "Mellifluous and honey-tongued Shakespeare": "I say," writes Meres, "that the Muses would speak with Shakespeare's fine filed phrase, if they would speak English." Since Meres also mentions Shakespeare's "sugared sonnets among his private friends," it is assumed that many of Shakespeare's sonnets (not published until 1609) were also written in the 1590s.

The Globe

A stylized representation of the Globe theater.
From Claes Jansz Visscher, *Londinum florentissima
Britanniae urbs . . .* [c. 1625].

In 1599, Shakespeare's company built a theater for themselves across the river from London, naming it the Globe. The plays that are considered by many to be Shakespeare's major tragedies (*Hamlet, Othello, King Lear,* and *Macbeth*) were written while the company was resident in this theater, as were such comedies as *Twelfth Night* and *Measure for Measure.* Many of Shakespeare's plays were performed at court (both for Queen Elizabeth I and, after her death in 1603, for King James I), some were presented at the Inns of Court (the residences of London's legal societies), and some were doubtless performed in other towns, at the universities, and at great houses when the King's Men went on tour; otherwise, his plays from 1599 to 1608 were, so far as we know, performed only at the Globe. Between 1608 and 1612, Shakespeare wrote several plays—among them *The Winter's Tale* and *The Tempest*—presumably for the company's new indoor Blackfriars theater, though the plays seem to have been performed also at the Globe and at court. Surviving documents describe a performance of *The Winter's Tale* in 1611 at the Globe, for example, and performances of *The Tempest* in 1611 and 1613 at the royal palace of Whitehall.

Shakespeare wrote very little after 1612, the year in which he probably wrote *King Henry VIII.* (It was at a performance of *Henry VIII* in 1613 that the Globe caught fire and burned to the ground.) Sometime between 1610 and 1613 he seems to have returned to live in Stratford-upon-Avon, where he owned a large house and considerable property, and where his wife and his two daughters and their husbands lived. (His son Hamnet had died in 1596.) During his professional years in London, Shakespeare had presumably derived income from the acting company's profits as well as from his own career as an actor, from the sale of his play manuscripts to the acting company, and, after

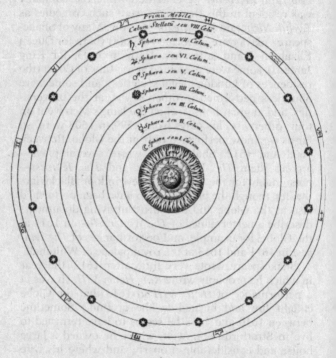

The following labels appear in the diagram from outermost to innermost:

Primu Mobile

Cælum Stellatū seu VIII Cælū.

♄ Sphæra seu VII. Cælum.

♃ Sphæra seu VI. Cælum.

♂ Sphæra seu V. Cælum.

☉ Sphæra seu IIII. Cælum.

♀ Sphæra seu III. Cælum.

☿ Sphæra seu II. Cælum.

☾ Sphæra seu I. Cælum.

The Ptolemaic system.
From Marcus Manilius, *The sphere of . . .* (1675).

1599, from his shares as an owner of the Globe. It was presumably that income, carefully invested in land and other property, which made him the wealthy man that surviving documents show him to have become. It is also assumed that William Shakespeare's growing wealth and reputation played some part in inclining the crown, in 1596, to grant John Shakespeare, William's father, the coat of arms that he had so long sought. William Shakespeare died in Stratford on April 23, 1616 (according to the epitaph carved under his bust in Holy Trinity Church) and was buried on April 25. Seven years after his death, his collected plays were published as *Mr. William Shakespeares Comedies, Histories, & Tragedies* (the work now known as the First Folio).

The years in which Shakespeare wrote were among the most exciting in English history. Intellectually, the discovery, translation, and printing of Greek and Roman classics were making available a set of works and worldviews that interacted complexly with Christian texts and beliefs. The result was a questioning, a vital intellectual ferment, that provided energy for the period's amazing dramatic and literary output and that fed directly into Shakespeare's plays. The Ghost in *Hamlet,* for example, is wonderfully complicated in part because he is a figure from Roman tragedy—the spirit of the dead returning to seek revenge—who at the same time inhabits a Christian hell (or purgatory); Hamlet's description of humankind reflects at one moment the Neoplatonic wonderment at mankind ("What a piece of work is a man!") and, at the next, the Christian disparagement of human sinners ("And yet, to me, what is this quintessence of dust?").

As intellectual horizons expanded, so also did geographical and cosmological horizons. New worlds—both North and South America—were explored, and in them were found human beings who lived and worshiped in ways radically different from those of Renaissance Europeans and Englishmen. The universe during these years also seemed to shift and expand. Copernicus had earlier theorized that the earth was not the center of the cosmos but revolved as a planet around the sun. Galileo's telescope, created in 1609, allowed scientists to see that Copernicus had been correct: the universe was not organized with the earth at the center, nor was it so nicely circumscribed as people had, until that time, thought. In terms of expanding horizons, the impact of these discoveries on people's beliefs—religious, scientific, and philosophical—cannot be overstated.

London, too, rapidly expanded and changed during the years (from the early 1590s to around 1610) that Shakespeare lived there. London—the center of England's government, its economy, its royal court, its overseas trade—was, during these years, becoming an exciting metropolis, drawing to it thousands of new citizens every year. Troubled by overcrowding, by poverty, by recurring epidemics of the plague, London was also a mecca for the wealthy and the aristocratic, and for those who sought advancement at court, or power in government or finance or trade. One hears in Shakespeare's plays the voices of London—the struggles for power, the fear of venereal disease, the language of buying and selling. One hears as well the voices of Stratford-upon-Avon—references to the nearby Forest of Arden, to sheepherding, to small-town gossip, to village fairs and markets. Part of the richness of Shakespeare's work is the influence felt there of the various worlds in which he lived: the world of metropolitan London, the world of small-town and rural England, the world of the theater, and the worlds of craftsmen and shepherds.

That Shakespeare inhabited such worlds we know from surviving London and Stratford documents, as well as from the evidence of the plays and poems themselves. From such records we can sketch the dramatist's life. We know from his works that he was a voracious reader. We know from legal and business documents that he was a multifaceted theater man who became a wealthy landowner. We know a bit about his family life and a fair amount about his legal and financial dealings. Most scholars today depend upon such evidence as they draw their picture of the world's greatest playwright. Such, however, has not always been the case. Until the late eighteenth century, the William Shakespeare who lived in most biographies was the creation of legend and tradition. This was the Shakespeare who was supposedly caught poaching deer at Charlecote, the estate of Sir Thomas Lucy close by Stratford; this was the Shakespeare who fled from Sir Thomas's vengeance and made his way in London by taking care of horses outside a playhouse; this was the Shakespeare who reportedly could barely read but whose natural gifts were extraordinary, whose father was a butcher who allowed his gifted son sometimes to help in the butcher shop, where William supposedly killed calves "in a high style," making a speech for the occasion. It was this legendary William Shakespeare whose Falstaff (in *1* and *2 Henry IV*) so pleased Queen Elizabeth that she demanded a play about Falstaff in love, and demanded that it be written in fourteen days (hence the existence of *The Merry Wives of Windsor*). It was this legendary Shakespeare who reached the top of his acting career in the roles of the Ghost in *Hamlet* and old Adam in *As You Like It*—and who died of a fever contracted by drinking too hard at "a merry meeting" with the poets Michael Drayton and Ben Jonson. This legendary Shakespeare is a rambunctious, undisciplined man, as attractively "wild" as his plays were seen by earlier generations to be. Unfortunately, there is no trace of evidence to support these wonderful stories.

Perhaps in response to the disreputable Shakespeare of legend—or perhaps in response to the fragmentary and, for some, all-too-ordinary Shakespeare documented by surviving records—some people since the mid–nineteenth century have argued that William Shakespeare could not have written the plays that bear his name. These persons have put forward some dozen names as more likely authors, among them Queen Elizabeth, Sir Francis Bacon, Edward de Vere (earl of Oxford), and Christopher Marlowe. Such attempts to find what for these people is a more believable author of the plays is a tribute to the regard in which the plays are held. Unfortunately for their claims, the documents that exist that provide evidence for the facts of Shakespeare's life tie him inextricably to the body of plays and poems that bear his name. Unlikely as it seems to those who want the works to have been written by an aristocrat, a university graduate, or an "important" person, the plays and poems seem clearly to have been produced by a man from Stratford-upon-Avon with a very good "grammar school" education and a life of experience in London and in the world of the London theater. How this particular man produced the works that dominate the cultures of much of the world almost four hundred years after his death is one of life's mysteries—and one that will continue to tease our imaginations as we continue to delight in his plays and poems.

Shakespeare's Theater

The actors of Shakespeare's time performed plays in a great variety of locations. They played at court (that is, in the great halls of such royal residences as Whitehall, Hampton Court, and Greenwich); they played in halls at the universities of Oxford and Cambridge, and at the Inns of Court (the residences in London of the legal societies); and they also played in the private houses of great lords and civic officials. Sometimes acting companies went on tour from London into the provinces, often (but not only) when outbreaks of bubonic plague in the capital forced the closing of theaters to reduce the possibility of contagion in crowded audiences. In the provinces the actors usually staged their plays in churches (until around 1600) or in guildhalls. Though surviving records show only a handful of occasions when actors played at inns while on tour, London inns were important playing places up until the 1590s.

The building of theaters in London had begun only shortly before Shakespeare wrote his first plays in the 1590s. These theaters were of two kinds: outdoor or public playhouses that could accommodate large numbers of playgoers, and indoor or private theaters for much smaller audiences. What is usually regarded as the first London outdoor public playhouse was called simply the Theatre. James Burbage—the father of Richard Burbage, who was perhaps the most famous actor in Shakespeare's company—built it in 1576 in an area north of the city of London called Shoreditch. Among the more famous of the other public playhouses that capitalized on the new fashion were the Curtain and the Fortune (both also built north of the city), and the Rose, the Swan, the Globe, and the

Hope (all located on the Bankside, a region just across the Thames south of the city of London). All these play-houses had to be built outside the jurisdiction of the city of London because many civic officials were hostile to the performance of drama and repeatedly petitioned the royal council to abolish it.

The theaters erected on the Bankside (a region under the authority of the Church of England, whose head was the monarch) shared the neighborhood with houses of prostitution and with the Paris Garden, where the blood sports of bearbaiting and bullbaiting were carried on. There may have been no clear distinction between playhouses and buildings for such sports, for the Hope was used for both plays and baiting, and Philip Henslowe, owner of the Rose and, later, partner in the ownership of the Fortune, was also a partner in a monopoly on baiting. All these forms of entertainment were easily accessible to Londoners by boat across the Thames or over London Bridge.

Evidently Shakespeare's company prospered on the Bankside. They moved there in 1599. Threatened by difficulties in renewing the lease on the land where their first playhouse (the Theatre) had been built, Shakespeare's company took advantage of the Christmas holiday in 1598 to dismantle the Theatre and transport its timbers across the Thames to the Bankside, where, in 1599, these timbers were used in the building of the Globe. The weather in late December 1598 is recorded as having been especially harsh. It was so cold that the Thames was "nigh [nearly] frozen," and there was heavy snow. Perhaps the weather aided Shakespeare's company in eluding their landlord, the snow hiding their activity and the freezing of the Thames allowing them to slide the timbers across to the Bankside without paying tolls for repeated trips over London Bridge. Attractive as this narrative is, it remains just as likely that the heavy snow hampered transport of the timbers in wagons through the London streets to the river. It also must be remembered that the Thames was, according to report, only "nigh frozen" and therefore as impassable as it ever was. Whatever the precise circumstances of this fascinating event in English theater history, Shakespeare's company was able to begin playing at their new Globe theater on the Bankside in 1599. After the first Globe burned down in 1613 during the staging of Shakespeare's *Henry VIII* (its thatch roof was set alight by cannon fire called for by the performance), Shakespeare's company immediately rebuilt on the same location. The second Globe seems to have been a grander structure than its predecessor. It remained in use until the beginning of the English Civil War in 1642, when Parliament officially closed the theaters. Soon thereafter it was pulled down.

The public theaters of Shakespeare's time were very different buildings from our theaters today. First of all, they were open-air playhouses. As recent excavations of the Rose and the Globe confirm, some were polygonal or roughly circular in shape; the Fortune, however, was square. The most recent estimates of their size put the diameter of these buildings at 72 feet (the Rose) to 100 feet (the Globe), but they were said to hold vast audiences of two or three thousand, who must have been squeezed together quite tightly. Some of these spectators paid extra to sit or stand in the two or three levels of roofed galleries that extended, on the upper levels, all the way around the theater and surrounded an open space. In this space were the stage and, perhaps, the tiring house (what we would call dressing rooms), as well as the so-called yard. In the yard stood the spectators who chose to pay less, the ones whom Hamlet contemptuously called "groundlings." For a roof they had only the sky, and so they were exposed to all kinds of weather. They stood on a floor that was sometimes made of mortar and sometimes of ash mixed with the shells of hazelnuts, which, it has recently been discovered, were standard flooring material in the period.

Unlike the yard, the stage itself was covered by a roof. Its ceiling, called "the heavens," is thought to have been elaborately painted to depict the sun, moon, stars, and planets. Just how big the stage was remains hard to determine. We have a single sketch of part of the interior of the Swan. A Dutchman named Johannes de Witt visited this theater around 1596 and sent a sketch of it back to his friend, Arend van Buchel. Because van Buchel found de Witt's letter and sketch of interest, he copied both into a book. It is van Buchel's copy, adapted, it seems, to the shape and size of the page in his book, that survives. In this sketch, the stage appears to be a large rectangular platform that thrusts far out into the yard, perhaps even as far as the center of the circle formed by the surrounding galleries. This drawing, combined with the specifications for the size of the stage in the building contract for the Fortune, has led scholars to conjecture that the stage on which Shakespeare's plays were performed must have measured approximately 43 feet in width and 27 feet in depth, a vast acting area. But the digging up of a large part of the Rose by archaeologists has provided evidence of a quite different stage design. The Rose stage was a platform tapered at the corners and much shallower than what seems to be depicted in the van Buchel sketch. Indeed, its measurements seem to be about 37.5 feet across at its widest point and only 15.5 feet deep. Because the surviving indications of stage size and design differ from each other so much, it is possible that the stages in other playhouses, like the

Theatre, the Curtain, and the Globe (the outdoor play-houses where Shakespeare's plays were performed), were different from those at both the Swan and the Rose.

After about 1608 Shakespeare's plays were staged not only at the Globe but also at an indoor or private playhouse in Blackfriars. This theater had been constructed in 1596 by James Burbage in an upper hall of a former Dominican priory or monastic house. Although Henry VIII had dissolved all English monasteries in the 1530s (shortly after he had founded the Church of England), the area remained under church, rather than hostile civic, control. The hall that Burbage had purchased and renovated was a large one in which Parliament had once met. In the private theater that he constructed, the stage, lit by candles, was built across the narrow end of the hall, with boxes flanking it. The rest of the hall offered seating room only. Because there was no provision for standing room, the largest audience it could hold was less than a thousand, or about a quarter of what the Globe could accommodate. Admission to Blackfriars was correspondingly more expensive. Instead of a penny to stand in the yard at the Globe, it cost a minimum of sixpence to get into Blackfriars. The best seats at the Globe (in the Lords' Room in the gallery above and behind the stage) cost sixpence; but the boxes flanking the stage at Blackfriars were half a crown, or five times sixpence. Some spectators who were particularly interested in displaying themselves paid even more to sit on stools on the Blackfriars stage.

Whether in the outdoor or indoor playhouses, the stages of Shakespeare's time were different from ours. They were not separated from the audience by the dropping of a curtain between acts and scenes. Therefore the playwrights of the time had to find other ways of signaling to the audience that one scene (to be imagined as occurring in one location at a given time) had ended and the next (to be imagined at perhaps a different location at a later time) had begun. The customary way used by Shakespeare and many of his contemporaries was to have everyone onstage exit at the end of one scene and have one or more different characters enter to begin the next. In a few cases, where characters remain onstage from one scene to another, the dialogue or stage action makes the change of location clear, and the characters are generally to be imagined as having moved from one place to another. For example, in *Romeo and Juliet,* Romeo and his friends remain onstage in Act 1 from scene 4 to scene 5, but they are represented as having moved between scenes from the street that leads to Capulet's house into the house itself. The new location is signaled in part by the appearance onstage of Capulet's servingmen carrying napkins, something they would not take into the streets. Playwrights had to be quite resourceful in the use of hand properties, like the napkin, or in the use of dialogue to specify where the action was taking place in their plays because, in contrast to most of today's theaters, the playhouses of Shakespeare's time did not use movable scenery to dress the stage and make the setting precise. As another consequence of this difference, however, the playwrights of Shakespeare's time did not have to specify exactly where the action of their plays was set when they did not choose to do so, and much of the action of their plays is tied to no specific place.

Usually Shakespeare's stage is referred to as a "bare stage," to distinguish it from the stages of the past two or three centuries with their elaborate sets. But the stage in Shakespeare's time was not completely bare. Philip Henslowe, owner of the Rose, lists in his inventory of stage properties a rock, three tombs, and two mossy banks. Stage directions in plays of the time also call for such things as thrones (or "states"), banquets (presumably tables with plaster replicas of food on them), and beds and tombs to be pushed onto the stage. Thus the stage often held more than the actors.

The actors did not limit their performing to the stage alone. Occasionally they went beneath the stage, as the Ghost appears to do in the first act of *Hamlet*. From there they could emerge onto the stage through a trapdoor. They could retire behind the hangings across the back of the stage (or the front of the tiring house), as, for example, the actor playing Polonius does when he hides behind the arras. Sometimes the hangings could be drawn back during a performance to "discover" one or more actors behind them. When performance required that an actor appear "above," as when Juliet is imagined to stand at the window of her chamber in the famous and misnamed "balcony scene," then the actor probably climbed the stairs to the gallery over the back of the stage and temporarily shared it with some of the spectators. The stage was also provided with ropes and winches so that actors could descend from, and re-ascend to, the "heavens."

Perhaps the greatest difference between dramatic performances in Shakespeare's time and ours was that in Shakespeare's England the roles of women were played by boys. (Some of these boys grew up to take male roles in their maturity.) There were no women in the acting companies, only in the audience. It had not always been so in the history of the English stage. There are records of women on English stages in the thirteenth and fourteenth centuries, two hundred years before Shakespeare's plays were performed. After the accession of James I in 1603, the queen of England and her ladies took part in entertainments at court called masques, and with the reopening of the theaters in 1660 at the restoration of Charles II, women again took their place on the public stage.

The chief competitors for the companies of adult actors such as the one to which Shakespeare belonged and for which he wrote were companies of exclusively boy actors. The competition was most intense in the early 1600s. There were then two principal children's companies: the Children of Paul's (the choirboys from St. Paul's Cathedral, whose private playhouse was near the cathedral); and the Children of the Chapel Royal (the choirboys from the monarch's private chapel, who performed at the Blackfriars theater built by Burbage in 1596, which Shakespeare's company had been stopped from using by local residents who objected to crowds). In *Hamlet* Shakespeare writes of "an aerie [nest] of children, little eyases [hawks], that cry out on the top of question and are most tyrannically clapped for 't. These are now the fashion and . . . berattle the common stages [attack the public theaters]." In the long run, the adult actors prevailed. The Children of Paul's dissolved around 1606. By about 1608 the Children of the Chapel Royal had been forced to stop playing at the Blackfriars theater, which was then taken over by the King's company of players, Shakespeare's own troupe.

Acting companies and theaters of Shakespeare's time seem to have been organized in different ways. With the building of the Globe, Shakespeare's company apparently managed itself, with the principal actors, Shakespeare among them, having the status of "sharers" and the right to a share in the takings, as well as the responsibility for a part of the expenses. Five of the sharers, including Shakespeare, owned the Globe. As actor, as sharer in an acting company and in ownership of theaters, and as playwright, Shakespeare was about as involved in the theatrical industry as one could imagine. Although Shakespeare and his fellows prospered, their status under the law was conditional upon the protection of powerful patrons. "Common players"—those who did not have patrons or masters—were classed in the language of the law with "vagabonds and sturdy beggars." So the actors had to secure for themselves the official rank of servants of patrons. Among the patrons under whose protection Shakespeare's company worked were the lord chamberlain and, after the accession of King James in 1603, the king himself.

In the early 1990s we seemed on the verge of learning a great deal more about the theaters in which Shakespeare and his contemporaries performed—or, at least, opening up new questions about them. At that time about 70 percent of the Rose had been excavated, as had about 10 percent of the second Globe, the one built in 1614. It was then hoped that more would become available for study. However, excavation was halted at that point, and it is not known if or when it will resume.

The second Part of Henry the Sixt,
with the death of the Good Duke
HVMFREY.

Actus Primus. Scœna Prima.

Flourish of Trumpets: Then Hoboyes.

*Enter King, Duke Humfrey, Salisbury, Warwicke, and Beau-
ford on the one side.
The Queene, Suffolke, Yorke, Somerset, and Buckingham,
on the other.*

Suffolke.

AS by your high Imperiall Maiesty,
I had in charge at my depart for France,
As Procurator to your Excellence,
To marry Princes Margaret for your Grace;
So in the Famous Ancient City, Tours,
In presence of the Kings of France, and Sicill,
The Dukes of Orleance, Calaber, Britaigne, and Alanson,
Seuen Earles, twelue Barons, & twenty reuerend Bishops
I haue perform'd my Taske, and was espous'd,
And humbly now vpon my bended knee,
In sight of England, and her Lordly Peeres,
Deliuer vp my Title in the Queene
To your most gracious hands, that are the Substance
Of that great Shadow I did represent:
The happiest Gift, that euer Marquesse gaue,
The Fairest Queene, that euer King receiu'd.

King. Suffolke arise. Welcome Queene Margaret,
I can expresse no kinder signe of Loue
Then this kinde kisse: O Lord, that lends me life,
Lend me a heart repleate with thankfulnesse:
For thou hast giuen me in this beauteous Face
A world of earthly blessings to my soule,
If Simpathy of Loue vnite our thoughts.

Queen. Great King of England, & my gracious Lord,
The mutuall conference that my minde hath had,
By day, by night: waking, and in my dreames,
In Courtly company, or at my Beades,
With you mine *Alder liefest* Soueraigne,
Makes me the bolder to salute my King,
With ruder termes, such as my wit affoords,
And ouer ioy of heart doth minister.

King. Her sight did rauish, but her grace in Speech,
Her words yclad with wisedomes Maiesty,
Makes me from Wondring, fall to Weeping ioyes,
Such is the Fulnesse of my hearts content.
Lords, with one cheerefull voice, Welcome my Loue.

All. Long liue Qu. Margaret, Englands happines.

Queene. We thanke you all. *Florish*

Suf. My Lord Protector, so it please your Grace,
Heere are the Articles of contracted peace,
Betweene our Soueraigne, and the French King Charles,
For eighteene moneths concluded by consent.

Glo. Reads. Inprimis, *It is agreed betweene the French K.
Charles, and William de la Pole Marquesse of Suffolke, Am-
bassador for Henry King of England, That the said Henry shal
espouse the Lady Margaret, daughter vnto Reignier King of
Naples, Sicillia, and Ierusalem, and Crowne her Queene of
England, ere the thirtieth of May next ensuing.*

*Item, That the Duchy of Aniou, and the County of Maine,
shall be released and deliuered to the King her father.*

King. Vnkle, how now?

Glo. Pardon me gracious Lord,
Some sodaine qualme hath strucke me at the heart,
And dim'd mine eyes; that I can reade no further.

King. Vnckle of Winchester, I pray read on.

Win. Item, *It is further agreed betweene them, That the
Duchesse of Anion and Maine, shall be released and deliuered
ouer to the King her Father, and shee sent ouer of the King of
Englands owne proper Cost and Charges, without hauing any
Dowry.*

King. They please vs well. Lord Marques kneel down,
We heere create thee the first Duke of Suffolke,
And girt thee with the Sword. Cosin of Yorke,
We heere discharge your Grace from being Regent
I'th parts of France, till terme of eighteene Moneths
Be full expyr'd. Thankes Vncle Winchester,
Gloster, Yorke, Buckingham, Somerset,
Salisburie, and Warwicke.
We thanke you all for this great fauour done,
In entertainment to my Princely Queene.
Come, let vs in, and with all speede prouide
To see her Coronation be perform'd.

Exit King, Queene, and Suffolke.

Manet the rest.

Glo. Braue Peeres of England, Pillars of the State,
To you Duke Humfrey must vnload his greefe:
Your greefe, the common greefe of all the Land.
What? did my brother Henry spend his youth,
His valour, coine, and people in the warres?
Did he so often lodge in open field:
In Winters cold, and Summers parching heate,
To conquer France, his true inheritance?
And did my brother Bedford toyle his wits,

To

The Publication of Shakespeare's Plays

Eighteen of Shakespeare's plays found their way into print during the playwright's lifetime, but there is nothing to suggest that he took any interest in their publication. These eighteen appeared separately in editions called quartos. Their pages were not much larger than the one you are now reading, and these little books were sold unbound for a few pence. The earliest of the quartos that still survive were printed in 1594, the year that both *Titus Andronicus* and a version of the play now called *Henry VI, Part 2* became available. While almost every one of these early quartos displays on its title page the name of the acting company that performed the play, only about half provide the name of the playwright, Shakespeare. The first quarto edition to bear the name Shakespeare on its title page is *Love's Labor's Lost* of 1598. A few of these quartos were popular with the book-buying public of Shakespeare's lifetime; for example, quarto *Richard II* went through five editions between 1597 and 1615. But most of the quartos were far from best sellers; *Love's Labor's Lost* (1598), for instance, was not reprinted in quarto until 1631. After Shakespeare's death, two more of his plays appeared in quarto format: *Othello* in 1622 and *The Two Noble Kinsmen*, coauthored with John Fletcher, in 1634.

In 1623, seven years after Shakespeare's death, *Mr. William Shakespeares Comedies, Histories, & Tragedies* was published. This printing offered readers in a single book thirty-six of the thirty-eight plays now thought to have been written by Shakespeare, including eighteen that had never been printed before. And it offered them

in a style that was then reserved for serious literature and scholarship. The plays were arranged in double columns on pages nearly a foot high. This large
page size is called "folio," as opposed to the smaller
"quarto," and the 1623 volume is usually called the
Shakespeare First Folio. It is reputed to have sold for
the lordly price of a pound. (One copy at the Folger
Shakespeare Library is marked fifteen shillings—that
is, three-quarters of a pound.)

In a preface to the First Folio entitled "To the great
Variety of Readers," two of Shakespeare's former fellow actors in the King's Men, John Heminge and Henry
Condell, wrote that they themselves had collected their
dead companion's plays. They suggested that they had
seen his own papers: "we have scarce received from
him a blot in his papers." The title page of the Folio
declared that the plays within it had been printed
"according to the True Original Copies." Comparing
the Folio to the quartos, Heminge and Condell disparaged the quartos, advising their readers that "before
you were abused with divers stolen and surreptitious
copies, maimed, and deformed by the frauds and
stealths of injurious impostors." Many Shakespeareans
of the eighteenth and nineteenth centuries believed
Heminge and Condell and regarded the Folio plays as
superior to anything in the quartos.

Once we begin to examine the Folio plays in detail,
it becomes less easy to take at face value the word of
Heminge and Condell about the superiority of the
Folio texts. For example, of the first nine plays in the
Folio (one-quarter of the entire collection), four were
essentially reprinted from earlier quarto printings that
Heminge and Condell had disparaged; and four have
now been identified as printed from copies written in
the hand of a professional scribe of the 1620s named
Ralph Crane; the ninth, *The Comedy of Errors*, was

apparently also printed from a manuscript, but one whose origin cannot be readily identified. Evidently, then, eight of the first nine plays in the First Folio were not printed, in spite of what the Folio title page announces, "according to the True Original Copies," or Shakespeare's own papers, and the source of the ninth is unknown. Because today's editors have been forced to treat Heminge and Condell's pronouncements with skepticism, they must choose whether to base their own editions upon quartos or the Folio on grounds other than Heminge and Condell's story of where the quarto and Folio versions originated.

Editors have often fashioned their own narratives to explain what lies behind the quartos and Folio. They have said that Heminge and Condell meant to criticize only a few of the early quartos, the ones that offer much shorter and sometimes quite different, often garbled, versions of plays. Among the examples of these are the 1600 quarto of *Henry V* (the Folio offers a much fuller version) or the 1603 *Hamlet* quarto (in 1604 a different, much longer form of the play got into print as a quarto). Early-twentieth-century editors speculated that these questionable texts were produced when someone in the audience took notes from the plays' dialogue during performances and then employed "hack poets" to fill out the notes. The poor results were then sold to a publisher and presented in print as Shakespeare's plays. More recently this story has given way to another in which the shorter versions are said to be re-creations from memory of Shakespeare's plays by actors who wanted to stage them in the provinces but lacked manuscript copies. Most of the quartos offer much better texts than these so-called bad quartos. Indeed, in most of the quartos we find texts that are at least equal to or better than what is printed in the Folio. Many Shakespeare enthusiasts persuaded themselves that most of the quartos were set into type directly from Shakespeare's own papers, although there is nothing on which to base this conclusion except the desire for it to be true. Thus speculation continues about how the Shakespeare plays got to be printed. All that we have are the printed texts.

The book collector who was most successful in bringing together copies of the quartos and the First Folio was Henry Clay Folger, founder of the Folger Shakespeare Library in Washington, D.C. While it is estimated that there survive around the world only about 230 copies of the First Folio, Mr. Folger was able to acquire more than seventy-five copies, as well as a large number of fragments, for the library that bears his name. He also amassed a substantial number of quartos. For example, only fourteen copies of the First Quarto of *Love's Labor's Lost* are known to exist, and three are at the Folger Shakespeare Library. As a consequence of Mr. Folger's labors, scholars visiting the Folger Library have been able to learn a great deal about sixteenth- and seventeenth-century printing and, particularly, about the printing of Shakespeare's plays. And Mr. Folger did not stop at the First Folio, but collected many copies of later editions of Shakespeare, beginning with the Second Folio (1632), the Third (1663–64), and the Fourth (1685). Each of these later folios was based on its immediate predecessor and was edited anonymously. The first editor of Shakespeare whose name we know was Nicholas Rowe, whose first edition came out in 1709. Mr. Folger collected this edition and many, many more by Rowe's successors.

An Introduction to This Text

Henry VI, Part 2 was first printed, in a version far different from the one edited here, in 1594 as a quarto with the title *The First part of the Contention betwixt the two famous Houses of Yorke and Lancaster, with the death of the good Duke Humphrey: And the banishment and death of the Duke of Suffolke, and the Tragicall end of the proud Cardinall of Winchester, with the notable Rebellion of Iacke Cade: and the Duke of Yorkes first claime vnto the Crowne.* This quarto was reprinted in 1600 and again, with a half-dozen corrections that bring its text closer to the First Folio version, in 1619. In the 1623 collection of Shakespeare's plays now known as the First Folio there appeared a much fuller and very different text, this one titled *The second Part of Henry the Sixt, with the death of the Good Duke HVMFREY*.

The relation between Folio and quarto texts of this play has been a matter of speculation and discussion for centuries. In the eighteenth century it came to be believed that the quarto was the non-Shakespearean source for the Folio play. Then, early in the twentieth century, the text printed in the quarto was properly recognized as being later than the text printed in the Folio, from which it was derived. However, the process of derivation remains a vexed question. Particular passages printed in the quarto—1.1.61–66; 2.1.74 SD, 127–66 SD; 2.3.60 SD–2.4.0 SD; 4.5.0 SD–4.6.6—reproduce the Folio text verbatim or nearly verbatim. Nevertheless, the closeness of the quarto to the Folio in these passages may not mean that the quarto manuscript reproduced the Folio manuscript most carefully here; instead, it may indicate that the Folio typesetters consulted the printed quarto for these passages, perhaps because they found the manuscript being used as printer's copy deficient in these places. Some editors and critics have invoked the theory of memorial reconstruction to account for the quarto's relationship to the Folio. However, *The First part of the Contention* does not differ from *The second Part of Henry the Sixt* in the same way that the 1602 quarto of *The Merry Wives of Windsor* does from the Folio text of that play—the quarto of *Wives* being the only one that seems in any substantial way a memorial reconstruction of its Folio counterpart. Thus memorial reconstruction seems irrelevant to the case of *Henry VI, Part 2*, where the nature of the quarto text remains an unresolved question.

The present edition is based directly on the First Folio text of 1623,* and resorts to the quarto only for occasional readings when the sense of the Folio breaks down. For the convenience of the reader, we have modernized the punctuation and the spelling of the Folio. Sometimes we go so far as to modernize certain old forms of words; for example, usually when *a* means *he*, we change it to *he;* we change *mo* to *more*, and *ye* to *you*. But it is not our practice in editing any of the plays to modernize words that sound distinctly different from modern forms. For example, when the early printed texts read *sith* or *apricocks* or *porpentine*, we have not modernized to *since*, *apricots*, *porcupine*. When the forms *an, and,* or *and if* appear instead of the modern form *if,* we have reduced *and* to *an* but have not changed any of these forms to their modern equivalent, *if*. We also modernize and, where necessary, correct passages in foreign languages, unless an apparent

---

* We have also consulted the computerized text of the First Folio provided by the Text Archive of the Oxford University Computing Centre, to which we are grateful.

error in the early printed text can be reasonably explained as a joke.

Whenever we change the wording of the First Folio or add anything to its stage directions, we mark the change by enclosing it in superior half-brackets (⌐ ⌐). We want our readers to be immediately aware when we have intervened. (Only when we correct an obvious typographical error in the First Folio does the change not get marked.) Whenever we change either the First Folio's wording or its punctuation so that meaning changes, we list the change in the textual notes at the back of the book, even if all we have done is fix an obvious error.

We regularize spellings of a number of the proper names in the dialogue and stage directions, as is the usual practice in editions of the play. For example, the First Folio uses the forms "*Salisbury*," "*Salsbury*," "*Salsburie*," and "*Salisburie*," but this edition uses only "*Salisbury*." However, it is not our practice in this play to render all names of French characters or places in modern French. Instead, to accommodate metrical considerations in the play's verse, we retain the First Folio's anglicized spellings of, for example, "Alanson" for Alençon, "Orleance" for Orléans, and "Britaigne" for Brittany. (For more detail, see the longer note to 1.1.7–8 on page 252.)

This edition differs from many earlier ones in its efforts to aid the reader in imagining the play as a performance rather than as a series of actual events. Thus some stage directions are edited with reference to the stage. For example, in 2.4 of *Henry VI, Part 1*, the prequel to *Henry VI, Part 2*, a group of noblemen quarrel over a case at law and divide into two parties. They identify themselves as members of their parties by plucking and wearing roses of different colors. One party is led by Richard Plantagenet, subsequently cre-

ated the duke of York, and wears the white rose. His
chief follower is Warwick. The opposing party is
headed by the duke of Somerset, whose principal sup-
porter is Suffolk; they wear the red rose. Once these
parties have formed in this scene, thereafter in stage
productions each time they enter in *Henry VI, Parts 1,
2,* or *3,* their members square off against each other
belligerently as they display the roses that signal their
allegiances. To emphasize this stage presentation of
factionalism in our edition, we reorganize the First
Folio's entrance directions in scenes where such factionalism is prominent so that members of each
faction enter together wearing the rose appropriate to
their faction. In 1.3 of *Henry VI, Part 2,* for example,
when Suffolk enters at line 5 SD, we indicate that he is
wearing the red rose, and, at line 103 SD we indicate
that York and Warwick enter wearing the white rose
and Somerset wearing the red. Through this intervention we hope to help our readers stage the play in their
own imaginations in a way that more closely approxi-
mates an experience in the theater.

Whenever it is reasonably certain, in our view, that a
speech is accompanied by a particular action, we provide a stage direction describing the action, setting the
added direction in brackets to signal that it is not
found in the Folio. (Occasional exceptions to this rule
occur when the action is so obvious that to add a stage
direction would insult the reader). Stage directions for
the entrance of a character in mid-scene are, with rare
exceptions, placed so that they immediately precede
the character's participation in the scene, even though
these entrances may appear somewhat earlier in the
early printed texts. Whenever we move a stage direction, we record this change in the textual notes. Latin
stage directions (e.g., *Exeunt*) are translated into English (e.g., *They exit*).

We expand the often severely abbreviated forms of names used as speech headings in early printed texts into the full names of the characters. We also regularize the speakers' names in speech headings, using only a single designation for each character, even though the early printed texts sometimes use a variety of designations. Such variety is evident in connection with several characters. Humphrey, duke of Gloucester, is sometimes "*Glo.*" and sometimes "*Hum.*" in the Folio speech prefixes, but always "GLOUCESTER" in this edition. One of Jack Cade's followers in the Act 4 rebellion is Dick the butcher, who sometimes in the Folio speaks as "*But.*" and sometimes as "*Dicke.*" but speaks only as "DICK" in our edited text.

In the present edition, as well, we mark with a dash any change of address within a speech, unless a stage direction intervenes. When the -ed ending of a word is to be pronounced, we mark it with an accent. Like editors for the past two centuries, we print metrically linked lines in the following way:

KING HENRY
  Uncle, how now?
GLOUCESTER   Pardon me, gracious lord.
                          (1.1.56–57)

However, when there are a number of short verse-lines that can be linked in more than one way, we do not, with rare exceptions, indent any of them.

The Explanatory Notes

The notes that appear on the pages facing the text are designed to provide readers with the help that they may need to enjoy the play. Whenever the meaning of a word in the text is not readily accessible in a good contemporary dictionary, we offer the meaning in a note. Sometimes we provide a note even when the relevant meaning is to be found in the dictionary but when the word has acquired since Shakespeare's time other potentially confusing meanings. In our notes, we try to offer modern synonyms for Shakespeare's words. We also try to indicate to the reader the connection between the word in the play and the modern synonym. For example, Shakespeare sometimes uses the word *head* to mean *source*, but, for modern readers, there may be no connection evident between these two words. We provide the connection by explaining Shakespeare's usage as follows: "**head:** fountainhead, source." On some occasions, a whole phrase or clause needs explanation. Then, when space allows, we rephrase in our own words the difficult passage, and add at the end synonyms for individual words in the passage. When scholars have been unable to determine the meaning of a word or phrase, we acknowledge the uncertainty. Bible quotations are from the Geneva Bible (1560), modernized.

HENRY VI
Part 2

English Ancestry of King Henry VI

[Characters in this play appear in bold]

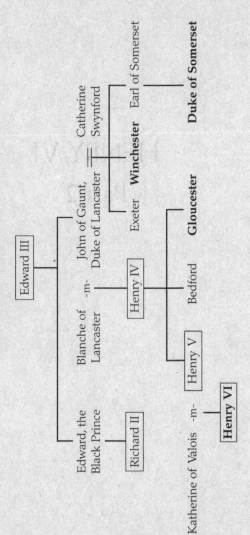

Characters in the Play

KING HENRY VI
QUEEN MARGARET

Humphrey, Duke of GLOUCESTER, the king's uncle,
  and Lord Protector
DUCHESS of Gloucester, Dame Eleanor Cobham
CARDINAL Beaufort, Bishop of Winchester, the king's
  great-uncle

Duke of SOMERSET
Duke of SUFFOLK, William de la Pole, earlier Marquess
  of SUFFOLK
BUCKINGHAM
Lord CLIFFORD
YOUNG CLIFFORD, his son

Duke of YORK, Richard Plantagenet
Earl of SALISBURY
Earl of WARWICK, Salisbury's son
EDWARD, Earl of March } *sons of the Duke of York*
RICHARD

Jack CADE, leader of the Kentish rebellion
BEVIS
John HOLLAND
DICK the butcher } *followers of Jack Cade*
SMITH the weaver
MICHAEL
GEORGE

Lord SCALES
Lord SAYE
Sir Humphrey STAFFORD } *King Henry's supporters against Cade*
His BROTHER,
  William Stafford

3

Sir John HUME, a priest
John SOUTHWELL, a priest
Margery JOURDAIN, a witch
Roger BOLINGBROKE, a conjurer
SPIRIT

Sir John STANLEY } *custodians of the Duchess*
SHERIFF   } *of Gloucester*

Thomas HORNER, the Duke of York's armorer
Peter THUMP, Horner the armorer's man or prentice
Two or Three PETITIONERS
Three NEIGHBORS of Horner's
Three PRENTICES, friends of Thump

A MAN of Saint Albans
Sander SIMPCOX, supposed recipient of a miracle
His WIFE
MAYOR of Saint Albans
A BEADLE of Saint Albans

LIEUTENANT, captain of a ship
Ship's MASTER
Master's MATE
Walter WHITMORE, a ship's officer
Two GENTLEMEN, prisoners

MESSENGERS
SERVANTS
A HERALD
POST, or messenger
Two or three MURDERERS of Gloucester
VAUX
CLERK of Chartham
Two or Three CITIZENS
Alexander IDEN, a gentleman of Kent

Servants, Guards, Falconers, Attendants, Townsmen
of Saint Albans, Bearers, Drummers, Commoners,
Rebels, a Sawyer, Soldiers, Officers, Matthew Gough,
and Others

HENRY VI
Part 2

ACT 1

1.1 King Henry meets his consort Queen Margaret, brought by Suffolk from France. The nobles fall into dissension, with the Cardinal, Buckingham, and Somerset opposing Gloucester, and with Salisbury and Warwick supporting him. Alone, York discloses his secret ambition for the crown.

---

0 SD. **Flourish:** fanfare to announce the approach of royalty; **hautboys:** powerful woodwinds used in outdoor ceremonials (an early form of the oboe) See picture, page 212.

1–2. **As . . . charge:** i.e., **as I** was commanded **by your Majesty imperial:** See longer note, page 251.

2. **depart:** departure

3. **procurator:** agent, deputy, proxy

4. **To marry . . . Grace:** For the background on this marriage in *Henry VI, Part 1*, see longer note, page 251.

6. **Sicil:** Sicily (See line 51.)

7–8. **Orleance:** Orléans; **Calaber:** Calabria; **Britaigne:** Brittany; **Alanson:** Alençon (For these Folio spellings, see longer note, page 252.)

11. **espoused:** married (by proxy)

13. **peers:** nobles

14. **title in:** right to possession of

15. **that are the substance:** i.e., you who **are the** solid or real thing, as proverbially opposed to image or semblance called the **shadow** (line 16)

17. **happiest:** most fortunate

18. **fairest:** most beautiful

ACT 1

Scene 1

Flourish of trumpets, then hautboys.
Enter King ⌜Henry,⌝ Duke Humphrey ⌜of Gloucester,⌝
Salisbury, Warwick, and ⌜Cardinal⌝ Beaufort, on the one
side; Queen ⌜Margaret,⌝ Suffolk, York, Somerset, and
Buckingham, on the other.

SUFFOLK
  As by your high imperial Majesty
  I had in charge at my depart for France,
  As procurator to your Excellence,
  To marry Princess Margaret for your Grace,
  So, in the famous ancient city Tours,   5
  In presence of the Kings of France and Sicil,
  The Dukes of Orleance, Calaber, Britaigne, and
    Alanson,
  Seven earls, twelve barons, and twenty reverend
    bishops,   10
  I have performed my task and was espoused;
                                          ⌜He kneels.⌝
  And humbly now upon my bended knee,
  In sight of England and her lordly peers,
  Deliver up my title in the Queen
  To your most gracious hands, that are the substance   15
  Of that great shadow I did represent:
  The happiest gift that ever marquess gave,
  The fairest queen that ever king received.

7

20. **kinder:** more natural
21. **kind:** affectionate
22. **that:** i.e., who
23. **Lend:** grant, give (In line 22, **lends me** means "grants me temporary possession.")
25. **A world:** a vast quantity or infinity
26. **sympathy:** harmony, correspondence
28. **mutual conference:** intimate conversation
30. **courtly company:** i.e., the **company** of courtiers; **at my beads:** i.e., alone at prayer **beads:** rosary (See picture, page 40.)
31. **alderliefest:** very dear
32. **salute:** greet, address
33. **ruder:** less polished; **wit:** mind, intelligence; **affords:** supplies
34. **overjoy:** too great joy; **minister:** impart
35. **Her sight:** i.e., the **sight** of **her; ravish:** overpower with delight
36. **yclad:** clad, clothed
37. **wond'ring:** admiration
39. **cheerful:** joyous (but with likely wordplay on *cheer*, meaning "encourage by shouts and cries")
40. **happiness:** good fortune
41. **We:** the royal "we," which Henry has not yet used
42. **so it . . . Grace:** a polite formula requesting agreement
43. **are . . . peace:** is the peace treaty
45. **concluded:** agreed, settled

KING HENRY
　　Suffolk, arise.—Welcome, Queen Margaret.
　　　　　　　　　　　　　　　　　　⌈*Suffolk rises.*⌉
　　I can express no kinder sign of love　　　　　　　　　20
　　Than this kind kiss.　　　　⌈*He kisses her.*⌉
　　　　　　　　　　O Lord, that lends me life,
　　Lend me a heart replete with thankfulness!
　　For Thou hast given me in this beauteous face
　　A world of earthly blessings to my soul,　　　　　　25
　　If sympathy of love unite our thoughts.
QUEEN MARGARET
　　Great king of England and my gracious lord,
　　The mutual conference that my mind hath had
　　By day, by night, waking and in my dreams,
　　In courtly company or at my beads,　　　　　　　　30
　　With you, mine alderliefest sovereign,
　　Makes me the bolder to salute my king
　　With ruder terms, such as my wit affords
　　And overjoy of heart doth minister.
KING HENRY
　　Her sight did ravish, but her grace in speech,　　　35
　　Her words yclad with wisdom's majesty,
　　Makes me from wond'ring fall to weeping joys,
　　Such is the fullness of my heart's content.
　　Lords, with one cheerful voice welcome my love.
ALL *kneel.*
　　Long live Queen Margaret, England's happiness!　40
QUEEN MARGARET　　We thank you all.
　　　　　　　　　　　　　　Flourish. ⌈*All rise.*⌉
SUFFOLK, ⌈*to Gloucester*⌉
　　My Lord Protector, so it please your Grace,
　　Here are the articles of contracted peace
　　Between our sovereign and the French king Charles,
　　For eighteen months concluded by consent.　　　45
　　　　　　　　　　　⌈*He hands Gloucester a paper.*⌉

46. **Imprimis:** in the first place (used to introduce the first of a number of items)

49. **espouse:** marry

52. **ere:** before; **Item:** also (used to introduce each article after the first in a document)

54. **released:** surrendered, made over

56. **Uncle:** See genealogical chart, page 2. **how now:** i.e., **how** is it **now**

58. **qualm:** fit of sickness or faintness

59. **that:** i.e., so **that**

60. **Uncle:** i.e., great-uncle (See chart, page 2.) **read on:** See longer note, page 252.

64. **sent over:** i.e., transported from France to England

64–65. **of the . . . charges:** i.e., at the expense **of the King of England   own proper:** personal

67. **They:** i.e., the clauses of the treaty

69. **girt:** gird; **Cousin:** a term of address used among nobles and aristocrats

71. **regent:** At 4.1.163–64 of *Henry VI, Part 1*, the king had created York **regent of France;** the king now leaves the office open for **eighteen months.**

72. **th' parts of France:** i.e., the **parts of France** under English control

73. **full:** i.e., fully

77. **entertainment to:** i.e., treatment or reception of; **princely:** royal

GLOUCESTER (*reads*)   *Imprimis, it is agreed between the*
    French king Charles and William de la Pole, Mar-
    quess of Suffolk, ambassador for Henry, King of En-
    gland, that the said Henry shall espouse the Lady
    Margaret, daughter unto Reignier, King of Naples,   50
    Sicilia, and Jerusalem, and crown her Queen of En-
    gland ere the thirtieth of May next ensuing. Item,
    that the duchy of Anjou and the county of Maine
    shall be released and delivered to the King her
    father—   ⌜*He drops the paper.*⌝   55

KING HENRY
    Uncle, how now?

GLOUCESTER   Pardon me, gracious lord.
    Some sudden qualm hath struck me at the heart
    And dimmed mine eyes, that I can read no further.

KING HENRY
    Uncle of Winchester, I pray read on.   60

CARDINAL ⌜*picks up the paper and reads*⌝   *Item, it is fur-*
    ther agreed between them that the ⌜*duchies*⌝ *of*
    Anjou and Maine shall be released and delivered to
    the King her father, and she sent over of the King of
    England's own proper cost and charges, without   65
    having any dowry.

KING HENRY
    They please us well.—Lord Marquess, kneel down.
                        ⌜*Suffolk kneels.*⌝
    We here create thee the first Duke of Suffolk
    And girt thee with the sword. ⌜*Suffolk rises.*⌝ Cousin
    of York,   70
    We here discharge your Grace from being regent
    I' th' parts of France till term of eighteen months
    Be full expired.—Thanks, Uncle Winchester,
    Gloucester, York, Buckingham, Somerset,
    Salisbury, and Warwick;   75
    We thank you all for this great favor done
    In entertainment to my princely queen.

78. **in:** i.e., go **in; provide:** prepare

80. **peers:** nobles (with wordplay on *piers* or **pillars**); **state:** government

83. **What:** interjection to introduce a question; **brother Henry: Henry** V (See picture, page 20.)

85. **lodge:** encamp

87. **true inheritance:** rightful possession (See longer note, page 253.)

88. **Bedford:** Duke of **Bedford,** whose brother, Henry V, when dying, made him regent of France; **toil:** tire; **wits:** mental faculties

89. **policy:** statecraft, political skill

92. **France and Normandy:** For the military service of some of these figures in **France,** not all of it glorious, see *Henry VI, Part 1*, 4.3, 4.4, 5.3.

93. **uncle Beaufort:** the Cardinal

94. **council of the realm:** Privy Council

95. **Studied:** deliberated

96. **to and fro:** i.e., for and against

99. **despite:** contemptuous defiance

103. **league:** agreement

104. **Fatal:** fateful, ominous

105. **Blotting:** obliterating, effacing

106. **Razing:** erasing; **characters:** graphic symbols, printed or written letters

107. **monuments:** (1) written documents; (2) commemorative structures

108. **as:** i.e., **as** if

109. **passionate:** hot-tempered, angry

Come, let us in, and with all speed provide
To see her coronation be performed.

King, Queen, and Suffolk exit.
The rest remain.

GLOUCESTER
Brave peers of England, pillars of the state,   80
To you Duke Humphrey must unload his grief,
Your grief, the common grief of all the land.
What, did my brother Henry spend his youth,
His valor, coin, and people in the wars?
Did he so often lodge in open field,   85
In winter's cold and summer's parching heat,
To conquer France, his true inheritance?
And did my brother Bedford toil his wits
To keep by policy what Henry got?
Have you yourselves, Somerset, Buckingham,   90
Brave York, Salisbury, and victorious Warwick,
Received deep scars in France and Normandy?
Or hath mine uncle Beaufort and myself,
With all the learnèd council of the realm,
Studied so long, sat in the Council House,   95
Early and late, debating to and fro
How France and Frenchmen might be kept in awe,
And ⌜had⌝ his Highness in his infancy
Crowned in Paris in despite of foes?
And shall these labors and these honors die?   100
Shall Henry's conquest, Bedford's vigilance,
Your deeds of war, and all our counsel die?
O peers of England, shameful is this league,
Fatal this marriage, cancelling your fame,
Blotting your names from books of memory,   105
Razing the characters of your renown,
Defacing monuments of conquered France,
Undoing all, as all had never been!
CARDINAL
Nephew, what means this passionate discourse,

110. **peroration:** eloquent speech; **circumstance:** detail

111. **For:** i.e., as **for; still:** always

114. **rules the roast:** i.e., presides over the dinner table, has full authority

116. **large:** i.e., grand; **style:** title (See lines 50–51 above.)

117. **Agrees not:** does not correspond

118. **by . . . all:** See 2 Corinthians 5.15: "And he **died for all.**"

120. **wherefore:** why

126. **arms:** (1) weapons; (2) limbs

129. **Mort Dieu:** God's death (French)

130. **For:** i.e., as **for; suffocate:** suffocated

134. **I . . . but:** i.e., **I** always **read** that

136. **his own:** i.e., **his own sums** (line 135)

137. **match with:** marry; **vantages:** profits

138. **proper jest:** fine joke (sarcastic)

139. **fifteenth:** tax amounting to one-fifteenth of everyone's annual profit or income (or, perhaps, property) In *Henry VI, Part 1*, Henry authorizes Suffolk to "gather up a tenth" (5.5.93).

140. **charges:** expenses

This peroration with such circumstance?   110
For France, 'tis ours, and we will keep it still.
GLOUCESTER
  Ay, uncle, we will keep it if we can,
  But now it is impossible we should.
  Suffolk, the new-made duke that rules the roast,
  Hath given the duchy of Anjou and Maine   115
  Unto the poor King Reignier, whose large style
  Agrees not with the leanness of his purse.
SALISBURY
  Now, by the death of Him that died for all,
  These counties were the keys of Normandy.
  But wherefore weeps Warwick, my valiant son?   120
WARWICK
  For grief that they are past recovery;
  For, were there hope to conquer them again,
  My sword should shed hot blood, mine eyes no
      tears.
  Anjou and Maine? Myself did win them both!   125
  Those provinces these arms of mine did conquer.
  And are the cities that I got with wounds
  Delivered up again with peaceful words?
  Mort Dieu!
YORK
  For Suffolk's duke, may he be suffocate   130
  That dims the honor of this warlike isle!
  France should have torn and rent my very heart
  Before I would have yielded to this league.
  I never read but England's kings have had
  Large sums of gold and dowries with their wives;   135
  And our King Henry gives away his own
  To match with her that brings no vantages.
GLOUCESTER
  A proper jest, and never heard before,
  That Suffolk should demand a whole fifteenth
  For costs and charges in transporting her!   140

141. **starved:** died

149. **out:** i.e., come **out**

151. **ancient bickerings:** long-standing wrangling or altercations (Such altercations are shown in *Henry VI, Part 1*, 1.3, 3.1.)

152. **Lordings:** lords, sirs (possibly contemptuous)

158. **next of blood:** i.e., as the only surviving brother of Henry V, the nearest blood relation to the king

159. **heir apparent:** actually, *heir presumptive*, who would become monarch only if Henry VI died without issue

163. **Look to it:** beware; **smoothing:** plausible

164. **wise and circumspect:** See Ephesians 5.15: "Take heed therefore that ye walk circumspectly, not as fools, but as **wise**."

169. **maintain:** keep vigorous

171. **fear me:** i.e., **fear; for:** in spite of; **gloss:** deceptive appearance

172. **found:** discovered on inspection to be

16

She should have stayed in France and starved in
   France
Before—

CARDINAL
My lord of Gloucester, now you grow too hot.
It was the pleasure of my lord the King.　　　　145

GLOUCESTER
My lord of Winchester, I know your mind.
'Tis not my speeches that you do mislike,
But 'tis my presence that doth trouble you.
Rancor will out. Proud prelate, in thy face
I see thy fury. If I longer stay,　　　　150
We shall begin our ancient bickerings.—
Lordings, farewell; and say, when I am gone,
I prophesied France will be lost ere long.
                      Gloucester exits.

CARDINAL
So, there goes our Protector in a rage.
'Tis known to you he is mine enemy,　　　　155
Nay, more, an enemy unto you all,
And no great friend, I fear me, to the King.
Consider, lords, he is the next of blood
And heir apparent to the English crown.
Had Henry got an empire by his marriage,　　　　160
And all the wealthy kingdoms of the West,
There's reason he should be displeased at it.
Look to it, lords. Let not his smoothing words
Bewitch your hearts; be wise and circumspect.
What though the common people favor him,　　　　165
Calling him "Humphrey, the good Duke of
   Gloucester,"
Clapping their hands and crying with loud voice
"Jesu maintain your royal Excellence!"
With "God preserve the good Duke Humphrey!"　　　　170
I fear me, lords, for all this flattering gloss,
He will be found a dangerous Protector.

174. **He:** Henry VI; **of himself:** i.e., by **himself**
177. **hoise:** remove; **seat:** office (i.e., as Protector)
178. **brook:** endure, tolerate
179. **presently:** immediately, instantly
181. **greatness:** eminence; **place:** position; **grief:** trouble
183. **insolence:** arrogance
184. **Than all:** i.e., **than** that of **all**
185. **displaced:** removed from office
186. **Or thou:** i.e., either you
188. **before:** ahead (**Pride** refers to the Cardinal, **Ambition** to Somerset and Buckingham.)
189. **preferment:** advancement
191. **never saw but:** i.e., always **saw** that
192. **bear him:** conduct himself
195. **stout:** fierce; **as:** i.e., **as** if
196. **demean:** conduct
199. **plainness:** honesty, directness of language; **housekeeping:** hospitality
201. **Excepting none but:** i.e., except for
202. **brother:** i.e., brother-in-law

Henry VI.
From John Speed, *The theatre of the empire of Great Britaine . . .* (1627 [i.e., 1631]).

BUCKINGHAM
  Why should he, then, protect our sovereign,
  He being of age to govern of himself?—
  Cousin of Somerset, join you with me,   175
  And all together, with the Duke of Suffolk,
  We'll quickly hoise Duke Humphrey from his seat.

CARDINAL
  This weighty business will not brook delay.
  I'll to the Duke of Suffolk presently.   *Cardinal exits.*

SOMERSET
  Cousin of Buckingham, though Humphrey's pride   180
  And greatness of his place be grief to us,
  Yet let us watch the haughty cardinal.
  His insolence is more intolerable
  Than all the princes' in the land besides.
  If Gloucester be displaced, he'll be Protector.   185

BUCKINGHAM
  Or thou or I, Somerset, will be ⌈Protector,⌉
  Despite Duke Humphrey or the Cardinal.
                     Buckingham and Somerset exit.

SALISBURY
  Pride went before; Ambition follows him.
  While these do labor for their own preferment,
  Behooves it us to labor for the realm.   190
  I never saw but Humphrey, Duke of Gloucester,
  Did bear him like a noble gentleman.
  Oft have I seen the haughty cardinal,
  More like a soldier than a man o' th' Church,
  As stout and proud as he were lord of all,   195
  Swear like a ruffian and demean himself
  Unlike the ruler of a commonweal.—
  Warwick, my son, the comfort of my age,
  Thy deeds, thy plainness, and thy housekeeping
  Hath won the greatest favor of the Commons,   200
  Excepting none but good Duke Humphrey.—
  And, brother York, thy acts in Ireland,

203. **civil discipline:** civilized orderliness
204. **late:** recent
206. **honored of:** i.e., **honored** by
211. **cherish:** hold dear, make much of
212. **tend:** foster
214. **common profit:** i.e., general or public good
216. **cause:** reason
217. **the main:** the chief matter in hand, the most important eventuality (called, at the time, "the **main chance**") See line 221, below.
225. **Stands on a tickle point:** is in a precarious position
226. **concluded on:** determined (In *Henry VI, Part 1*, the king gave Suffolk the authority freely to "agree to any covenants" [5.5.88].) **articles:** treaty
227. **peers:** nobles
228. **change:** exchange; **fair:** beautiful
231–32. **make ... pillage:** i.e., sell their plunder for pennies

Henry V.
From John Taylor, *All the workes of . . .* (1630).

In bringing them to civil discipline,
Thy late exploits done in the heart of France,
When thou wert regent for our sovereign,   205
Have made thee feared and honored of the people.
Join we together for the public good
In what we can to bridle and suppress
The pride of Suffolk and the Cardinal,
With Somerset's and Buckingham's ambition;   210
And, as we may, cherish Duke Humphrey's deeds
While they do tend the profit of the land.

WARWICK
So God help Warwick, as he loves the land
And common profit of his country!

YORK
And so says York—⌐*aside*⌐ for he hath greatest   215
  cause.

SALISBURY
Then let's make haste away and look unto the main.

WARWICK
Unto the main? O father, Maine is lost!
That Maine which by main force Warwick did win
And would have kept so long as breath did last!   220
Main chance, father, you meant; but I meant Maine,
Which I will win from France or else be slain.
                              Warwick and Salisbury exit.
                              York remains.

YORK
Anjou and Maine are given to the French;
Paris is lost; the state of Normandy
Stands on a tickle point now they are gone.   225
Suffolk concluded on the articles,
The peers agreed, and Henry was well pleased
To change two dukedoms for a duke's fair daughter.
I cannot blame them all. What is 't to them?
'Tis thine they give away, and not their own.   230
Pirates may make cheap pennyworths of their
  pillage,

234. **Still:** continually; **reveling:** making merry

235. **Whileas:** while; **silly:** helpless, pitiable

236. **wrings . . . hands:** i.e., he, being **hapless** (unlucky, unfortunate), **wrings his hands**

237. **stands aloof:** holds back, keeps clear

239. **Ready to starve:** likely to die

240. **bite his tongue:** keep silent (proverbial)

242. **Methinks:** it seems to me

244. **proportion:** relation

245–46. **As . . . Calydon:** See longer note, page 253.

248. **Cold:** gloomy, dispiriting; **hope of:** i.e., **hope of** ruling

251. **take the Nevilles' parts:** support Warwick and his father, Salisbury

253. **advantage:** an occasion or opportunity

254. **mark . . . hit:** i.e., target I am aiming at (a metaphor from archery)

255. **Lancaster:** Henry VI; **right:** i.e., **right** to the throne

256. **childish:** perhaps, immature, puerile (However, because Henry became king while yet an infant, York may mean this word literally.)

258. **churchlike:** i.e., churchman's, priest's; **humors:** disposition; **fits not:** i.e., are not appropriate

259. **be still:** i.e., take no action for; **time do serve:** an occasion presents itself

260. **wake:** be on guard

261. **state:** government

262. **Till:** while; **surfeiting:** indulging to excess

263. **dear-bought:** expensively purchased

265. **be fall'n at jars:** quarrels

(continued)

And purchase friends, and give to courtesans,
Still reveling like lords till all be gone;
Whileas the silly owner of the goods   235
Weeps over them, and wrings his hapless hands,
And shakes his head, and trembling stands aloof,
While all is shared and all is borne away,
Ready to starve, and dare not touch his own.
So York must sit and fret and bite his tongue 240
While his own lands are bargained for and sold.
Methinks the realms of England, France, and
 Ireland
Bear that proportion to my flesh and blood
As did the fatal brand Althaea burnt   245
Unto the Prince's heart of Calydon.
Anjou and Maine both given unto the French!
Cold news for me, for I had hope of France,
Even as I have of fertile England's soil.
A day will come when York shall claim his own; 250
And therefore I will take the Nevilles' parts
And make a show of love to proud Duke Humphrey,
And, when I spy advantage, claim the crown,
For that's the golden mark I seek to hit.
Nor shall proud Lancaster usurp my right, 255
Nor hold the scepter in his childish fist,
Nor wear the diadem upon his head,
Whose churchlike humors fits not for a crown.
Then, York, be still awhile till time do serve.
Watch thou and wake, when others be asleep, 260
To pry into the secrets of the state
Till Henry, surfeiting in joys of love
With his new bride and England's dear-bought
 queen,
And Humphrey with the peers be fall'n at jars. 265
Then will I raise aloft the milk-white rose,
With whose sweet smell the air shall be perfumed,
And in my standard bear the arms of York,
To grapple with the house of Lancaster;

266. **milk-white rose:** badge of the House of York (For *Henry VI, Part 1*'s fictional account of how the **milk-white rose** became the badge of the House of York, see its 2.4.)

268. **standard:** military flag, a rallying point in battle; **arms of York:** i.e., the **York** coat-of-arms

269. **grapple:** struggle; battle or encounter hand-to-hand (suggesting wordplay on **arms** [line 268] as limbs)

270. **force perforce:** by violent means

271. **bookish rule:** i.e., **rule** or government based in reading or theory

1.2 The Duchess of Gloucester's dream of becoming queen is rebuked by her husband but encouraged by the treacherous priest John Hume.

———————————

1. **corn:** grain (See picture, page 30.)

2. **Ceres':** In mythology, Ceres was the goddess of grain. (See picture, page 94.)

4. **As:** i.e., **as** if

5. **sullen:** dull, gloomy

8. **Enchased:** adorned

11. **reach:** grasp, clutch

12. **is 't:** i.e., **is** it (referring to the reach of Gloucester's **hand** [line 11])

13. **heaved:** lifted (without any sense of great exertion)

15. **abase:** cast down

16. **vouchsafe:** bestow in a condescending manner; **unto:** i.e., to

(continued)

And force perforce I'll make him yield the crown,   270
Whose bookish rule hath pulled fair England down.
                              York exits.

⌜Scene 2⌝

Enter Duke Humphrey ⌜of Gloucester⌝ and his wife
        ⌜*the Duchess*⌝ *Eleanor.*

DUCHESS
  Why droops my lord like over-ripened corn
  Hanging the head at Ceres' plenteous load?
  Why doth the great Duke Humphrey knit his brows,
  As frowning at the favors of the world?
  Why are thine eyes fixed to the sullen earth,   5
  Gazing on that which seems to dim thy sight?
  What seest thou there? King Henry's diadem,
  Enchased with all the honors of the world?
  If so, gaze on and grovel on thy face
  Until thy head be circled with the same.   10
  Put forth thy hand; reach at the glorious gold.
  What, is 't too short? I'll lengthen it with mine;
  And, having both together heaved it up,
  We'll both together lift our heads to heaven
  And never more abase our sight so low   15
  As to vouchsafe one glance unto the ground.
GLOUCESTER
  O Nell, sweet Nell, if thou dost love thy lord,
  Banish the canker of ambitious thoughts!
  And may that ⌜hour⌝ when I imagine ill
  Against my king and nephew, virtuous Henry,   20
  Be my last breathing in this mortal world!
  My troublous dreams this night doth make me sad.
DUCHESS
  What dreamed my lord? Tell me, and I'll requite it
  With sweet rehearsal of my morning's dream.

17. **Nell:** diminutive form of Eleanor
18. **canker:** ulcer, spreading sore
19. **imagine ill:** devise harm
22. **troublous:** troublesome; **this night:** last night
24. **rehearsal:** recounting; **morning's dream:** Such dreams were reputed to be true.
25. **Methought:** it seemed to me; **staff:** rod borne as the Protector's **badge** of **office**
26. **broke:** i.e., broken
28. **wand:** i.e., **staff**
32. **bode:** portend, presage
33. **argument:** manifestation
36. **list:** listen
37. **seat of majesty:** the royal throne
39. **chair:** throne
43. **chide:** scold
44. **dame:** lady; **ill-nurtured:** badly trained or educated
48. **compass:** scope
49. **hammering:** devising, contriving
53. **choleric:** enraged
56. **checked:** reproached, reprimanded

GLOUCESTER

   Methought this staff, mine office badge in court,   25

   Was broke in twain—by whom I have forgot,

   But, as I think, it was by th' Cardinal—

   And on the pieces of the broken wand

   Were placed the heads of Edmund, Duke of

      Somerset,   30

   And William de la Pole, first Duke of Suffolk.

   This was my dream. What it doth bode God knows.

DUCHESS

   Tut, this was nothing but an argument

   That he that breaks a stick of Gloucester's grove

   Shall lose his head for his presumption.   35

   But list to me, my Humphrey, my sweet duke:

   Methought I sat in seat of majesty,

   In the cathedral church of Westminster

   And in that chair where kings and queens were

      crowned,   40

   Where Henry and Dame Margaret kneeled to me

   And on my head did set the diadem.

GLOUCESTER

   Nay, Eleanor, then must I chide outright.

   Presumptuous dame, ill-nurtured Eleanor,

   Art thou not second woman in the realm   45

   And the Protector's wife, beloved of him?

   Hast thou not worldly pleasure at command,

   Above the reach or compass of thy thought?

   And wilt thou still be hammering treachery

   To tumble down thy husband and thyself   50

   From top of honor to disgrace's feet?

   Away from me, and let me hear no more!

DUCHESS

   What, what, my lord? Are you so choleric

   With Eleanor for telling but her dream?

   Next time I'll keep my dreams unto myself   55

   And not be checked.

57. **pleased:** in good humor

59. **Saint Albans:** town in Hertfordshire, twenty miles north of London (See picture, page 68.)

60. **Whereas:** where; **hawk:** hunt game with trained hawks or falcons (See picture, page 78.)

62. **presently:** immediately

63. **Follow:** wordplay on such meanings as "act as an attendant or servant" and "go behind"; **go before:** take precedence (i.e., over the queen) Proverbial: "They that cannot **go before** must come behind."

65. **next of blood:** See note to 1.1.158.

66. **tedious:** annoying; **stumbling blocks:** obstacles (with implied wordplay on **blocks** as *blockheads* or *heads* in line 67)

69. **Fortune's:** The goddess Fortuna or Fortune was thought to control individuals' rise to and fall from power in the world. (See picture, page 38.)

70. **Sir:** conventional title for a priest

73. **Grace:** "Your **Grace**" was the courtesy title of a duchess.

75. **Your . . . multiplied:** See 1 Peter 1.2: "**Grace** and peace **be multiplied** unto you." **multiplied:** i.e., made greater

77. **cunning witch:** See longer note, page 254.

78. **conjurer:** sorcerer

79. **undertake:** pledge; **do me good:** be beneficial to me

GLOUCESTER
  Nay, be not angry. I am pleased again.

                    Enter Messenger.

MESSENGER
  My Lord Protector, 'tis his Highness' pleasure
  You do prepare to ride unto Saint Albans,
  Whereas the King and Queen do mean to hawk.   60
GLOUCESTER
  I go.—Come, Nell, thou wilt ride with us?
DUCHESS
  Yes, my good lord. I'll follow presently.
                    Gloucester exits, ⌈with Messenger.⌉
  Follow I must; I cannot go before
  While Gloucester bears this base and humble mind.
  Were I a man, a duke, and next of blood,   65
  I would remove these tedious stumbling blocks
  And smooth my way upon their headless necks;
  And, being a woman, I will not be slack
  To play my part in Fortune's pageant.—
  Where are you there? Sir John! Nay, fear not, man.   70
  We are alone; here's none but thee and I.

                    Enter ⌈Sir John⌉ Hume.

HUME
  Jesus preserve your royal Majesty!
DUCHESS
  What sayst thou? "Majesty"? I am but "Grace."
HUME
  But by the grace of God and Hume's advice,
  Your Grace's title shall be multiplied.   75
DUCHESS
  What sayst thou, man? Hast thou as yet conferred
  With Margery Jourdain, the cunning witch,
  With Roger Bolingbroke, the conjurer?
  And will they undertake to do me good?

81. **underground:** the underworld

83. **propounded him:** offered to him for consideration

91. **Marry:** i.e., indeed (originally an oath on the name of the Virgin Mary) Proverbial: "**Marry, and shall.**" **how now:** i.e., **how** is it **now**

92. **mum:** a command to be silent (Proverbial: "**No** word **but mum.**")

93. **asketh:** requires

96. **flies:** that **flies; coast:** direction

100. **aspiring humor:** ambitious disposition

102. **buzz:** privately communicate; **conjurations:** spells, charms, incantations; **in:** i.e., into

103. **a crafty ... broker:** proverbial **crafty:** underhanded, scheming **knave:** unprincipled, devious man **broker:** agent, middleman

105–6. **go ... call:** be on the point of calling

107. **at last:** ultimately

108. **wrack:** wreck, destruction

109. **her attainture:** the stain of her dishonor; **fall:** i.e., **fall** from power

110. **Sort how it will:** i.e., however it turns out

"Over-ripened corn." (1.2.1)
From Geoffrey Whitney, *A choice of emblemes . . .* (1586).

HUME
  This they have promisèd: to show your Highness   80
  A spirit raised from depth of underground
  That shall make answer to such questions
  As by your Grace shall be propounded him.
DUCHESS
  It is enough. I'll think upon the questions.
  When from Saint Albans we do make return,   85
  We'll see these things effected to the full.
  Here, Hume, take this reward.
                            ⌜*She gives him money.*⌝
                          Make merry, man,
  With thy confederates in this weighty cause.
                                  Duchess exits.
HUME
  Hume must make merry with the Duchess' gold.   90
  Marry, and shall! But, how now, Sir John Hume?
  Seal up your lips, and give no words but "mum";
  The business asketh silent secrecy.
  Dame Eleanor gives gold to bring the witch;
  Gold cannot come amiss, were she a devil.   95
  Yet have I gold flies from another coast—
  I dare not say, from the rich cardinal
  And from the great and new-made Duke of Suffolk,
  Yet I do find it so. For, to be plain,
  They, knowing Dame Eleanor's aspiring humor,   100
  Have hirèd me to undermine the Duchess
  And buzz these conjurations in her brain.
  They say a crafty knave does need no broker,
  Yet am I Suffolk and the Cardinal's broker.
  Hume, if you take not heed, you shall go near   105
  To call them both a pair of crafty knaves.
  Well, so it stands; and thus I fear at last
  Hume's knavery will be the Duchess' wrack,
  And her attainture will be Humphrey's fall.
  Sort how it will, I shall have gold for all.   110
                                  He exits.

1.3   Queen Margaret and Suffolk dismiss petitioners seeking Gloucester's aid and then conspire against Gloucester. Somerset and York then clash, as do Gloucester and Suffolk. The accusation that York's armorer has declared York the rightful king puts York under suspicion of treason.

———————

0 SD. **man:** servant

1. **My masters:** sirs, gentlemen; **close:** i.e., **close** together; or, perhaps, quiet and unobserved

2. **by and by:** immediately; soon

3. **supplications:** formal petitions; **in the quill:** in a body, in concert

5 SD. **red rose:** badge of the house of Lancaster, to which Henry VI belongs (For the fictional account of how the **red rose** became the badge of the House of Lancaster, see *Henry VI, Part 1*, 2.4; for Henry VI's personal adoption of the **red rose,** see *Henry VI, Part 1*, 4.1.)

6. **methinks:** it seems to me

7. **sure:** i.e., surely

10. **fellow:** term of address to a lower-class person

17. **an 't please your Grace:** a formula of politeness

18. **man:** follower

23. **enclosing:** fencing in as private property

24. **commons:** undivided land belonging to the community as a whole; **Melford:** Long **Melford** in Suffolk

25–26. **petitioner of:** i.e., **petitioner** on behalf **of**

⌜Scene 3⌝

*Enter three or four Petitioners, ⌜Peter,⌝ the
Armorer's man, being one.*

FIRST PETITIONER My masters, let's stand close. My
Lord Protector will come this way by and by, and
then we may deliver our supplications in the quill.

SECOND PETITIONER Marry, the Lord protect him, for
he's a good man! Jesu bless him!   5

*Enter Suffolk, ⌜wearing the red rose,⌝
and Queen ⌜Margaret.⌝*

⌜FIRST PETITIONER⌝ Here he comes, methinks, and the
Queen with him. I'll be the first, sure.
                                                      ⌜He steps forward.⌝

SECOND PETITIONER Come back, fool! This is the Duke
of Suffolk, and not my Lord Protector.

SUFFOLK How now, fellow? Wouldst anything with   10
me?

FIRST PETITIONER I pray, my lord, pardon me. I took
you for my Lord Protector.

QUEEN MARGARET ⌜*takes a petition and reads.*⌝ *To my
Lord Protector.* Are your supplications to his lord-   15
ship? Let me see them.—What is thine?

FIRST PETITIONER Mine is, an 't please your Grace,
against John Goodman, my Lord Cardinal's man,
for keeping my house, and lands, and wife and all,
from me.   20

SUFFOLK Thy wife too? That's some wrong indeed.—
What's yours? ⌜*Taking a petition.*⌝ What's here?
⌜*(Reads.)*⌝ *Against the Duke of Suffolk for enclosing
the commons of Melford.* How now, sir knave?

SECOND PETITIONER Alas, sir, I am but a poor petitioner   25
of our whole township.

PETER, ⌜*showing his petition*⌝ Against my master,

32. **forsooth:** truly
33. **he:** i.e., **the Duke of York** (lines 30–31)
36. **Take . . . in:** i.e., arrest **this fellow**
36–37. **send . . . pursuivant:** i.e., have **his master** sent **for** by an officer
37. **presently:** immediately
38. **matter:** business, affair; **before:** in the presence of
40. **grace:** favor
41. **suits:** petitions; **sue to:** petition
42. **base:** menial, unworthy; **cullions:** rascals (literally, testicles)
44. **guise:** style
45. **Is this:** i.e., are these
47. **Albion's:** England's
48. **still:** always
49. **governance:** control, mastery
50. **style:** ceremonial designation
52. **Pole:** i.e., de la **Pole,** Suffolk's family name
53. **rann'st atilt:** engaged in mounted combat with lances
55. **had:** i.e., would have
56. **courtship:** courtliness of manners; **proportion:** figure, shape

Thomas Horner, for saying that the Duke of York
was rightful heir to the crown.

QUEEN MARGARET What sayst thou? Did the Duke of   30
York say he was rightful heir to the crown?

PETER That my ⌜master⌝ was? No, forsooth. My master said that he was and that the King was an
usurper.

SUFFOLK, ⌜*calling*⌝ Who is there?   35

Enter Servant.

Take this fellow in, and send for his master with a
pursuivant presently.—We'll hear more of your
matter before the King.
                              ⌜*Peter*⌝ *exits* ⌜*with Servant.*⌝

QUEEN MARGARET
And as for you that love to be protected
Under the wings of our Protector's grace,   40
Begin your suits anew, and sue to him.
                              Tear the supplication.
Away, base cullions.—Suffolk, let them go.

ALL Come, let's be gone.   ⌜*They*⌝ *exit.*

QUEEN MARGARET
My lord of Suffolk, say, is this the guise,
Is this the fashions in the court of England?   45
Is this the government of Britain's isle
And this the royalty of Albion's king?
What, shall King Henry be a pupil still
Under the surly Gloucester's governance?
Am I a queen in title and in style,   50
And must be made a subject to a duke?
I tell thee, Pole, when in the city Tours
Thou rann'st atilt in honor of my love
And stol'st away the ladies' hearts of France,
I thought King Henry had resembled thee   55
In courage, courtship, and proportion.
But all his mind is bent to holiness,

58. **Ave Marys:** Hail Marys (prayers to the Virgin Mary); **beads:** rosary (See picture, page 40.)

59. **champions:** men of valor

60. **saws:** sayings, proverbs; **sacred writ:** the Bible

61. **tiltyard:** enclosed space for combat

62. **brazen images:** brass statues; **canonized:** accent on second syllable

63. **I would:** i.e., I wish

65. **triple crown:** papal tiara

66. **state:** high position, office; **his holiness:** (1) **his** piety; (2) **his Holiness,** the pope's title

67. **patient:** calm

69. **work:** effect, bring about; **full:** complete; **content:** pleasure, satisfaction

70. **Beaufort:** i.e., the Cardinal

71. **imperious:** overbearing, domineering

74. **he . . . all:** i.e., the most powerful of those you named

76. **simple:** ordinary; **peers:** nobles

78. **dame:** lady

79. **sweeps it:** moves majestically

82. **Strangers:** foreigners; **take her for:** i.e., assume she is

83. **She . . . back:** proverbial for wearing very expensive clothes: "He wears a whole lordship **on** his **back.**" **revenues:** accent on second syllable

86. **Contemptuous:** perhaps, disdainful; or, perhaps, contemptible; **callet:** strumpet

87. **vaunted:** boasted; **minions:** favorites

88. **very train:** i.e., **train** alone; **her . . . gown:** i.e., the **worst gown** she wears

To number Ave Marys on his beads;
His champions are the prophets and apostles,
His weapons holy saws of sacred writ,   60
His study is his tiltyard, and his loves
Are brazen images of canonized saints.
I would the College of the Cardinals
Would choose him pope and carry him to Rome
And set the triple crown upon his head!   65
That were a state fit for his holiness.

SUFFOLK
Madam, be patient. As I was cause
Your Highness came to England, so will I
In England work your Grace's full content.

QUEEN MARGARET
Besides the haughty Protector, have we Beaufort   70
The imperious churchman, Somerset, Buckingham,
And grumbling York; and not the least of these
But can do more in England than the King.

SUFFOLK
And he of these that can do most of all
Cannot do more in England than the Nevilles;   75
Salisbury and Warwick are no simple peers.

QUEEN MARGARET
Not all these lords do vex me half so much
As that proud dame, the Lord Protector's wife.
She sweeps it through the court with troops of
    ladies,   80
More like an empress than Duke Humphrey's wife.
Strangers in court do take her for the Queen.
She bears a duke's revenues on her back,
And in her heart she scorns our poverty.
Shall I not live to be avenged on her?   85
Contemptuous baseborn callet as she is,
She vaunted 'mongst her minions t' other day
The very train of her worst wearing gown

89. **better worth:** of greater **worth**

90. **gave:** i.e., **gave** Reignier, the queen's father

91. **limed a bush:** i.e., smeared **a bush** with birdlime, to which birds' feet stick

93. **light:** descend and settle; **lays:** songs

95. **let her rest:** i.e., think no more about her

96. **am bold:** i.e., will presume

97. **fancy not:** do not like

99. **in disgrace:** i.e., into **disgrace**

100. **late:** recent

101. **make . . . benefit:** i.e., do little to further his good

103. **happy:** fortunate

103 SD. **Sennet:** trumpet fanfare to signal a ceremonial entrance or exit

105. **Or:** either; **all's one:** i.e., it's all the same

106. **ill . . . himself:** conducted **himself** badly

107. **regentship:** rule (i.e., of France)

108. **place:** position, office

"Fortune's pageant" (1.2.69)
From Giovanni Boccaccio, *A treatise . . . shewing . . .
the falles of . . . princes . . .* (1554).

Was better worth than all my father's lands
Till Suffolk gave two dukedoms for his daughter.   90

SUFFOLK
  Madam, myself have limed a bush for her
  And placed a choir of such enticing birds
  That she will light to listen to the lays
  And never mount to trouble you again.
  So let her rest. And, madam, list to me,   95
  For I am bold to counsel you in this:
  Although we fancy not the Cardinal,
  Yet must we join with him and with the lords
  Till we have brought Duke Humphrey in disgrace.
  As for the Duke of York, this late complaint   100
  Will make but little for his benefit.
  So, one by one, we'll weed them all at last,
  And you yourself shall steer the happy helm.

Sound a sennet. Enter King ⌈Henry,⌉ Duke Humphrey
⌈of Gloucester,⌉ Cardinal, ⌈Somerset, wearing the red
rose,⌉ Buckingham, Salisbury; York and Warwick, ⌈both
wearing the white rose;⌉ and the Duchess ⌈of
Gloucester.⌉

KING HENRY
  For my part, noble lords, I care not which;
  Or Somerset or York, all's one to me.   105

YORK
  If York have ill demeaned himself in France,
  Then let him be denied the regentship.

SOMERSET
  If Somerset be unworthy of the place,
  Let York be regent; I will yield to him.

WARWICK
  Whether your Grace be worthy, yea or no,   110
  Dispute not that. York is the worthier.

CARDINAL
  Ambitious Warwick, let thy betters speak.

113. **field:** battlefield

114. **in this presence:** i.e., here attending on the king; or, perhaps, **in this** presence-chamber, the room in which the king receives guests

116. **Peace:** quiet

117. **preferred:** advanced; or, more favored

120. **censure:** opinion

125. **leave:** lay aside; **insolence:** arrogance

127. **wrack:** wreck, ruin

128. **Dauphin:** heir to the French throne (accent on first syllable)

130. **bondmen:** slaves

131. **racked:** oppressed (i.e., with excessive taxes); **bags:** i.e., money **bags**

132. **lank and lean:** loose from emptiness

135. **execution:** infliction of punishment (including capital punishment) specified by judicial sentence

A rosary. (1.1.30; 1.3.58)
From Cesare Vecellio, *Habiti antichi et moderni* . . . [1598].

WARWICK
  The Cardinal's not my better in the field.

BUCKINGHAM
  All in this presence are thy betters, Warwick.

WARWICK
  Warwick may live to be the best of all.   115

SALISBURY
  Peace, son.—And show some reason, Buckingham,
  Why Somerset should be preferred in this.

QUEEN MARGARET
  Because the King, forsooth, will have it so.

GLOUCESTER
  Madam, the King is old enough himself
  To give his censure. These are no women's matters.   120

QUEEN MARGARET
  If he be old enough, what needs your Grace
  To be Protector of his Excellence?

GLOUCESTER
  Madam, I am Protector of the realm,
  And at his pleasure will resign my place.

SUFFOLK
  Resign it, then, and leave thine insolence.   125
  Since thou wert king—as who is king but thou?—
  The commonwealth hath daily run to wrack,
  The Dauphin hath prevailed beyond the seas,
  And all the peers and nobles of the realm
  Have been as bondmen to thy sovereignty.   130

CARDINAL, ⌈*to Gloucester*⌉
  The Commons hast thou racked; the clergy's bags
  Are lank and lean with thy extortions.

SOMERSET, ⌈*to Gloucester*⌉
  Thy sumptuous buildings and thy wife's attire
  Have cost a mass of public treasury.

BUCKINGHAM, ⌈*to Gloucester*⌉
  Thy cruelty in execution   135
  Upon offenders hath exceeded law
  And left thee to the mercy of the law.

139. **suspect:** suspicion

140. **hop . . . head:** i.e., be beheaded (proverbial)

141. **minion:** a term of contempt like "creature"

143. **cry you mercy:** beg your pardon

146. **set . . . face:** proverbial **commandments:** i.e., fingernails

147. **against her will:** unintentional

148. **Look to 't:** beware; **in time:** i.e., before it is too late

149. **hamper:** entangle, bind; **dandle:** toy with

150. **most . . . breeches:** proverbial, meaning "the one who is in control (the greatest **master**) is a woman"

153. **listen after:** endeavor to hear; **how he proceeds:** i.e., what he goes on to say

154. **tickled:** provoked; **fume:** angry mood

156. **choler:** anger; **overblown:** blown over or away

157. **about:** around

158. **affairs:** matters, business

159. **objections:** charges, accusations

QUEEN MARGARET, ⌈*to Gloucester*⌉
    Thy sale of offices and towns in France,
    If they were known, as the suspect is great,
    Would make thee quickly hop without thy head.   140
                         Gloucester exits.
                ⌈*Queen Margaret drops her fan.*⌉
    ⌈*To Duchess.*⌉ Give me my fan. What, minion, can
      you not?   *She gives the Duchess a box on the ear.*
    I cry you mercy, madam. Was it you?

DUCHESS
    Was 't I? Yea, I it was, proud Frenchwoman.
    Could I come near your beauty with my nails,   145
    ⌈I'd⌉ set my ten commandments in your face.

KING HENRY
    Sweet aunt, be quiet. 'Twas against her will.

DUCHESS
    Against her will, good king? Look to 't in time.
    She'll hamper thee and dandle thee like a baby.
    Though in this place most master wear no breeches,   150
    She shall not strike Dame Eleanor unrevenged.
                  Eleanor, ⌈*the Duchess,*⌉ *exits.*

BUCKINGHAM, ⌈*aside to Cardinal*⌉
    Lord Cardinal, I will follow Eleanor
    And listen after Humphrey how he proceeds.
    She's tickled now; her fume needs no spurs;
    She'll gallop far enough to her destruction.   155
                        Buckingham exits.

    Enter Humphrey, ⌈*Duke of Gloucester.*⌉

GLOUCESTER
    Now, lords, my choler being overblown
    With walking once about the quadrangle,
    I come to talk of commonwealth affairs.
    As for your spiteful false objections,
    Prove them, and I lie open to the law;   160
    But God in mercy so deal with my soul

162. **duty:** homage, reverence
164. **meetest:** most appropriate
166. **election:** choice; **leave:** permission
168. **unmeet:** inappropriate
170. **for:** because; **in pride:** i.e., without losing my self-respect
171. **place:** position, office
172. **keep me:** hold me back
173. **discharge:** payment; **furniture:** armor
175. **Last time:** perhaps alluding to *Henry VI, Part 1*, 4.3 (but see longer note, page 254); **danced . . . will:** i.e., was forced to wait for him to act
177. **fact:** crime, deed
182. **excuse himself:** i.e., can clear **himself** of blame
183. **for:** i.e., as
184. **what are:** i.e., who are

An armorer at work. (2.3.52)
From Hartmann Schopper, *PANOPLIA omnium illiberalium mechanicarum aut sedentariarum* (1568).

As I in duty love my king and country!
But, to the matter that we have in hand:
I say, my sovereign, York is meetest man
To be your regent in the realm of France.   165

SUFFOLK
Before we make election, give me leave
To show some reason, of no little force,
That York is most unmeet of any man.

YORK
I'll tell thee, Suffolk, why I am unmeet:
First, for I cannot flatter thee in pride;   170
Next, if I be appointed for the place,
My lord of Somerset will keep me here
Without discharge, money, or furniture
Till France be won into the Dauphin's hands.
Last time I danced attendance on his will   175
Till Paris was besieged, famished, and lost.

WARWICK
That can I witness, and a fouler fact
Did never traitor in the land commit.

SUFFOLK   Peace, headstrong Warwick!

WARWICK
Image of pride, why should I hold my peace?   180

Enter ⌜Horner, the⌝ Armorer, and his Man
⌜Peter, under guard.⌝

SUFFOLK
Because here is a man accused of treason.
Pray God the Duke of York excuse himself!

YORK
Doth anyone accuse York for a traitor?

KING HENRY
What mean'st thou, Suffolk? Tell me, what are
    these?   185

186. **Please ... Majesty:** a formula of politeness; **this:** referring to Peter

188. **His:** i.e., his master Horner's

192. **An 't ... Majesty:** a formula of politeness

195. **ten bones:** i.e., fingers

196. **garret:** watchtower

198. **Base:** unworthy; **dunghill:** fit for a heap of dung; **villain:** scoundrel; **mechanical:** manual laborer

203. **prentice:** apprentice

204. **correct:** chastise; **his fault:** i.e., a mistake he made

205. **be even:** get **even**

206. **good witness of:** i.e., reliable witness(es) to

207. **cast away:** ruin; **for:** because of

210. **doom:** decree

212. **this breeds:** i.e., **this** accusation of treason **breeds**

215. **he:** i.e., Horner

Men in doublet and hose. (2.1.164; 4.7.51)
From [Robert Greene,] *A quip for an vpstart courtier* . . . (1620).

SUFFOLK
  Please it your Majesty, this is the man
  That doth accuse his master of high treason.
  His words were these: that Richard, Duke of York,
  Was rightful heir unto the English crown,
  And that your Majesty was an usurper.   190

KING HENRY Say, man, were these thy words?

HORNER An 't shall please your Majesty, I never said
    nor thought any such matter. God is my witness, I
    am falsely accused by the villain.

PETER By these ten bones, my lords, he did speak 195
    them to me in the garret one night as we were
    scouring my lord of York's armor.

YORK, ⌜*to Horner*⌝
  Base dunghill villain and mechanical,
  I'll have thy head for this thy traitor's speech!—
  I do beseech your royal Majesty,   200
  Let him have all the rigor of the law.

HORNER Alas, my lord, hang me if ever I spake the
    words. My accuser is my prentice; and when I did
    correct him for his fault the other day, he did vow
    upon his knees he would be even with me. I have 205
    good witness of this. Therefore I beseech your
    Majesty, do not cast away an honest man for a
    villain's accusation!

KING HENRY
  Uncle, what shall we say to this in law?

GLOUCESTER
  This doom, my lord, if I may judge: 210
  Let Somerset be regent o'er the French,
  Because in York this breeds suspicion;
  And let these have a day appointed them
  For single combat in convenient place,
  For he hath witness of his servant's malice.   215
  This is the law, and this Duke Humphrey's doom.

223. **Sirrah:** term of address to a social inferior; **or you:** i.e., either you

226. **sent away:** i.e., embarked (to France)

1.4 The Duchess of Gloucester watches while a spirit is conjured up to prophesy the fates of her rivals, but she is caught in the act by Buckingham and York.

───────────

1. **my masters:** sirs, gentlemen

3–4. **provided:** prepared

4–5. **exorcisms:** conjurations, calling up of spirits

6. **Fear:** doubt

8–9. **convenient:** appropriate

14. **read you:** i.e., **read** from the conjuring book; **us to:** i.e., **us** get **to**

A conjuror in a circle. (1.4.24 SD)
From Christopher Marlowe, *The tragicall historie of . . . Doctor Faustus . . .* (1631).

SOMERSET
  I humbly thank your royal Majesty.
HORNER
  And I accept the combat willingly.
PETER   Alas, my lord, I cannot fight; for God's sake pity
  my case! The spite of man prevaileth against me. O   220
  Lord, have mercy upon me! I shall never be able to
  fight a blow. O Lord, my heart!
GLOUCESTER
  Sirrah, or you must fight or else be hanged.
KING HENRY   Away with them to prison; and the day of
  combat shall be the last of the next month.—   225
  Come, Somerset, we'll see thee sent away.
                         Flourish. They exit.

⌜Scene 4⌝

Enter the Witch ⌜*Margery Jourdain,*⌝ *the two Priests*
⌜*Hume and Southwell,*⌝ *and Bolingbroke,* ⌜*a conjurer.*⌝

HUME   Come, my masters. The Duchess, I tell you,
  expects performance of your promises.
BOLINGBROKE   Master Hume, we are therefore provided. Will her Ladyship behold and hear our exorcisms?   5
HUME   Ay, what else? Fear you not her courage.
BOLINGBROKE   I have heard her reported to be a
  woman of an invincible spirit. But it shall be convenient, Master Hume, that you be by her aloft
  while we be busy below; and so, I pray you, go, in   10
  God's name, and leave us.   *Hume exits.*
  Mother Jourdain, be you prostrate and grovel on
  the earth. ⌜*She lies face downward.*⌝ John Southwell, read you; and let us to our work.

15. **Well said:** i.e., **well** done
16. **gear:** business
17. **their times:** i.e., when to act
18. **silent:** time of silence
19. **Troy:** city that, in legend, was burned by the Greeks the **night** they penetrated its walls (See picture, page 54.)
20. **bandogs:** ferocious chained guard dogs
21. **break up:** burst open
23. **Whom we raise:** i.e., the spirit that we conjure up
24. **make fast:** bind; **hallowed verge:** sanctified boundary (i.e., **the circle** in 24 SD)
24 SD. **ceremonies belonging:** appropriate **ceremonies; the circle:** See picture, page 48, and see longer note, page 255. **Conjuro te:** I conjure you (Latin); **riseth:** i.e., as if from under the ground
25. **Adsum:** I am here (Latin)
26. **Asmath:** a near anagram of *Sathan* or *Satan* (Editors often spell this name "Asnath" in order to make the anagram perfect.)
28. **tremblest:** See James 2.19: "the devils also believe and tremble." **that: that** which
30. **That:** i.e., I wish **that**
32–33. **The duke . . . death:** The words constitute a riddle, since who shall **depose** whom and who shall **outlive** whom is ambiguous.

     Enter Eleanor, ⌈*Duchess of Gloucester,*
       with Hume,⌉ *aloft.*

DUCHESS　Well said, my masters, and welcome all. To　　15
    this gear, the sooner the better.
BOLINGBROKE
    Patience, good lady. Wizards know their times.
    Deep night, dark night, the silent of the night,
    The time of night when Troy was set on fire,
    The time when screech owls cry and bandogs howl,　　20
    And spirits walk, and ghosts break up their graves—
    That time best fits the work we have in hand.
    Madam, sit you, and fear not. Whom we raise
    We will make fast within a hallowed verge.

     Here ⌈*they*⌉ *do the ceremonies belonging, and*
    make the circle. Bolingbroke or Southwell reads
    "Conjuro te, etc." It thunders and lightens terribly;
       then the Spirit riseth.

SPIRIT　*Adsum.*　　　　　　　　　　　　　　　　25
JOURDAIN　Asmath,
    By the eternal God, whose name and power
    Thou tremblest at, answer that I shall ask,
    For till thou speak, thou shalt not pass from hence.
SPIRIT
    Ask what thou wilt. That I had said and done!　　30
BOLINGBROKE, ⌈*reading from a paper, while Southwell*
    writes⌉
    First of the King: What shall of him become?
SPIRIT
    The duke yet lives that Henry shall depose,
    But him outlive and die a violent death.
BOLINGBROKE, ⌈*reads*⌉
    What fates await the Duke of Suffolk?
SPIRIT
    By water shall he die and take his end.　　　　35
BOLINGBROKE ⌈*reads*⌉
    What shall befall the Duke of Somerset?

39. **castles mounted:** perhaps, towering **castles;** or, perhaps, **castles** elevated in situation

40. **Have done:** get finished

41. **burning lake:** In Revelation 20.10, Satan is flung into a **lake** of fire.

42. **False:** lying, treacherous; **avoid:** depart

43. **Lay hands upon:** seize; **trash:** worthless writing

44. **Beldam:** hag, witch

44–45. **at an inch:** close at hand

46. **What:** an interjection to introduce a question

47. **commonweal:** state

48. **piece of pains:** bit of trouble

50. **guerdoned:** rewarded; **good deserts:** meritorious actions

52. **Injurious:** insulting

54. **clapped up close:** strictly confined in prison

55. **asunder:** apart; **shall:** i.e., **shall** go

56. **take her to thee:** apprehend her

57. **trinkets:** tools, implements; **forthcoming:** made available to a court of law

Iris, goddess of the rainbow. (3.2.422)
From Natale Conti, . . . *Mythologiae* . . . (1616).

SPIRIT   Let him shun castles.
Safer shall he be upon the sandy plains
Than where castles mounted stand.
Have done, for more I hardly can endure.   40
BOLINGBROKE
Descend to darkness and the burning lake!
False fiend, avoid!
    Thunder and lightning. Spirit exits, ⌐descending.⌐

*Enter the Duke of York and the Duke of Buckingham
with their Guard ⌐and Sir Humphrey Stafford,⌐ and
break in.*

YORK
Lay hands upon these traitors and their trash.
    ⌐*The Guard arrest Margery Jourdain and her
    accomplices and seize their papers.*⌐
⌐*To Jourdain.*⌐ Beldam, I think we watched you at an
  inch.
⌐*To the Duchess, aloft.*⌐   What, madam, are you   45
  there? The King and commonweal
Are deeply indebted for this piece of pains.
My Lord Protector will, I doubt it not,
See you well guerdoned for these good deserts.   50
DUCHESS
Not half so bad as thine to England's king,
Injurious duke, that threatest where's no cause.
BUCKINGHAM
True, madam, none at all. What call you this?
    ⌐*He holds up the papers seized.*⌐
Away with them! Let them be clapped up close
And kept asunder.—You, madam, shall with us.—   55
Stafford, take her to thee.   ⌐*Stafford exits.*⌐
We'll see your trinkets here all forthcoming.
All away!   ⌐*Jourdain, Southwell, and Bolingbroke*⌐
    exit ⌐*under guard, below; Duchess and Hume
    exit, under guard, aloft.*⌐

59. **methinks:** it seems to me

60. **plot:** scheme (with wordplay on "piece of ground")

61. **devil's writ:** i.e., **devil's** writing (as opposed to *Holy Writ*)

65. **just:** exactly

65–66. **Aio . . . posse:** York quotes the ambiguous Latin oracle provided by Apollo when Pyrrhus asked if he could conquer Rome; the oracle can mean both "I proclaim that you, the descendant of Aeacus, can conquer the Romans," and "I proclaim that the Romans can conquer you, the descendant of Aeacus."

75. **hardly attained:** acquired with difficulty; **hardly understood:** scarcely **understood**

76. **in progress:** proceeding

78. **news:** regarded as a plural

80. **sorry:** painful, dismal

81. **leave:** permission

82. **post:** messenger; **his:** i.e., the king's

Burning Troy. (1.4.19)
From Thomas Heywood, *The Iron Age . . .* (1632).

YORK
　　Lord Buckingham, methinks you watched her well.
　　A pretty plot, well chosen to build upon!　　　　　　　60
　　Now, pray, my lord, let's see the devil's writ.
　　　　　　　　⌐*Buckingham hands him the papers.*⌐
　　What have we here?
　　⌐*(Reads.)*⌐ *The duke yet lives that Henry shall depose,*
　　But him outlive and die a violent death.
　　Why, this is just *Aio* ⌐*te,*⌐ *Aeacida,*　　　　　　65
　　Romanos vincere posse. Well, to the rest:
　　⌐*(Reads.)*⌐ *Tell me what fate awaits the Duke of*
　　　　Suffolk?
　　By water shall he die and take his end.
　　What shall betide the Duke of Somerset?　　　　　70
　　Let him shun castles;
　　Safer shall he be upon the sandy plains
　　Than where castles mounted stand.
　　Come, come, my ⌐lord,⌐ these oracles
　　Are hardly attained and hardly understood.　　　　75
　　The King is now in progress towards Saint Albans;
　　With him the husband of this lovely lady.
　　Thither goes these news as fast as horse can carry
　　　　them—
　　A sorry breakfast for my Lord Protector.　　　　　80
BUCKINGHAM
　　Your Grace shall give me leave, my lord of York,
　　To be the post, in hope of his reward.
YORK　At your pleasure, my good lord.
　　　　　　　　　　　　⌐*Buckingham exits.*⌐
　　Who's within there, ho!

　　　　　　　　Enter a Servingman.

　　Invite my lords of Salisbury and Warwick　　　　　85
　　To sup with me tomorrow night. Away!
　　　　　　　　　　　　　　They exit.

HENRY VI
Part 2

ACT 2

2.1   King Henry and his court are hunting when they are interrupted by an announcement of a miracle in nearby Saint Albans. Gloucester exposes the miracle as a sham. Buckingham then brings news of the Duchess's arrest.

---

0 SD. **hallowing:** shouting to urge on the dogs to drive the water fowl up into the air

1. **flying at the brook:** i.e., hawking for fowl driven from the shelter of the banks of **the brook**

2. **sport:** recreation, diversion; **these seven years' day:** in the past **seven** years

3. **by your leave:** a polite formula asking pardon for taking a liberty

4. **ten . . . gone out:** i.e, I would have bet **ten to one the old** falcon **Joan** would not have hawked (Literally, *go out* means "march as a soldier, take the battlefield.")

5. **point:** position (to attack the prey); **made:** i.e., took (See picture, page 64.)

6. **pitch:** height (See picture, page 78.)

8. **fain of climbing:** i.e., eager to climb

9. **an it like:** if it please

10. **tower:** mount up

13. **base:** poor

15. **would:** wishes to

17. **Were it not good:** i.e., would **it not** be **good** if

⌜ACT 2⌝

⌜Scene 1⌝

Enter King ⌜Henry,⌝ Queen ⌜Margaret, Gloucester the Lord⌝ Protector, Cardinal, and Suffolk, ⌜and Attendants,⌝ with Falconers hallowing.

QUEEN MARGARET
Believe me, lords, for flying at the brook
I saw not better sport these seven years' day.
Yet, by your leave, the wind was very high,
And, ten to one, old Joan had not gone out.

KING HENRY, ⌜to Gloucester⌝
But what a point, my lord, your falcon made,   5
And what a pitch she flew above the rest!
To see how God in all his creatures works!
Yea, man and birds are fain of climbing high.

SUFFOLK
No marvel, an it like your Majesty,
My Lord Protector's hawks do tower so well;   10
They know their master loves to be aloft
And bears his thoughts above his falcon's pitch.

GLOUCESTER
My lord, 'tis but a base ignoble mind
That mounts no higher than a bird can soar.

CARDINAL
I thought as much. He would be above the clouds.   15

GLOUCESTER
Ay, my Lord Cardinal, how think you by that?
Were it not good your Grace could fly to heaven?

59

18–20. **treasury . . . heart:** See Matthew 6.19–21: "Lay not up treasures for yourselves upon **earth**. . . . But lay up treasures for yourselves in **heaven**. . . . For where your **treasure** is, there will your **heart** be also." **Beat:** hammer, insist

21. **Pernicious:** wicked, evil

22. **smooth'st it:** i.e., adopts such a flattering manner

23. **is your priesthood:** i.e., have you as a priest

24. **peremptory:** intolerant of debate or contradiction

25. **Tantaene . . . irae:** Is there such anger in the minds of heavenly creatures? (Latin; Virgil, *Aeneid* 1.11)

26. **hot:** angry

28. **well becomes:** is fully appropriate to

29. **good:** just

32. **lordly:** haughty, disdainful

35. **peace:** quiet

36. **whet not on:** do **not** urge **on; furious:** menacingly violent

37. **blessèd . . . peacemakers:** Matthew 5.9.

38–39. **peace . . . sword:** Matthew 10.34: "I came not to send **peace,** but the **sword.**"

40. **Faith:** a mild oath

43. **Make . . . matter:** i.e., do not gather up others of your faction for the occasion

44. **In thine own person:** alone; **answer:** provide satisfaction for; **thy abuse:** i.e., your injurious words

KING HENRY
  The treasury of everlasting joy.
CARDINAL, ⌐*to Gloucester*¬
  Thy heaven is on earth; thine eyes and thoughts
  Beat on a crown, the treasure of thy heart.   20
  Pernicious Protector, dangerous peer,
  That smooth'st it so with king and commonweal!
GLOUCESTER
  What, cardinal, is your priesthood grown
    peremptory?
  Tantaene animis caelestibus irae?   25
  Churchmen so hot? Good uncle, hide such malice.
  With such holiness, can you do it?
SUFFOLK
  No malice, sir, no more than well becomes
  So good a quarrel and so bad a peer.
GLOUCESTER
  As who, my lord?   30
SUFFOLK   Why, as you, my lord,
  An 't like your lordly ⌐Lord¬ Protectorship.
GLOUCESTER
  Why, Suffolk, England knows thine insolence.
QUEEN MARGARET
  And thy ambition, Gloucester.
KING HENRY   I prithee peace,   35
  Good queen, and whet not on these furious peers,
  For blessèd are the peacemakers on earth.
CARDINAL
  Let me be blessèd for the peace I make
  Against this proud Protector with my sword!
GLOUCESTER, ⌐*aside to Cardinal*¬
  Faith, holy uncle, would 't were come to that!   40
CARDINAL, ⌐*aside to Gloucester*¬   Marry, when thou
    dar'st!
GLOUCESTER, ⌐*aside to Cardinal*¬
  Make up no factious numbers for the matter.
  In thine own person answer thy abuse.

45. **peep:** show yourself; **An if:** i.e., **if**

49. **your man:** i.e., your falconer; **put up:** caused to rise from cover

51. **two-hand sword:** long **sword** (See picture, below.)

52. **Are you advised:** i.e., **are you** agreed (literally, have you considered); or, perhaps, do you understand

58. **shave your crown: shave your** tonsure (with wordplay on "cut off your head")

59. **fence:** use of the sword

60. **Medice, teipsum:** Physician, heal yourself (Latin)

61. **see to 't well:** take good care

62. **stomachs:** tempers

65. **compound:** settle

70. **Saint Alban's shrine:** St. Alban was martyred at Verulamium (now St. Albans) for sheltering Christians. (For a view of St. Albans, see picture, page 68.)

Early modern weapons, including the
two-hand sword. (2.1.51)
From Louis de Gaya, *A treatise of the arms . . .* (1678).

CARDINAL, ⌜*aside to Gloucester*⌝
  Ay, where thou dar'st not peep. An if thou dar'st, 45
  This evening, on the east side of the grove.

KING HENRY
  How now, my lords?

CARDINAL   Believe me, cousin Gloucester,
  Had not your man put up the fowl so suddenly,
  We had had more sport. ⌜(*Aside to Gloucester.*)⌝ 50
    Come with thy two-hand sword.

GLOUCESTER
  True, uncle. ⌜(*Aside to Cardinal.*)⌝ Are you advised?
    The east side of the grove.

CARDINAL, ⌜*aside to Gloucester*⌝
  I am with you.

KING HENRY   Why, how now, uncle Gloucester? 55

GLOUCESTER
  Talking of hawking; nothing else, my lord.
  ⌜(*Aside to Cardinal.*)⌝ Now, by God's mother, priest,
    I'll shave your crown for this,
  Or all my fence shall fail.

CARDINAL, ⌜*aside to Gloucester*⌝ *Medice, teipsum;* 60
  Protector, see to 't well; protect yourself.

KING HENRY
  The winds grow high; so do your stomachs, lords.
  How irksome is this music to my heart!
  When such strings jar, what hope of harmony?
  I pray, my lords, let me compound this strife. 65

    Enter ⌜*a man from St. Albans*⌝ *crying "A miracle!"*

GLOUCESTER   What means this noise?—
  Fellow, what miracle dost thou proclaim?

MAN   A miracle, a miracle!

SUFFOLK
  Come to the King, and tell him what miracle.

MAN
  Forsooth, a blind man at Saint Alban's shrine 70

74. **light in darkness:** See Psalm 112.4: "Unto the righteous ariseth **light in darkness.**"

74 SD. **brethren:** fellow citizens

75. **comes:** i.e., come; **on:** i.e., in

77–78. **Great . . . multiplied:** John 9.41: "If you were blind, you should not have **sin**; but now you say 'We see': therefore your **sin** remaineth." **earthly vale:** "This wretched earth and **vale** of all misery" (*Homily against Willful Rebellion*, a text read annually in English churches)

79. **Stand by:** i.e., **stand** aside

81. **circumstance:** details

82. **glorify the Lord:** Matthew 5.16: "**Glorify** your Father which is in heaven."

83. **restored:** recovered, returned to health

84. **an 't:** i.e., if it

88–89. **couldst . . . told:** i.e., would have been able to state more knowledgeably

91. **Berwick:** a town near the Scottish border

93. **unhallowed:** i.e., without saying a prayer (literally, without keeping it holy)

94. **still:** always

A falcon in flight. (2.1.5–6)
From George Turberville, *The booke of faulconrie . . .* (1575).

Within this half hour hath received his sight,
A man that ne'er saw in his life before.

KING HENRY

Now, God be praised, that to believing souls
Gives light in darkness, comfort in despair.

*Enter the Mayor of Saint Albans, and his brethren,
bearing the man ⌜Simpcox⌝ between two in a chair,
⌜followed by Simpcox's Wife and Others.⌝*

CARDINAL

Here comes the townsmen on procession   75
To present your Highness with the man.

KING HENRY

Great is his comfort in this earthly vale,
Although by his sight his sin be multiplied.

GLOUCESTER

Stand by, my masters.—Bring him near the King.
His Highness' pleasure is to talk with him.   80
         ⌜*The two bearers bring the chair forward.*⌝

KING HENRY

Good fellow, tell us here the circumstance,
That we for thee may glorify the Lord.
What, hast thou been long blind and now restored?

SIMPCOX   Born blind, an 't please your Grace.

WIFE   Ay, indeed, was he.   85

SUFFOLK   What woman is this?

WIFE   His wife, an 't like your Worship.

GLOUCESTER   Hadst thou been his mother, thou couldst
    have better told.

KING HENRY   Where wert thou born?   90

SIMPCOX

At Berwick in the North, an 't like your Grace.

KING HENRY

Poor soul, God's goodness hath been great to thee.
Let never day nor night unhallowed pass,
But still remember what the Lord hath done.

99. **Simon:** i.e., Simpcox (a name derived from **Simon**)

100. **offer:** make an offering (i.e., of money)

103. **lame:** See longer note, page 255.

111. **But that:** i.e., only the once

112. **bought . . . dear:** Proverbial: "**Dear bought** and far fetched are dainties for ladies."

113. **Mass:** i.e., by the **Mass** (a strong oath)

116. **damsons:** small plums

118. **subtle:** crafty, cunning; **serve:** be accepted, be valid

119. **Wink:** close your eyes

121. **clear as day:** proverbial

124. **red as blood:** proverbial

the Abby

Westminster Abbey. (1.2.38)
From John Seller, *A book of the prospects of the remarkable places in . . . London . . .* [c. 1700?].

QUEEN MARGARET
　Tell me, good fellow, cam'st thou here by chance,　　95
　Or of devotion to this holy shrine?

SIMPCOX
　God knows, of pure devotion, being called
　A hundred times and oftener in my sleep
　By good Saint Alban, who said "Simon, come,
　Come, offer at my shrine, and I will help thee."　　100

WIFE
　Most true, forsooth, and many time and oft
　Myself have heard a voice to call him so.

CARDINAL　What, art thou lame?

SIMPCOX　Ay, God Almighty help me!

SUFFOLK　How cam'st thou so?　　105

SIMPCOX　A fall off of a tree.

WIFE　A plum tree, master.

GLOUCESTER　How long hast thou been blind?

SIMPCOX　O, born so, master.

GLOUCESTER　What, and wouldst climb a tree?　　110

SIMPCOX　But that in all my life, when I was a youth.

WIFE　Too true, and bought his climbing very dear.

GLOUCESTER　Mass, thou lov'dst plums well, that
　　wouldst venture so.

SIMPCOX　Alas, good master, my wife desired some　115
　　damsons, and made me climb, with danger of my
　　life.

GLOUCESTER
　A subtle knave, but yet it shall not serve.—
　Let me see thine eyes. Wink now. Now open them.
　In my opinion, yet thou seest not well.　　120

SIMPCOX　Yes, master, clear as day, I thank God and
　　Saint ⌈Alban.⌉

GLOUCESTER
　Sayst thou me so? What color is this cloak of?

SIMPCOX　Red, master, red as blood.

126. **coal black as jet:** proverbial

129. **a many:** i.e., **many**

140–44. **If . . . impossible:** Proverbial: "**Blind** men can judge no **colors**." **several:** different **suddenly:** on the spur of the moment, promptly **nominate:** name

146. **cunning:** learning, skill

148. **that:** i.e., if only

150. **beadles:** parish officers who punish minor offenders

152. **presently:** immediately

153. **straight:** straightaway, right now

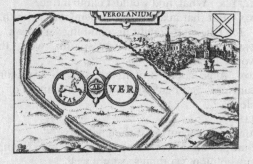

St. Albans. (1.2.59, 85; 1.4.76; 2.1.149; 5.2.69; 5.3.31)
From John Speed, *The theatre of the empire of Great Britaine . . .* (1627 [i.e., 1631]).

68

GLOUCESTER
　Why, that's well said. What color is my gown of?   125
SIMPCOX　Black, forsooth, coal black as jet.
KING HENRY
　Why, then, thou know'st what color jet is of.
SUFFOLK
　And yet, I think, jet did he never see.
GLOUCESTER
　But cloaks and gowns, before this day, a many.
WIFE
　Never, before this day, in all his life.   130
GLOUCESTER　Tell me, sirrah, what's my name?
SIMPCOX　Alas, master, I know not.
GLOUCESTER, ⌈*pointing*⌉　What's his name?
SIMPCOX　I know not.
GLOUCESTER, ⌈*pointing to someone else*⌉　Nor his?   135
SIMPCOX　No, indeed, master.
GLOUCESTER　What's thine own name?
SIMPCOX　Sander Simpcox, an if it please you, master.
GLOUCESTER　Then, Sander, sit there, the lying'st knave
　in Christendom. If thou hadst been born blind,　140
　thou mightst as well have known all our names as
　thus to name the several colors we do wear. Sight
　may distinguish of colors; but suddenly to nomi-
　nate them all, it is impossible.—My lords, Saint
　Alban here hath done a miracle; and would you　145
　not think ⌈his⌉ cunning to be great that could
　restore this cripple to his legs again?
SIMPCOX　O master, that you could!
GLOUCESTER　My masters of Saint Albans, have you not
　beadles in your town and things called whips?　150
MAYOR　Yes, my lord, if it please your Grace.
GLOUCESTER　Then send for one presently.
MAYOR　Sirrah, go fetch the beadle hither straight.
　　　　　　　　　　　　　　⌈*A man*⌉ *exits.*

154. **by and by:** immediately

156. **leap me:** i.e., **leap** (the ethical dative)

158. **alone:** i.e., without help

159. **go about:** contrive, endeavor

160–61. **find your legs:** i.e., recover the use of **your legs**

164. **doublet:** tight-fitting jacket (See page 46.)

167. **bearest:** i.e., puts up with **this**

168. **villain:** scoundrel

169. **knave:** rascal; **drab:** slut

170. **for pure need:** out of utter necessity

174. **fly away:** flee

176. **whole towns to fly:** a reference to Suffolk's giving away Anjou and Maine

"God's mother." (2.1.57)
From Richard Day, *A booke of Christian prayers* . . . (1590).

GLOUCESTER   Now fetch me a stool hither by and by.
⌐*One brings a stool.*⌐ Now, sirrah, if you mean to   155
save yourself from whipping, leap me over this
stool, and run away.
SIMPCOX   Alas, master, I am not able to stand alone.
You go about to torture me in vain.

Enter a Beadle with whips.

GLOUCESTER   Well, sir, we must have you find your   160
legs.—Sirrah beadle, whip him till he leap over
that same stool.
BEADLE   I will, my lord.—Come on, sirrah, off with
your doublet quickly.
SIMPCOX   Alas, master, what shall I do? I am not able to   165
stand.

*After the Beadle hath hit him once, he leaps
over the stool and runs away; and they follow
and cry "A miracle!"*

KING HENRY
O God, seest Thou this, and bearest so long?
QUEEN MARGARET
It made me laugh to see the villain run.
GLOUCESTER, ⌐*to the Beadle*⌐
Follow the knave, and take this drab away.
WIFE   Alas, sir, we did it for pure need.   170
GLOUCESTER
Let them be whipped through every market town
Till they come to Berwick, from whence they came.
⌐*The Beadle, Mayor, Wife, and the others from
Saint Albans*⌐ *exit.*

CARDINAL
Duke Humphrey has done a miracle today.
SUFFOLK
True, made the lame to leap and fly away.
GLOUCESTER
But you have done more miracles than I.   175
You made in a day, my lord, whole towns to fly.

177. **tidings:** news
178. **unfold:** disclose, reveal
179. **sort:** band, group; **naughty:** wicked; **lewdly:** evilly; **bent:** inclined
180. **countenance:** patronage; **confederacy:** conspiracy, collusion
182. **head:** leader; **rout:** disreputable crowd
183. **practiced:** plotted; **dangerously:** injuriously; **state:** government
185. **fact:** act (i.e., of committing the crime)
187. **Demanding of:** asking about
189. **at large:** fully
190. **by this means:** thus, in this way
191. **forthcoming:** apprehended, awaiting trial
192. **turned:** blunted
194. **like:** i.e., likely; **hour:** appointed time (i.e., to fight)
195. **leave to afflict:** stop afflicting
198. **meanest groom:** lowliest male servant
199. **mischiefs:** evils; **work . . . ones:** i.e., do **the wicked ones** bring about
200. **confusion:** destruction
201. **tainture:** defilement
202. **look thyself:** make sure you
203. **for:** i.e., as **for**
203–4. **to heaven . . . How:** i.e., I call on **heaven** to corroborate **how** fully

Enter Buckingham.

KING HENRY
  What tidings with our cousin Buckingham?
BUCKINGHAM
  Such as my heart doth tremble to unfold:
  A sort of naughty persons, lewdly bent,
  Under the countenance and confederacy   180
  Of Lady Eleanor, the Protector's wife,
  The ringleader and head of all this rout,
  Have practiced dangerously against your state,
  Dealing with witches and with conjurers,
  Whom we have apprehended in the fact,   185
  Raising up wicked spirits from under ground,
  Demanding of King Henry's life and death
  And other of your Highness' Privy Council,
  As more at large your Grace shall understand.
CARDINAL
  And so, my Lord Protector, by this means   190
  Your lady is forthcoming yet at London.
  ⌜*Aside to Gloucester.*⌝ This news, I think, hath turned
      your weapon's edge;
  'Tis like, my lord, you will not keep your hour.
GLOUCESTER
  Ambitious churchman, leave to afflict my heart.   195
  Sorrow and grief have vanquished all my powers,
  And, vanquished as I am, I yield to thee,
  Or to the meanest groom.
KING HENRY
  O God, what mischiefs work the wicked ones,
  Heaping confusion on their own heads thereby!   200
QUEEN MARGARET
  Gloucester, see here the tainture of thy nest,
  And look thyself be faultless, thou wert best.
GLOUCESTER
  Madam, for myself, to heaven I do appeal

204. **commonweal:** state

207. **have forgot:** i.e., has forgotten

208. **conversed:** consorted

209. **pitch, defile:** Proverbial: "He that toucheth **pitch** shall be defiled with it."

213. **for this night:** i.e., tonight; **repose us:** i.e., rest

216. **answers:** defenses

217. **poise:** weigh; **equal:** impartial; **scales:** a weighing instrument consisting of a bar with a pan suspended from each end (See picture, page 96.)

218. **Whose beam:** the transverse bar of which; **sure:** i.e., level (literally, firm, steady)

2.2 York persuades Salisbury and Warwick of the validity of his claim to the throne.

----

2. **leave:** permission

3. **close:** private, secluded; **walk:** footwalk, path

4. **craving:** asking; **title:** right, entitlement

5. **is infallible:** unfailingly holds good

How I have loved my king and commonweal;
And, for my wife, I know not how it stands.   205
Sorry I am to hear what I have heard.
Noble she is; but if she have forgot
Honor and virtue, and conversed with such
As, like to pitch, defile nobility,
I banish her my bed and company   210
And give her as a prey to law and shame
That hath dishonored Gloucester's honest name.

KING HENRY
Well, for this night we will repose us here.
Tomorrow toward London back again,
To look into this business thoroughly,   215
And call these foul offenders to their answers,
And poise the cause in Justice' equal scales,
Whose beam stands sure, whose rightful cause
   prevails.

                              Flourish. They exit.

┌Scene 2┐

Enter York, Salisbury, and Warwick.

YORK
Now, my good lords of Salisbury and Warwick,
Our simple supper ended, give me leave,
In this close walk, to satisfy myself
In craving your opinion of my title,
Which is infallible, to England's crown.   5

SALISBURY
My lord, I long to hear it at full.

WARWICK
Sweet York, begin; and if thy claim be good,
The Nevilles are thy subjects to command.

YORK   Then thus:
Edward the Third, my lords, had seven sons: 10

21–30. Who . . . traitorously: This story is shown in Shakespeare's *Richard II*. **all you:** i.e., you two

33. by force . . . right: proverbial

35. issue: offspring

37. line: i.e., **line** of descent (See genealogical charts, page xvi and page 2.)

42–45. This Edmund . . . died: See longer note, page 255.

Henry IV. (2.2.25)
From John Speed, *The theatre of the empire of Great Britaine . . .* (1627 [i.e., 1631]).

The first, Edward the Black Prince, Prince of Wales;
The second, William of Hatfield; and the third,
Lionel, Duke of Clarence; next to whom
Was John of Gaunt, the Duke of Lancaster;
The fifth was Edmund Langley, Duke of York; 15
The sixth was Thomas of Woodstock, Duke of
  Gloucester;
William of Windsor was the seventh and last.
Edward the Black Prince died before his father
And left behind him Richard, his only son, 20
Who, after Edward the Third's death, reigned as
  king
Till Henry Bolingbroke, Duke of Lancaster,
The eldest son and heir of John of Gaunt,
Crowned by the name of Henry the Fourth, 25
Seized on the realm, deposed the rightful king,
Sent his poor queen to France, from whence she
  came,
And him to Pomfret; where, as all you know,
Harmless Richard was murdered traitorously. 30
WARWICK   Father, the Duke hath told the truth.
Thus got the house of Lancaster the crown.
YORK
Which now they hold by force and not by right;
For Richard, the first son's heir, being dead,
The issue of the next son should have reigned. 35
SALISBURY
But William of Hatfield died without an heir.
YORK
The third son, Duke of Clarence, from whose line
I claim the crown, had issue, Philippa, a daughter,
Who married Edmund Mortimer, Earl of March.
Edmund had issue, Roger, Earl of March; 40
Roger had issue: Edmund, Anne, and Eleanor.
SALISBURY
This Edmund, in the reign of Bolingbroke,

57. **proceedings:** i.e., line of descent, pedigree

60. **fails:** dies out, becomes extinct; **his: John of Gaunt's**

61. **flourishes:** grows vigorously and luxuriantly (With **flourishes** begins an extended metaphor in which **Lionel's issue** [line 60] is conventionally compared to a tree; the metaphor continues with **slips** [shoots] and **stock** [trunk] in line 62.)

64. **plot:** piece of ground

68. **We:** the royal "**we**"

70. **that:** i.e., until such time **that**

72. **suddenly:** without preparation

73. **advice:** consultation

75. **Wink at:** i.e., ignore; **insolence:** arrogance

Hawking. (1.2.60)
From Erasmo di Valvasone, *La caccia . . .* [1602].

As I have read, laid claim unto the crown
And, but for Owen Glendower, had been king,
Who kept him in captivity till he died.   45
But to the rest.

YORK   His eldest sister, Anne,
My mother, being heir unto the crown,
Married Richard, Earl of Cambridge, who was ⌈son⌉
To Edmund Langley, Edward the Third's fifth son.   50
By her I claim the kingdom. She was heir
To Roger, Earl of March, who was the son
Of Edmund Mortimer, who married Philippa,
Sole daughter unto Lionel, Duke of Clarence.
So, if the issue of the elder son   55
Succeed before the younger, I am king.

WARWICK
What plain proceedings is more plain than this?
Henry doth claim the crown from John of Gaunt,
The fourth son; York claims it from the third.
Till Lionel's issue fails, his should not reign.   60
It fails not yet, but flourishes in thee
And in thy sons, fair slips of such a stock.
Then, father Salisbury, kneel we together,
And in this private plot be we the first
That shall salute our rightful sovereign   65
With honor of his birthright to the crown.

SALISBURY, WARWICK, ⌈*kneeling*⌉
Long live our sovereign Richard, England's king!

YORK
We thank you, lords. ⌈*They rise.*⌉ But I am not your
    king
Till I be crowned, and that my sword be stained   70
With heart-blood of the house of Lancaster;
And that's not suddenly to be performed,
But with advice and silent secrecy.
Do you as I do in these dangerous days:
Wink at the Duke of Suffolk's insolence,   75

76. **Beaufort's:** i.e., the Cardinal's
77. **crew:** gang, mob
80. **'Tis that:** i.e., it is **that** which

2.3 King Henry sentences the Duchess to public penance and exile, and removes Gloucester from his office as Lord Protector. Then York's armorer is effectively convicted by being killed in a trial by combat with his accuser.

---

0 SD. **State:** persons of rank who form the government

5. **adjudged to:** i.e., determined to require (See Exodus 22.18: "Thou shalt not suffer a witch to live.")

8. **Smithfield:** place of execution of heretics in London (See picture, page 82.)

9. **strangled:** hanged (See picture, below.)

"The gallows." (2.3.9)
From *Warhafftige vnnd eygentliche Beschreibung der . . . Verrätherey . . .* (1606).

At Beaufort's pride, at Somerset's ambition,
At Buckingham, and all the crew of them,
Till they have snared the shepherd of the flock,
That virtuous prince, the good Duke Humphrey.
'Tis that they seek; and they, in seeking that,   80
Shall find their deaths, if York can prophesy.

SALISBURY
My lord, break we off. We know your mind at full.

WARWICK
My heart assures me that the Earl of Warwick
Shall one day make the Duke of York a king.

YORK
And, Neville, this I do assure myself: 85
Richard shall live to make the Earl of Warwick
The greatest man in England but the King.

They exit.

⌜Scene 3⌝

*Sound trumpets. Enter King ⌜Henry⌝ and State
⌜(Queen Margaret, Gloucester, York, Salisbury, Suffolk,
and Others)⌝ with Guard, to banish the Duchess ⌜of
Gloucester, who is accompanied by Margery Jourdain,
Southwell, Hume, and Bolingbroke, all guarded.⌝*

KING HENRY
Stand forth, Dame Eleanor Cobham, Gloucester's
   wife.
In sight of God and us, your guilt is great.
Receive the sentence of the law for ⌜sins⌝
Such as by God's book are adjudged to death.   5
⌜*To Jourdain, Southwell, Hume, and Bolingbroke.*⌝
You four, from hence to prison back again;
From thence unto the place of execution:
The witch in Smithfield shall be burnt to ashes,
And you three shall be strangled on the gallows.

10. **for:** because
12. **Despoilèd:** stripped; **honor:** title
13. **open:** public
15. **With:** i.e., in the custody of
16. **were:** would be
18. **justify:** acquit
20–21. **this dishonor . . . ground:** See Genesis 42.38: "You shall bring my gray head **with sorrow** unto the grave."
23. **Sorrow would:** i.e., **sorrow** requires; **ease:** comfort, freedom from annoyance
25. **staff:** rod borne as the Protector's badge of office
26–27. **God . . . feet:** See Psalm 71.5: "for thou art **my hope,** O Lord **God**"; Psalm 49.9: "**my guide** and **stay**"; Psalm 119.105: "Thy word is a **lantern** unto **my feet.**"
30. **of years:** i.e., who is of age
32. **govern:** steer
33. **King his:** king's
35. **willingly:** voluntarily

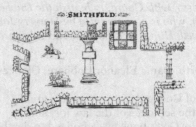

Smithfield. (2.3.8)
From Hugh Alley, *A caveat for the city of London . . .* (1598).

⌜*To Duchess*⌝ You, madam, for you are more nobly   10
    born,
Despoilèd of your honor in your life,
Shall, after three days' open penance done,
Live in your country here in banishment
With Sir John Stanley in the Isle of Man.   15

DUCHESS
Welcome is banishment. Welcome were my death.

GLOUCESTER
Eleanor, the law, thou seest, hath judged thee.
I cannot justify whom the law condemns.
    ⌜*Duchess and the other prisoners exit under guard.*⌝
Mine eyes are full of tears, my heart of grief.
Ah, Humphrey, this dishonor in thine age   20
Will bring thy head with sorrow to the ground.—
I beseech your Majesty give me leave to go;
Sorrow would solace, and mine age would ease.

KING HENRY
Stay, Humphrey, Duke of Gloucester. Ere thou go,
Give up thy staff. Henry will to himself   25
Protector be; and God shall be my hope,
My stay, my guide, and lantern to my feet.
And go in peace, Humphrey, no less beloved
Than when thou wert Protector to thy king.

QUEEN MARGARET
I see no reason why a king of years   30
Should be to be protected like a child.
God and King Henry govern England's realm!—
Give up your staff, sir, and the King his realm.

GLOUCESTER
My staff?—Here, noble Henry, is my staff.
    ⌜*He puts down his staff before Henry.*⌝
As willingly do I the same resign   35
As e'er thy father Henry made it mine;
And even as willingly at thy feet I leave it
As others would ambitiously receive it.

39. **dead and gone:** proverbial
40. **attend:** watch over
42. **scarce:** hardly
43. **shrewd:** severe; **maim:** injury; **pulls:** wrenches
45. **raught:** laid hold of
46. **best fits:** is most appropriate
47. **sprays:** shoots, branches
48. **pride:** glory; **her:** i.e., its
49. **let him go:** stop talking about him
51. **appellant and defendant:** challenger and defender
52. **lists:** place where they will fight their trial by combat
54. **therefor:** for that reason
55. **quarrel:** charge, accusation
56. **fit:** suitable
58. **worse bestead:** harder pressed
60 SD. **drinking to him so much:** giving him **so much** to drink; or, inviting him to drink by **drinking to** his good luck; **Drum:** drummer; **staff . . . to it:** combat flail, a **staff with a** long thin leather bag of sand attached to the end of it; **Prentices:** apprentices

84

Farewell, good king. When I am dead and gone,
May honorable peace attend thy throne.   40
                              Gloucester exits.
                     ⌜*Henry picks up the staff.*⌝

QUEEN MARGARET
Why, now is Henry king and Margaret queen,
And Humphrey, Duke of Gloucester, scarce himself,
That bears so shrewd a maim. Two pulls at once:
His lady banished and a limb lopped off.
This staff of honor raught, there let it stand   45
Where it best fits to be, in Henry's hand.

SUFFOLK
Thus droops this lofty pine and hangs his sprays;
Thus Eleanor's pride dies in her youngest days.

YORK
Lords, let him go.—Please it your Majesty,
This is the day appointed for the combat,   50
And ready are the appellant and defendant—
The armorer and his man—to enter the lists,
So please your Highness to behold the fight.

QUEEN MARGARET
Ay, good my lord, for purposely therefor
Left I the court to see this quarrel tried.   55

KING HENRY
I' God's name, see the lists and all things fit.
Here let them end it, and God defend the right!

YORK
I never saw a fellow worse bestead
Or more afraid to fight than is the appellant,
The servant of this armorer, my lords.   60

Enter at one door the Armorer ⌜*Horner*⌝ *and his
Neighbors, drinking to him so much that he is drunk;
and he enters with a Drum before him and his staff with
a sandbag fastened to it; and at the other door his man
* ⌜*Peter,*⌝ *with a Drum and sandbag, and Prentices
drinking to him.*

62. **sack:** Spanish or Canary wine

65. **charneco:** another kind of wine (perhaps Portuguese)

66. **double beer:** extra strong ale

68. **Let it come:** i.e., let the bowl of drink go around; **pledge:** drink to the health of

69. **fig for:** exclamation of contempt, often expressed by the gesture of thrusting the thumb between two fingers or into the mouth

73. **credit:** the good name, reputation

75. **draft:** swallow of drink

81. **fence:** fencing

91. **touching:** regarding

92. **take my death:** i.e., stake my life

93. **ill:** harm

94. **have at thee:** an expression signaling an attack; **downright blow:** i.e., **a blow** directed straight downward

95. **Dispatch:** make haste; **double:** i.e., slur, thicken (literally, repeat itself)

96. **Alarum:** call to arms

The obverse and reverse of a shilling. (4.7.22)
From Edward Hawkins, *The silver coins of England* . . . (1841).

FIRST NEIGHBOR   Here, neighbor Horner, I drink to you
    in a cup of sack; and fear not, neighbor, you shall
    do well enough.

SECOND NEIGHBOR   And here, neighbor, here's a cup of
    charneco.   65

THIRD NEIGHBOR   And here's a pot of good double beer,
    neighbor. Drink, and fear not your man.

HORNER   Let it come, i' faith, and I'll pledge you all.
    And a fig for Peter!   ⌜*They drink.*⌝

FIRST PRENTICE   Here, Peter, I drink to thee, and be not   70
    afraid.

SECOND PRENTICE   Be merry, Peter, and fear not thy
    master. Fight for credit of the prentices.

PETER   I thank you all. Drink, and pray for me, I pray
    you, for I think I have taken my last draft in this   75
    world. Here, Robin, an if I die, I give thee my
    apron.—And, Will, thou shalt have my hammer.—
    And here, Tom, take all the money that I have. ⌜*He*
    distributes his possessions.⌝ O Lord, bless me, I
    pray God, for I am never able to deal with my   80
    master. He hath learnt so much fence already.

SALISBURY   Come, leave your drinking, and fall to
    blows. Sirrah, what's thy name?

PETER   Peter, forsooth.

SALISBURY   Peter? What more?   85

PETER   Thump.

SALISBURY   Thump? Then see thou thump thy master
    well.

HORNER   Masters, I am come hither, as it were, upon
    my man's instigation, to prove him a knave and   90
    myself an honest man; and touching the Duke of
    York, I will take my death I never meant him any
    ill, nor the King, nor the Queen.—And therefore,
    Peter, have at thee with a downright blow!

YORK   Dispatch. This knave's tongue begins to double.   95
    Sound, trumpets. Alarum to the combatants!

96 SD. **They . . . down:** See longer note, page 256.

97. **Hold:** stop

99. **in thy master's way:** i.e., that impeded your master

100–101. **in this presence:** i.e., **in** the **presence** of the king

106. **Which he:** whom Horner

2.4 Gloucester watches his Duchess's public humiliation as she goes into exile. He is summoned to Parliament.

—————

0 SD. **mourning cloaks:** black hooded cloaks worn in funeral processions

1. **Thus . . . cloud:** proverbial

2. **evermore:** always; **succeeds:** follows

3. **his:** its

4. **fleet:** pass rapidly

9. **Uneath:** scarcely; **flinty:** hard, stony

11. **ill:** badly, poorly; **abrook:** endure

⌜*Trumpet sounds.*⌝
They fight, and Peter strikes him down.

HORNER   Hold, Peter, hold! I confess, I confess treason.
⌜*He dies.*⌝

YORK   Take away his weapon.—Fellow, thank God and
the good wine in thy master's way.

PETER   O God, have I overcome mine enemies in this   100
presence? O Peter, thou hast prevailed in right!

KING HENRY
Go, take hence that traitor from our sight;
For by his death we do perceive his guilt.
And God in justice hath revealed to us
The truth and innocence of this poor fellow,   105
Which he had thought to have murdered
    wrongfully.—
Come, fellow, follow us for thy reward.
Sound a flourish. They exit, ⌜*bearing Horner's body.*⌝

⌜Scene 4⌝

Enter Duke Humphrey ⌜*of Gloucester*⌝ *and his Men,*
in mourning cloaks.

GLOUCESTER
Thus sometimes hath the brightest day a cloud,
And after summer evermore succeeds
Barren winter, with his wrathful nipping cold;
So cares and joys abound, as seasons fleet.
Sirs, what's o'clock?   5

SERVANT   Ten, my lord.

GLOUCESTER
Ten is the hour that was appointed me
To watch the coming of my punished duchess.
Uneath may she endure the flinty streets,
To tread them with her tender-feeling feet.   10
Sweet Nell, ill can thy noble mind abrook

12. **abject:** despicable, mean-spirited, low-class

13. **envious:** spiteful, malicious

14. **erst:** formerly

14–15. **thy proud ... streets:** The metaphor is of a Roman victor in war riding his **chariot,** his captives bound to its wheels, through the city's streets in a triumphal procession.

16. **soft:** wait

17 SD. **white sheet:** the traditional garment of the person doing public penance; **taper:** wax candle

18. **take:** i.e, rescue

19. **for:** i.e., upon pain of losing

21. **they:** i.e., **the people** (line 12), imagined offstage

22. **giddy:** (1) furious; (2) dizzy; (3) inconstant

23. **throw:** turn

24. **hateful:** (1) hate-filled; (2) hated, repulsive

25. **closet:** private chamber; **pent up:** shut in, closely confined; **rue:** pity

26. **ban:** curse

31. **Methinks:** it seems to me

32. **Mailed up:** wrapped (i.e., as if I were a hunting hawk wrapped in a handkerchief to keep it quiet)

33. **with a rabble:** by a mob

34. **deep-fet groans:** i.e., **groans** fetched from **deep** within myself

36. **start:** flinch; **envious:** malicious

The abject people gazing on thy face
With envious looks laughing at thy shame,
That erst did follow thy proud chariot wheels
When thou didst ride in triumph through the streets.   15
But, soft! I think she comes, and I'll prepare
My tearstained eyes to see her miseries.

*Enter the Duchess ⌜of Gloucester, barefoot, and⌝ in a
white sheet, ⌜with papers pinned to her back⌝ and a
taper burning in her hand, with ⌜Sir John Stanley,⌝
                the Sheriff, and Officers.*

SERVANT
   So please your Grace, we'll take her from the Sheriff.
GLOUCESTER
   No, stir not for your lives. Let her pass by.
DUCHESS
   Come you, my lord, to see my open shame?   20
   Now thou dost penance too. Look how they gaze!
   See how the giddy multitude do point,
   And nod their heads, and throw their eyes on thee.
   Ah, Gloucester, hide thee from their hateful looks,
   And, in thy closet pent up, rue my shame,   25
   And ban thine enemies, both mine and thine.
GLOUCESTER
   Be patient, gentle Nell. Forget this grief.
DUCHESS
   Ah, Gloucester, teach me to forget myself!
   For whilst I think I am thy married wife
   And thou a prince, Protector of this land,   30
   Methinks I should not thus be led along,
   Mailed up in shame, with papers on my back,
   And followed with a rabble that rejoice
   To see my tears and hear my deep-fet groans.
   The ruthless flint doth cut my tender feet,   35
   And when I start, the envious people laugh

37. **advisèd:** cautious, wary

39. **Trowest thou:** do you believe

42. **pomp:** (former) ostentatious display, magnificence

46. **As:** i.e., that; **forlorn:** desolate, abandoned

47. **wonder:** spectacle; **pointing-stock:** object of derision

48. **rascal:** lowborn; **follower:** pursuer

49. **mild:** unprovoked

50. **nothing:** anything

51. **sure:** surely

53. **her:** i.e., Queen Margaret

54. **Beaufort:** Cardinal **Beaufort; false:** treacherous

55. **limed . . . wings:** See note to 1.3.91.

56. **how thou canst:** i.e., however you can; **tangle:** entangle

58. **seek prevention of:** i.e., attempt to anticipate or forestall

59. **forbear:** refrain; **all awry:** completely wide (i.e., of the target)

60. **attainted:** accused, condemned

63. **procure:** cause; **scathe:** harm

65. **reproach:** disgrace

66. **were not:** would **not** be

67. **in danger:** i.e., would be **in danger**

68. **quiet:** calm, peace of mind

69. **sort:** adapt

70. **These few . . . worn:** Proverbial: "**A wonder** lasts but nine days." **worn: worn** out, exhausted

And bid me be advisèd how I tread.
Ah, Humphrey, can I bear this shameful yoke?
Trowest thou that e'er I'll look upon the world
Or count them happy that enjoys the sun? 40
No, dark shall be my light, and night my day.
To think upon my pomp shall be my hell.
Sometimes I'll say I am Duke Humphrey's wife
And he a prince and ruler of the land;
Yet so he ruled and such a prince he was 45
As he stood by whilst I, his forlorn duchess,
Was made a wonder and a pointing-stock
To every idle rascal follower.
But be thou mild, and blush not at my shame,
Nor stir at nothing till the ax of death 50
Hang over thee, as, sure, it shortly will.
For Suffolk, he that can do all in all
With her that hateth thee and hates us all,
And York and impious Beaufort, that false priest,
Have all limed bushes to betray thy wings; 55
And fly thou how thou canst, they'll tangle thee.
But fear not thou until thy foot be snared,
Nor never seek prevention of thy foes.

GLOUCESTER
Ah, Nell, forbear. Thou aimest all awry.
I must offend before I be attainted; 60
And had I twenty times so many foes,
And each of them had twenty times their power,
All these could not procure me any scathe
So long as I am loyal, true, and crimeless.
Wouldst have me rescue thee from this reproach? 65
Why, yet thy scandal were not wiped away,
But I in danger for the breach of law.
Thy greatest help is quiet, gentle Nell.
I pray thee, sort thy heart to patience;
These few days' wonder will be quickly worn. 70

72. **Holden:** i.e., to be held; **Bury:** i.e., **Bury** St. Edmunds, in Suffolk

73. **before:** in advance

74. **close dealing:** a secret way of acting

76. **commission:** command

77. **stays:** stops

81. **given in charge:** ordered

82. **Entreat:** treat; **in that:** because

83. **laugh:** perhaps, smile on (me), favor (me)

90. **afeard:** afraid

91. **this world's eternity:** i.e., that I would live forever

"Ceres' plenteous load." (1.2.2)
From Cesare Ripa, *Iconologia . . .* (1613).

Enter a Herald.

HERALD
  I summon your Grace to his Majesty's Parliament
  Holden at Bury the first of this next month.
GLOUCESTER
  And my consent ne'er asked herein before?
  This is close dealing. Well, I will be there.
                            ⌐*Herald exits.*⌐
  My Nell, I take my leave.—And, master sheriff,   75
  Let not her penance exceed the King's commission.
SHERIFF
  An 't please your Grace, here my commission stays,
  And Sir John Stanley is appointed now
  To take her with him to the Isle of Man.
GLOUCESTER
  Must you, Sir John, protect my lady here?   80
STANLEY
  So am I given in charge, may 't please your Grace.
GLOUCESTER
  Entreat her not the worse in that I pray
  You use her well. The world may laugh again,
  And I may live to do you kindness, if
  You do it her. And so, Sir John, farewell.   85
DUCHESS
  What, gone, my lord, and bid me not farewell?
GLOUCESTER
  Witness my tears. I cannot stay to speak.
                    Gloucester exits ⌐*with his Men.*⌐
DUCHESS
  Art thou gone too? All comfort go with thee,
  For none abides with me. My joy is death—
  Death, at whose name I oft have been afeard,   90
  Because I wished this world's eternity.—
  Stanley, I prithee, go, and take me hence.
  I care not whither, for I beg no favor;
  Only convey me where thou art commanded.

96. **used:** treated; **state:** rank

97. **I am but reproach:** i.e., my rank is only disgrace

98. **reproachfully:** disgracefully, shamefully

101. **better than I fare:** i.e., **fare better than I do**

102. **conduct:** escort, guide

103. **office:** duty

104. **is discharged:** has been performed

108. **shifted:** removed (with wordplay on *shift* as "change clothing")

110. **show:** display; **attire me how I can:** however I dress

Justice with her balance scales. (2.1.217)
From Thomas Peyton, *The glasse of time . . .* (1620).

STANLEY
　Why, madam, that is to the Isle of Man, 95
　There to be used according to your state.

DUCHESS
　That's bad enough, for I am but reproach.
　And shall I, then, be used reproachfully?

STANLEY
　Like to a duchess and Duke Humphrey's lady;
　According to that state you shall be used. 100

DUCHESS
　Sheriff, farewell, and better than I fare,
　Although thou hast been conduct of my shame.

SHERIFF
　It is my office; and, madam, pardon me.

DUCHESS
　Ay, ay, farewell. Thy office is discharged.
　　　　　　　⌜*The Sheriff and Officers exit.*⌝
　Come, Stanley, shall we go? 105

STANLEY
　Madam, your penance done, throw off this sheet,
　And go we to attire you for our journey.

DUCHESS
　My shame will not be shifted with my sheet.
　No, it will hang upon my richest robes
　And show itself, attire me how I can. 110
　Go, lead the way. I long to see my prison.
　　　　　　　　　　　　　They exit.

HENRY VI
Part 2

ACT 3

3.1   In Parliament Queen Margaret and the nobles level charges against Gloucester, but King Henry remains convinced of his uncle's innocence. Nonetheless, the King allows Suffolk and the Cardinal to hold him for trial. Fearing that Gloucester will not be convicted, the Queen, the Cardinal, Suffolk, and York conspire to murder him, and Suffolk and the Cardinal promise to carry out the killing. Word comes of an Irish uprising, and York, delighted to be provided with an army, agrees to quell it.

---

0 SD. **sennet:** trumpet fanfare to signal a ceremonial entrance or exit

1. **muse:** marvel that

2. **hindmost man:** last **man** to come

3. **occasion:** cause, reason

5. **strangeness:** coldness, aloofness

7. **insolent:** proud, haughty

9. **We:** the royal "we"; **since:** when

10. **glance:** cast, flash

12. **That:** i.e., so **that; submission:** deference, submissiveness

14. **give . . . day:** i.e., say "good morning"

17. **duty:** respect, reverence; **to us belongs:** pertains to me

18. **regarded:** i.e., paid any attention; **grin:** bare their teeth

⌈ACT 3⌉

⌈Scene 1⌉

Sound a sennet. Enter King ⌈Henry,⌉ Queen ⌈Margaret,⌉
Cardinal, Suffolk, York, Buckingham, Salisbury, and
Warwick, ⌈and Others⌉ to the Parliament.

KING HENRY
  I muse my lord of Gloucester is not come.
  'Tis not his wont to be the hindmost man,
  Whate'er occasion keeps him from us now.
QUEEN MARGARET
  Can you not see, or will you not observe,
  The strangeness of his altered countenance?   5
  With what a majesty he bears himself,
  How insolent of late he is become,
  How proud, how peremptory, and unlike himself?
  We know the time since he was mild and affable;
  And if we did but glance a far-off look,   10
  Immediately he was upon his knee,
  That all the court admired him for submission.
  But meet him now, and, be it in the morn
  When everyone will give the time of day,
  He knits his brow and shows an angry eye   15
  And passeth by with stiff unbowèd knee,
  Disdaining duty that to us belongs.
  Small curs are not regarded when they grin,
  But great men tremble when the lion roars—
  And Humphrey is no little man in England.   20

23. **Meseemeth:** it seems to me; **policy:** prudent course of action

24. **Respecting:** considering; **rancorous:** spiteful

25. **his advantage . . . decease:** i.e., the **advantage** (namely, the crown) that he would enjoy if you were to die

29. **make commotion:** cause insurrection or rebellion

32. **Suffer:** tolerate

33. **herbs:** plants; **want:** lack; **husbandry:** good gardening

35. **collect:** infer; deduce

36. **fond:** foolish

37. **supplant:** (1) remove; (2) uproot

38. **subscribe:** confess myself mistaken

40. **Reprove:** disprove; **allegation:** charge

41. **effectual:** pertinent; valid

43. **put:** appointed

45. **by his subornation:** i.e., through his corruption or instigation

46. **practices:** plots, conspiracies

47. **privy to:** intimately acquainted with

48. **by reputing of:** i.e., esteeming, thinking highly of

49. **successive heir:** i.e., **heir** next in order of succession

50. **vaunts:** boasts

51. **bedlam:** mad (**Bedlam** alludes to St. Mary of Bethlehem Hospital for the insane in London.)

52. **frame:** devise

53. **Smooth . . . deep:** proverbial

54. **show:** appearance

55. **The fox . . . lamb:** proverbial **he:** it **would:** wishes to

First, note that he is near you in descent,
And, should you fall, he is the next will mount.
Meseemeth then it is no policy,
Respecting what a rancorous mind he bears
And his advantage following your decease, 25
That he should come about your royal person
Or be admitted to your Highness' Council.
By flattery hath he won the Commons' hearts;
And when he please to make commotion,
'Tis to be feared they all will follow him. 30
Now 'tis the spring, and weeds are shallow-rooted;
Suffer them now, and they'll o'ergrow the garden
And choke the herbs for want of husbandry.
The reverent care I bear unto my lord
Made me collect these dangers in the Duke. 35
If it be fond, call it a woman's fear,
Which fear, if better reasons can supplant,
I will subscribe and say I wronged the Duke.
My ⌈lords⌉ of Suffolk, Buckingham, and York,
Reprove my allegation if you can, 40
Or else conclude my words effectual.

SUFFOLK
Well hath your Highness seen into this duke,
And, had I first been put to speak my mind,
I think I should have told your Grace's tale.
The Duchess by his subornation, 45
Upon my life, began her devilish practices;
Or if he were not privy to those faults,
Yet, by reputing of his high descent—
As next the King he was successive heir,
And such high vaunts of his nobility— 50
Did instigate the bedlam brainsick duchess
By wicked means to frame our sovereign's fall.
Smooth runs the water where the brook is deep,
And in his simple show he harbors treason.
The fox barks not when he would steal the lamb. 55

57. **Unsounded:** unfathomed

58–59. **Did . . . done:** The same charge is made against him at 1.3.135–37. **Devise:** order

61. **Levy:** collect as taxes

63. **By means whereof:** i.e., because of which

64. **to:** compared to

67. **at once:** (1) perhaps, once and for all; (2) without any more discussion; (3) to answer all of you together

68. **annoy:** hurt

69. **shall I:** i.e., if I were to; **conscience:** inward knowledge or conviction

72. **sucking lamb:** Proverbial: **"As innocent as** a **lamb." harmless dove:** proverbial

73. **given:** disposed

74. **work:** plot, contrive

75. **fond:** foolish; **affiance:** trust

76. **borrowed:** an allusion to the Aesop fable in which a crow dresses in the plumage of another bird

77. **he's disposèd as:** i.e., he has the disposition of

78–79. **His skin . . . wolves:** See Matthew 7.15: "Beware of false prophets, which come to you in sheep's clothing, but inwardly they are ravening **wolves."** (See picture, page 106.)

80. **Who . . . deceit:** i.e., **who** that intends **deceit cannot** adopt a disguise

82. **Hangs:** depends; **cutting short:** Proverbial: "Shorten by the head." **fraudful:** treacherous

No, no, my sovereign, Gloucester is a man
Unsounded yet and full of deep deceit.

CARDINAL
Did he not, contrary to form of law,
Devise strange deaths for small offenses done?

YORK
And did he not, in his protectorship,   60
Levy great sums of money through the realm
For soldiers' pay in France, and never sent it,
By means whereof the towns each day revolted?

BUCKINGHAM
Tut, these are petty faults to faults unknown,
Which time will bring to light in smooth Duke   65
    Humphrey.

KING HENRY
My lords, at once: the care you have of us
To mow down thorns that would annoy our foot
Is worthy praise; but, shall I speak my conscience,
Our kinsman Gloucester is as innocent   70
From meaning treason to our royal person
As is the sucking lamb or harmless dove.
The Duke is virtuous, mild, and too well given
To dream on evil or to work my downfall.

QUEEN MARGARET
Ah, what's more dangerous than this fond affiance?   75
Seems he a dove? His feathers are but borrowed,
For he's disposèd as the hateful raven.
Is he a lamb? His skin is surely lent him,
For he's inclined as is the ravenous wolves.
Who cannot steal a shape that means deceit?   80
Take heed, my lord; the welfare of us all
Hangs on the cutting short that fraudful man.

Enter Somerset.

SOMERSET
All health unto my gracious sovereign!

85. **interest in:** right or title to
86. **bereft:** robbed from
87. **Cold:** gloomy, dispiriting
90. **blossoms . . . bud:** proverbial   **blasted:** withered, blighted
92. **gear:** business
93. **sell:** i.e., exchange
95. **stayed:** tarried, delayed
100. **for:** because of
101. **unspotted:** pure, unblemished
105. **of France:** i.e., from the French king
106. **stayed:** held back
107. **By means whereof:** i.e., as a result of which
108. **What:** i.e., who

A wolf dressed as a sheep. (3.1.78–79)
From August Casimir Redel, *Annus symbolicus . . .* (c. 1695).

KING HENRY
  Welcome, Lord Somerset. What news from France?

SOMERSET
  That all your interest in those territories   85
  Is utterly bereft you. All is lost.

KING HENRY
  Cold news, Lord Somerset; but God's will be done.

YORK, ⌈*aside*⌉
  Cold news for me, for I had hope of France
  As firmly as I hope for fertile England.
  Thus are my blossoms blasted in the bud,   90
  And caterpillars eat my leaves away.
  But I will remedy this gear ere long,
  Or sell my title for a glorious grave.

              Enter Gloucester.

GLOUCESTER
  All happiness unto my lord the King!
  Pardon, my liege, that I have stayed so long.   95

SUFFOLK
  Nay, Gloucester, know that thou art come too soon,
  Unless thou wert more loyal than thou art.
  I do arrest thee of high treason here.

GLOUCESTER
  Well, Suffolk, thou shalt not see me blush
  Nor change my countenance for this arrest.   100
  A heart unspotted is not easily daunted.
  The purest spring is not so free from mud
  As I am clear from treason to my sovereign.
  Who can accuse me? Wherein am I guilty?

YORK
  'Tis thought, my lord, that you took bribes of France 105
  And, being Protector, stayed the soldiers' pay,
  By means whereof his Highness hath lost France.

GLOUCESTER
  Is it but thought so? What are they that think it?

111. **watched:** i.e., kept awake through

112. **studying:** applying my mind to acquiring

113. **That:** i.e., may **that; doit:** coin of little value; **wrested:** extorted, wrung

114. **groat:** coin worth four pennies (See picture, page 112.)

115. **brought:** i.e., produced as evidence

116. **proper:** private; **store:** supply, stock

117. **needy:** poor

118. **dispursèd:** paid out

119. **restitution:** i.e., reimbursement

120. **serves you well:** i.e., suits your interest

123. **Strange:** extreme

124. **That . . . tyranny:** i.e., as a result of which, **England** was disgraced as tyrannical

128. **lowly:** humble; **ransom:** means of freeing themselves from the penalty; **fault:** misdeed, offense

129. **bloody:** bloodthirsty

130. **felonious:** wicked; **fleeced:** plundered; **poor:** hapless; **passengers:** travelers

131. **condign:** merited, fitting

133. **Above:** more than; **felon:** felony; **what trespass else:** i.e., any other violation

134. **easy:** slight; **answered:** justified, defended against

135. **unto your charge:** to your responsibility

136. **purge:** clear, exculpate

138. **commit you to:** consign **you** officially **to** the custody of

139. **further:** later

I never robbed the soldiers of their pay
Nor ever had one penny bribe from France. 110
So help me God as I have watched the night—
Ay, night by night—in studying good for England!
That doit that e'er I wrested from the King,
Or any groat I hoarded to my use,
Be brought against me at my trial day! 115
No, many a pound of mine own proper store,
Because I would not tax the needy Commons,
Have I dispursèd to the garrisons
And never asked for restitution.

CARDINAL
It serves you well, my lord, to say so much. 120

GLOUCESTER
I say no more than truth, so help me God.

YORK
In your protectorship, you did devise
Strange tortures for offenders, never heard of,
That England was defamed by tyranny.

GLOUCESTER
Why, 'tis well known that whiles I was Protector, 125
Pity was all the fault that was in me;
For I should melt at an offender's tears,
And lowly words were ransom for their fault.
Unless it were a bloody murderer
Or foul felonious thief that fleeced poor passengers, 130
I never gave them condign punishment.
Murder indeed, that bloody sin, I tortured
Above the felon or what trespass else.

SUFFOLK
My lord, these faults are easy, quickly answered;
But mightier crimes are laid unto your charge 135
Whereof you cannot easily purge yourself.
I do arrest you in his Highness' name,
And here commit you to my Lord Cardinal
To keep until your further time of trial.

141. **suspense:** doubt as to your character and conduct

144. **with:** i.e., by

145. **rancor's:** malignant hatred's

146. **subornation:** corruption; **predominant:** prevalent, prevailing

147. **equity:** fairness; **exiled:** i.e., **exiled** from

148. **their complot:** the design of their conspiracy

149. **happy:** fortunate

150. **prove:** establish; **period:** end; **tyranny:** oppressive exercise of power

151. **expend:** spend; employ

152. **mine:** i.e., **my death** (line 149)

153. **For thousands:** i.e., **for** the deaths of **thousands**

154. **their plotted tragedy:** (1) the plot of **their tragedy;** (2) the **tragedy** that they have devised

155. **blab:** betray

156. **cloudy:** sullen, frowning

157. **Sharp:** harsh

158. **envious:** malicious

159. **dogged:** malicious, cruel, surly; **the moon:** what is impossible to get

160. **overweening:** presumptuous

161. **accuse:** accusation; **level:** aim

163. **Causeless:** without cause or reason

165. **liefest:** dearest

167. **conventicles:** secret meetings for sinister purposes

169. **want:** lack

170. **store:** abundance

171. **effected:** fulfilled

KING HENRY

    My lord of Gloucester, 'tis my special hope   140
    That you will clear yourself from all suspense.
    My conscience tells me you are innocent.

GLOUCESTER

    Ah, gracious lord, these days are dangerous.
    Virtue is choked with foul ambition,
    And charity chased hence by rancor's hand;   145
    Foul subornation is predominant,
    And equity exiled your Highness' land.
    I know their complot is to have my life;
    And if my death might make this island happy
    And prove the period of their tyranny,   150
    I would expend it with all willingness.
    But mine is made the prologue to their play;
    For thousands more, that yet suspect no peril,
    Will not conclude their plotted tragedy.
    Beaufort's red sparkling eyes blab his heart's malice,   155
    And Suffolk's cloudy brow his stormy hate;
    Sharp Buckingham unburdens with his tongue
    The envious load that lies upon his heart;
    And dogged York, that reaches at the moon,
    Whose overweening arm I have plucked back,   160
    By false accuse doth level at my life.—
    And you, my sovereign lady, with the rest,
    Causeless have laid disgraces on my head
    And with your best endeavor have stirred up
    My liefest liege to be mine enemy.   165
    Ay, all of you have laid your heads together—
    Myself had notice of your conventicles—
    And all to make away my guiltless life.
    I shall not want false witness to condemn me
    Nor store of treasons to augment my guilt.   170
    The ancient proverb will be well effected:
    "A staff is quickly found to beat a dog."

173. **railing:** abusiveness

176. **rated at:** angrily reproved

177. **scope:** complete freedom

179. **twit:** i.e., twitted, disparaged

180. **clerkly:** learnedly; **couched:** expressed

182. **state:** high rank, greatness, power

183. **give . . . chide:** Proverbial: "**Give** losers **leave to** speak."

184. **spoke:** i.e., spoken

185. **Beshrew:** curse; **played me false:** betrayed me

187. **wrest the sense:** twist the meaning

189. **sure:** securely

191. **firm:** robust

192–93. **Thus . . . first:** See Matthew 26.31: "I will smite **the shepherd,** and the sheep of the flock shall be scattered." **gnarling:** snarling

194. **false:** erroneous

195. **decay:** destruction, ruin

197. **ourself:** i.e., I (royal plural)

The obverse and reverse of a groat. (3.1.114)
From Edward Hawkins, *The silver coins of England . . .* (1841).

CARDINAL
  My liege, his railing is intolerable.
  If those that care to keep your royal person
  From treason's secret knife and traitor's rage   175
  Be thus upbraided, chid, and rated at,
  And the offender granted scope of speech,
  'Twill make them cool in zeal unto your Grace.

SUFFOLK
  Hath he not twit our sovereign lady here
  With ignominious words, though clerkly couched,   180
  As if she had suborned some to swear
  False allegations to o'erthrow his state?

QUEEN MARGARET
  But I can give the loser leave to chide.

GLOUCESTER
  Far truer spoke than meant. I lose, indeed;
  Beshrew the winners, for they played me false!   185
  And well such losers may have leave to speak.

BUCKINGHAM
  He'll wrest the sense and hold us here all day.
  Lord Cardinal, he is your prisoner.

CARDINAL, ⌜*to his Men*⌝
  Sirs, take away the Duke, and guard him sure.

GLOUCESTER
  Ah, thus King Henry throws away his crutch   190
  Before his legs be firm to bear his body.—
  Thus is the shepherd beaten from thy side,
  And wolves are gnarling who shall gnaw thee first.
  Ah, that my fear were false; ah, that it were!
  For, good King Henry, thy decay I fear.   195
      Gloucester exits, ⌜*guarded by Cardinal's Men.*⌝

KING HENRY
  My lords, what to your wisdoms seemeth best
  Do, or undo, as if ourself were here.

QUEEN MARGARET
  What, will your Highness leave the Parliament?

201. **engirt:** encircled

203. **uncle Humphrey:** addressed to the now-absent Gloucester

204. **map:** very picture, image

205. **yet ... come:** i.e., **the hour ... is yet to come**

206. **proved:** experienced; **feared:** doubted; **faith:** loyalty

207. **louring:** threatening; **estate:** exalted rank

209. **subversion:** ruin; **harmless:** innocent

215. **dam:** mother

218. **myself bewails:** I lament loudly; **case:** plight

220. **do him good:** be beneficial to him

223. **Who's:** i.e., whoever is

224. **Free:** noble

224–25. **cold ... beams:** proverbial

226. **cold in:** indifferent to, apathetic in

227. **show:** feigned appearance

228–29. **mournful ... passengers:** See Hakluyt: "[The crocodile's] nature is ever when he would have his prey, to cry and sob like a Christian body, to provoke them to come to him, and then he snatcheth at them." (See picture, page 146.) **relenting:** soft-tempered, pitying **passengers:** travelers

230. **rolled in:** curled up on

KING HENRY
  Ay, Margaret. My heart is drowned with grief,
  Whose flood begins to flow within mine eyes,   200
  My body round engirt with misery;
  For what's more miserable than discontent?
  Ah, uncle Humphrey, in thy face I see
  The map of honor, truth, and loyalty;
  And yet, good Humphrey, is the hour to come   205
  That e'er I proved thee false or feared thy faith.
  What louring star now envies thy estate
  That these great lords and Margaret our queen
  Do seek subversion of thy harmless life?
  Thou never didst them wrong nor no man wrong.   210
  And as the butcher takes away the calf
  And binds the wretch and beats it when it ⌜strains,⌝
  Bearing it to the bloody slaughterhouse,
  Even so remorseless have they borne him hence;
  And as the dam runs lowing up and down,   215
  Looking the way her harmless young one went,
  And can do naught but wail her darling's loss,
  Even so myself bewails good Gloucester's case
  With sad unhelpful tears, and with dimmed eyes
  Look after him and cannot do him good,   220
  So mighty are his vowèd enemies.
  His fortunes I will weep and, 'twixt each groan,
  Say "Who's a traitor, Gloucester he is none."
      He exits, ⌜*with Buckingham, Salisbury, Warwick,*
            and Others. Somerset steps aside. ⌝
QUEEN MARGARET, ⌜*to Cardinal, Suffolk, and York*⌝
  Free lords, cold snow melts with the sun's hot
    beams.   225
  Henry my lord is cold in great affairs,
  Too full of foolish pity; and Gloucester's show
  Beguiles him, as the mournful crocodile
  With sorrow snares relenting passengers,
  Or as the snake, rolled in a flow'ring bank,   230

231. **checkered:** multicolored; **slough:** skin; **sting:** wound

234. **wit:** intelligence

235. **rid:** removed from

236. **rid us:** free us

237. **worthy:** excellent; **policy:** political cunning

238. **want:** lack; **color:** pretext

239. **meet:** i.e., suitable, fitting that; **course:** due process

240. **mind:** opinion; **were:** i.e., would be

241. **still:** without ceasing

242. **haply rise:** perhaps rebel

243. **yet:** thus far; **trivial argument:** slight reason or evidence

245. **by this:** i.e., according to **this** way of thinking; **would not have him:** i.e., do **not** want **him** to

246. **fain:** i.e., willing, eager

247. **'Tis . . . death:** See lines 387–88 below.

250. **Were 't . . . one:** i.e., would it not be just the same as if; **empty:** hungry

251. **kite:** vulture (See picture, page 140.)

255. **surveyor:** supervisor; **fold:** i.e., sheepfold

256. **a crafty:** i.e., of being a cunning, wily

257. **guilt:** criminality; **idly:** carelessly; **posted over:** passed off

258. **purpose:** intention (i.e., to kill); **is not executed:** i.e., has not been carried out

259. **in that:** because

With shining checkered slough, doth sting a child
That for the beauty thinks it excellent.
Believe me, lords, were none more wise than I—
And yet herein I judge mine own wit good—
This Gloucester should be quickly rid the world,   235
To rid us from the fear we have of him.

CARDINAL
That he should die is worthy policy,
But yet we want a color for his death.
'Tis meet he be condemned by course of law.

SUFFOLK
But, in my mind, that were no policy.   240
The King will labor still to save his life,
The Commons haply rise to save his life,
And yet we have but trivial argument,
More than mistrust, that shows him worthy death.

YORK
So that, by this, you would not have him die.   245

SUFFOLK
Ah, York, no man alive so fain as I!

YORK
'Tis York that hath more reason for his death.
But, my Lord Cardinal, and you, my lord of Suffolk,
Say as you think, and speak it from your souls:
Were 't not all one an empty eagle were set   250
To guard the chicken from a hungry kite
As place Duke Humphrey for the King's Protector?

QUEEN MARGARET
So the poor chicken should be sure of death.

SUFFOLK
Madam, 'tis true; and were 't not madness then
To make the fox surveyor of the fold—   255
Who, being accused a crafty murderer,
His guilt should be but idly posted over
Because his purpose is not executed?
No, let him die in that he is a fox,

260. **By . . . flock:** See picture, page 224.

261. **chaps:** jaws

262. **As . . . liege:** i.e., just as Gloucester is **by nature** (line 260) the murderer threatening the king **proved by reasons:** i.e., demonstrated by the **reasons** just given (lines 254–61)

263. **stand on:** insist on; **quillets:** i.e., subtle distinctions about

264. **gins:** traps

267. **mates:** checkmates, defeats

268. **resolutely spoke:** i.e., boldly spoken

269. **resolute:** characterized by firmness of purpose; **except . . . done:** unless the words spoken are acted on

271. **But that:** i.e., **but** to prove **that; accordeth:** agrees

272. **Seeing:** since, because

274. **I will . . . priest:** proverbial for "I will kill him"

275. **would have:** wish to **have**

276. **due orders for:** i.e., Holy Orders to become

277. **censure well the deed:** i.e., judge **the deed** to be good

279. **I tender so:** i.e., I have such care for

283. **It skills not greatly:** i.e., **it** does **not** matter much; **impugns:** opposes, finds fault with; **doom:** decision; sentence

283 SD. **Post:** special messenger with dispatches

284. **amain:** in haste

285. **signify:** make known; **up:** risen in rebellion

287. **succors:** military assistance; **rage:** violence; **betime:** early

By nature proved an enemy to the flock,   260
Before his chaps be stained with crimson blood,
As Humphrey, proved by reasons, to my liege.
And do not stand on quillets how to slay him—
Be it by gins, by snares, by subtlety,
Sleeping or waking. 'Tis no matter how,   265
So he be dead; for that is good deceit
Which mates him first that first intends deceit.

QUEEN MARGARET
Thrice noble Suffolk, 'tis resolutely spoke.

SUFFOLK
Not resolute, except so much were done,
For things are often spoke and seldom meant;   270
But that my heart accordeth with my tongue,
Seeing the deed is meritorious,
And to preserve my sovereign from his foe,
Say but the word and I will be his priest.

CARDINAL
But I would have him dead, my lord of Suffolk,   275
Ere you can take due orders for a priest.
Say you consent and censure well the deed,
And I'll provide his executioner.
I tender so the safety of my liege.

SUFFOLK
Here is my hand. The deed is worthy doing.   280

QUEEN MARGARET   And so say I.

YORK
And I. And now we three have spoke it,
It skills not greatly who impugns our doom.

Enter a Post.

POST
Great lords, from Ireland am I come amain
To signify that rebels there are up   285
And put the Englishmen unto the sword.
Send succors, lords, and stop the rage betime,

288. **uncurable:** incurable

289. **being green:** i.e., (**the wound** [line 288]) **being** recent

290. **breach:** injury; **craves:** requires, demands; **expedient:** expeditious, speedy; **stop:** closing up

293. **meet:** appropriate

295. **far-fet:** far-fetched; **policy:** political cunning

299. **betimes:** speedily, forthwith

301. **staying:** delaying

302. **charactered:** inscribed

303. **Men's flesh:** i.e., men whose **flesh** is

304–5. **this spark . . . it with:** Proverbial: "Of a little **spark a** great **fire.**"

306. **still:** quiet

308. **happily:** perhaps

309. **naught:** nothing

311. **the . . . shame:** perhaps alluding to the motto of the Knights of the Garter: *Honi soit qui mal y pense* (French for "**Shame** be to him who thinks evil.")

312. **try . . . is:** i.e., see what luck you have

313. **uncivil:** barbarous; **kerns:** lightly armed foot soldiers (See picture, page 122.)

314. **temper:** moisten (so as to form a paste)

Before the wound do grow uncurable;
For, being green, there is great hope of help.
⌈*He exits.*⌉

CARDINAL
A breach that craves a quick expedient stop!   290
What counsel give you in this weighty cause?

YORK
That Somerset be sent as regent thither.
'Tis meet that lucky ruler be employed—
Witness the fortune he hath had in France.

SOMERSET, ⌈*advancing*⌉
If York, with all his far-fet policy,   295
Had been the regent there instead of me,
He never would have stayed in France so long.

YORK
No, not to lose it all, as thou hast done.
I rather would have lost my life betimes
Than bring a burden of dishonor home   300
By staying there so long till all were lost.
Show me one scar charactered on thy skin.
Men's flesh preserved so whole do seldom win.

QUEEN MARGARET
Nay, then, this spark will prove a raging fire
If wind and fuel be brought to feed it with.—   305
No more, good York.—Sweet Somerset, be still.—
Thy fortune, York, hadst thou been regent there,
Might happily have proved far worse than his.

YORK
What, worse than naught? Nay, then, a shame take
all!   310

SOMERSET
And, in the number, thee that wishest shame!

CARDINAL
My lord of York, try what your fortune is.
Th' uncivil kerns of Ireland are in arms
And temper clay with blood of Englishmen.

316. **choicely:** carefully
317. **hap:** fortune, luck
318. **so . . . Majesty:** i.e., if the king agrees
320. **establish:** ratify
323. **Whiles:** i.e., while; **take order:** make arrangements
324. **charge:** duty
328. **break off:** i.e., (let's) stop talking
329. **that event:** i.e., what we contemplate happening
333. **truly:** properly
334. **steel:** harden, strengthen; **fearful:** apprehensive
335. **misdoubt:** mistrust
336. **that:** i.e., **that** which
337. **Resign:** surrender, consign
338. **keep:** live, reside; **mean-born:** lowborn

An Irish kern. (3.1.313, 365–66; 4.9.26–27)
From John Derricke, *The image of Irelande, with a discouerie of woodkarne . . .* (1581; 1883 facsimile).

To Ireland will you lead a band of men,   315
Collected choicely, from each county some,
And try your hap against the Irishmen?

YORK
I will, my lord, so please his Majesty.

SUFFOLK
Why, our authority is his consent,
And what we do establish he confirms.   320
Then, noble York, take thou this task in hand.

YORK
I am content. Provide me soldiers, lords,
Whiles I take order for mine own affairs.

SUFFOLK
A charge, Lord York, that I will see performed.
But now return we to the false Duke Humphrey.   325

CARDINAL
No more of him, for I will deal with him,
That henceforth he shall trouble us no more.
And so break off; the day is almost spent.
Lord Suffolk, you and I must talk of that event.

YORK
My lord of Suffolk, within fourteen days   330
At Bristow I expect my soldiers,
For there I'll ship them all for Ireland.

SUFFOLK
I'll see it truly done, my lord of York.

All but York exit.

YORK
Now, York, or never, steel thy fearful thoughts
And change misdoubt to resolution.   335
Be that thou hop'st to be, or what thou art
Resign to death; it is not worth th' enjoying.
Let pale-faced fear keep with the mean-born man
And find no harbor in a royal heart.
Faster than springtime showers comes thought on   340
  thought,

342. **dignity:** high rank (i.e., kingship)

344. **Weaves tedious snares:** i.e., tiresomely and laboriously **weaves** snare after snare (a transferred epithet)

345. **politicly:** shrewdly, craftily (ironic)

346. **send me packing:** dismiss me

347. **fear me:** i.e., **fear** (ethical dative); **starvèd:** (nearly) frozen

348. **cherished:** given warmth; **sting:** i.e., bite (Proverbial: "To nourish a **snake** in one's bosom.")

351. **take it kindly:** i.e., accept (your gift) with pleasure

352. **You . . . hands:** Proverbial: "**Put** not a naked sword **in a madman's** hand."

353. **nourish:** maintain

354. **storm:** i.e., **storm** that

356. **fell:** deadly

357. **circuit:** i.e., circle

358. **transparent:** penetrating

359. **Do:** i.e., does; **mad-bred:** stirred up by a madman (See line 352 above.) **flaw:** short spell of rough weather; tumult, uproar

360. **minister of:** i.e., agent for

361. **seduced:** enticed

362. **Ashford:** a town in central Kent

363. **commotion:** insurrection; **full:** very

364. **title:** name (For the Mortimer claim to the English throne, see 2.2.37–56, above, and *Henry VI, Part 1*, 2.5.0 SD, where **John** and Edmund are merged.)

365. **stubborn:** ruthless, fierce

367. **till that:** until; **darts:** arrows

368. **porpentine:** porcupine (See picture, page 188.)

(continued)

And not a thought but thinks on dignity.
My brain, more busy than the laboring spider,
Weaves tedious snares to trap mine enemies.
Well, nobles, well, 'tis politicly done   345
To send me packing with an host of men.
I fear me you but warm the starvèd snake,
Who, cherished in your breasts, will sting your
    hearts.
'Twas men I lacked, and you will give them me;   350
I take it kindly. Yet be well assured
You put sharp weapons in a madman's hands.
Whiles I in Ireland nourish a mighty band,
I will stir up in England some black storm
Shall blow ten thousand souls to heaven or hell;   355
And this fell tempest shall not cease to rage
Until the golden circuit on my head,
Like to the glorious sun's transparent beams,
Do calm the fury of this mad-bred flaw.
And for a minister of my intent,   360
I have seduced a headstrong Kentishman,
John Cade of Ashford,
To make commotion, as full well he can,
Under the title of John Mortimer.
In Ireland have I seen this stubborn Cade   365
Oppose himself against a troop of kerns,
And fought so long till that his thighs with darts
Were almost like a sharp-quilled porpentine;
And in the end being rescued, I have seen
Him caper upright like a wild Morisco,   370
Shaking the bloody darts as he his bells.
Full often, like a shag-haired crafty kern,
Hath he conversèd with the enemy,
And undiscovered come to me again
And given me notice of their villainies.   375
This devil here shall be my substitute;
For that John Mortimer, which now is dead,

369. **in the end:** finally

370. **caper:** dance, leap; **Morisco:** morris dancer (Morris dancers performed in costume and wore bells on their legs.)

371. **as he:** i.e., **as** the morris dancer shakes

372. **shag-haired crafty kern:** wily Irish soldier with rough matted hair

374. **undiscovered:** undetected, unobserved

375. **notice:** information, intelligence

376. **This devil here:** i.e., **this** diabolical creature I just described; **substitute:** deputy

377. **For that:** because

379. **By this:** i.e., by means of Cade's rebellion

380. **affect:** like, favor

381. **taken:** captured; **racked:** torn apart on the rack, an instrument of torture (See picture, page 158.)

383. **moved:** persuaded

384. **great like:** very likely

385. **strength:** military power, army

386. **reap . . . sowed:** Proverbial: "One sows, another reaps." **rascal:** scoundrel

388. **put apart:** perhaps, killed; or, perhaps, deposed (euphemism); **the next for me:** Interpreted in relation to 2.2, the phrase suggests, "I will be **next** on the throne."

3.2 The news of Gloucester's murder makes King Henry faint and the Commons rise to demand Suffolk's exile. The King obliges them. News arrives of the Cardinal's imminent death.

(continued)

In face, in gait, in speech he doth resemble.
By this, I shall perceive the Commons' mind,
How they affect the house and claim of York.   380
Say he be taken, racked, and torturèd,
I know no pain they can inflict upon him
Will make him say I moved him to those arms.
Say that he thrive, as 'tis great like he will,
Why then from Ireland come I with my strength   385
And reap the harvest which that rascal sowed.
For, Humphrey being dead, as he shall be,
And Henry put apart, the next for me.
                                              He exits.

⌜Scene 2⌝

*Enter two or three running over the stage, from the
murder of Duke Humphrey.*

FIRST MURDERER
Run to my lord of Suffolk. Let him know
We have dispatched the Duke as he commanded.
SECOND MURDERER
O, that it were to do! What have we done?
Didst ever hear a man so penitent?

Enter Suffolk.

FIRST MURDERER Here comes my lord.   5
SUFFOLK Now, sirs, have you dispatched this thing?
FIRST MURDERER Ay, my good lord, he's dead.
SUFFOLK
Why, that's well said. Go, get you to my house;
I will reward you for this venturous deed.
The King and all the peers are here at hand.   10
Have you laid fair the bed? Is all things well,
According as I gave directions?
FIRST MURDERER 'Tis, my good lord.
SUFFOLK Away, be gone.   ⌜*The Murderers*⌝ *exit.*

2. **dispatched:** killed

3. **to do:** i.e., still to be done (and therefore to be avoided)

6. **dispatched:** got done, finished off

8. **well said: well** done

9. **venturous:** daring; risky

10. **peers:** nobles

11. **laid fair:** i.e., straightened, smoothed; **Is:** i.e., are

17. **If:** whether; **publishèd:** reported publicly

18. **presently:** immediately

20. **straiter:** more strictly or severely

21. **true evidence:** honest witnesses; **esteem:** reputation

22. **approved . . . culpable:** i.e., proved guilty of treason **practice:** treachery

25. **acquit him:** i.e., **acquit** or clear himself

31. **forfend:** forbid

32. **tonight:** last night

35. **Rear up:** lift into a vertical position; **Wring . . . nose:** See Shakespeare's *Venus and Adonis*, where Adonis, trying to revive the unconscious Venus, "wrings her **nose**" (line 475).

A basilisk. (3.2.54, 336)
From Edward Topsell, *The history of four-footed beasts and serpents . . .* (1658).

Sound trumpets. Enter King ⌐Henry,¬ Queen
⌐Margaret,¬ Cardinal, Somerset, with Attendants.

KING HENRY
  Go, call our uncle to our presence straight.   15
  Say we intend to try his Grace today
  If he be guilty, as 'tis publishèd.

SUFFOLK
  I'll call him presently, my noble lord.   *He exits.*

KING HENRY
  Lords, take your places; and, I pray you all,
  Proceed no straiter 'gainst our uncle Gloucester   20
  Than from true evidence of good esteem
  He be approved in practice culpable.

QUEEN MARGARET
  God forbid any malice should prevail
  That faultless may condemn a nobleman!
  Pray God he may acquit him of suspicion!   25

KING HENRY
  I thank thee, ⌐Meg.¬ These words content me much.

Enter Suffolk.

  How now? Why look'st thou pale? Why tremblest
    thou?
  Where is our uncle? What's the matter, Suffolk?

SUFFOLK
  Dead in his bed, my lord. Gloucester is dead.   30

QUEEN MARGARET   Marry, God forfend!

CARDINAL
  God's secret judgment. I did dream tonight
  The Duke was dumb and could not speak a word.
                      King ⌐Henry¬ swoons.

QUEEN MARGARET
  How fares my lord? Help, lords, the King is dead!

SOMERSET
  Rear up his body. Wring him by the nose.   35

36. **ope:** open

40. **Comfort:** i.e., take comfort

41. **comfort:** cheer up; console

42. **right now:** just **now; raven's note:** For the association of the croaking of the raven with death, see Shakespeare's *Macbeth* 1.5.45–47, "The raven himself is hoarse / That croaks the fatal entrance of Duncan / Under my battlements."

43. **dismal:** cheerless; fatal; **bereft:** i.e., deprived me of; **vital powers:** faculties of mind and body necessary to life

44. **chirping of a wren:** In *Macbeth*, the wren is described as "The most diminutive of birds" (4.2.12).

45. **hollow:** insincere

46. **first-conceivèd sound: sound first** heard

47. **poison . . . words:** Proverbial: "**poison** under sugar" and "**sugared words.**"

49. **as:** i.e., **as** if it were

50. **baleful:** malignant, deadly

51. **Tyranny:** violence, outrage

52. **fright:** frighten

54. **basilisk:** mythological reptile whose glance is fatal (See picture, page 128.)

56. **shade:** shadow (Proverbial: "shadow **of death.**")

58. **rate:** berate

61. **for:** i.e., as **for**

62. **liquid:** watery

63. **blood-consuming sighs: Sighs** were believed to draw **blood** from the heart.

QUEEN MARGARET
  Run, go, help, help! O Henry, ope thine eyes!
                                    ⌜*King Henry stirs.*⌝

SUFFOLK
  He doth revive again. Madam, be patient.

KING HENRY
  O heavenly God!

QUEEN MARGARET   How fares my gracious lord?

SUFFOLK
  Comfort, my sovereign! Gracious Henry, comfort!   40

KING HENRY
  What, doth my lord of Suffolk comfort me?
  Came he right now to sing a raven's note,
  Whose dismal tune bereft my vital powers,
  And thinks he that the chirping of a wren,
  By crying comfort from a hollow breast,   45
  Can chase away the first-conceivèd sound?
  Hide not thy poison with such sugared words.
  Lay not thy hands on me. Forbear, I say!
  Their touch affrights me as a serpent's sting.
  Thou baleful messenger, out of my sight!   50
  Upon thy eyeballs, murderous Tyranny
  Sits in grim majesty to fright the world.
  Look not upon me, for thine eyes are wounding.
  Yet do not go away. Come, basilisk,
  And kill the innocent gazer with thy sight;   55
  For in the shade of death I shall find joy,
  In life but double death, now Gloucester's dead.

QUEEN MARGARET
  Why do you rate my lord of Suffolk thus?
  Although the Duke was enemy to him,
  Yet he most Christian-like laments his death.   60
  And for myself, foe as he was to me,
  Might liquid tears or heart-offending groans
  Or blood-consuming sighs recall his life,
  I would be blind with weeping, sick with groans,

67. **deem of:** judge

69. **made . . . away:** i.e., killed **the Duke**

71. **princes':** rulers'; **my reproach:** disgrace or blame of me

74. **woe is me:** (1) alas; (2) I am grieved

75. **woe:** sorry

77. **leper:** See picture, page 136.

78. **adder . . . deaf:** See Psalm 58.4–5: "like the **deaf adder** that stoppeth his ear. Which heareth not the voice of the enchanter [snake charmer]." **waxen:** grown

79. **forlorn:** abandoned, desolate

83. **an alehouse sign:** therefore paltry, worthless, or despicable: "**an alehouse'** paltry **sign**" (5.2.68)

84. **nigh-wracked:** almost shipwrecked

85. **awkward:** unfavorable, adverse; **bank:** coast

86. **Drove:** i.e., driven; **clime:** region

87. **boded:** foretold; **but well forewarning:** i.e., **but** that accurately prophesying

91. **he:** Aeolus (line 94), mythological god of the winds; **brazen caves:** i.e., **caves** strong as brass

92. **bid them:** i.e., bade the winds

93. **turn our stern:** i.e., cast the ship

95. **office:** task

96. **pretty-vaulting sea:** i.e., attractively arching waves of the **sea**

Look pale as primrose with blood-drinking sighs, 65
And all to have the noble duke alive.
What know I how the world may deem of me?
For it is known we were but hollow friends.
It may be judged I made the Duke away;
So shall my name with slander's tongue be wounded 70
And princes' courts be filled with my reproach.
This get I by his death. Ay me, unhappy,
To be a queen and crowned with infamy!

KING HENRY
Ah, woe is me for Gloucester, wretched man!

QUEEN MARGARET
Be woe for me, more wretched than he is. 75
What, dost thou turn away and hide thy face?
I am no loathsome leper. Look on me.
What, art thou, like the adder, waxen deaf?
Be poisonous too, and kill thy forlorn queen.
Is all thy comfort shut in Gloucester's tomb? 80
Why, then, Dame ⌈Margaret⌉ was ne'er thy joy.
Erect his statue and worship it,
And make my image but an alehouse sign.
Was I for this nigh-wracked upon the sea
And twice by awkward wind from England's bank 85
Drove back again unto my native clime?
What boded this, but well forewarning wind
Did seem to say "Seek not a scorpion's nest,
Nor set no footing on this unkind shore"?
What did I then but cursed the gentle gusts 90
And he that loosed them forth their brazen caves
And bid them blow towards England's blessèd shore
Or turn our stern upon a dreadful rock?
Yet Aeolus would not be a murderer,
But left that hateful office unto thee. 95
The pretty-vaulting sea refused to drown me,
Knowing that thou wouldst have me drowned on
    shore

99. **salt as sea:** i.e., salty **as** the **sea** (proverbial)

100. **splitting rocks:** i.e., **rocks** that can split ships; **sinking sands:** i.e., sandbars or shoals, which wreck and sink ships

101. **ragged:** jagged

102. **Because:** in order that; **flinty heart:** proverbial

103. **perish:** kill

104. **ken:** see, descry; **chalky cliffs:** white **cliffs** of Dover

106. **hatches:** deck

107. **dusky:** dark

108. **earnest-gaping:** ardently staring

109. **jewel:** ornament made of gold or silver and precious stones

110. **bound in with:** surrounded by

114. **packing:** gone; **heart:** i.e., the **jewel**

115. **dusky spectacles:** dim instruments of seeing

116. **ken:** sight; **Albion's:** England's; **wishèd:** desired

117. **tempted:** enticed

118. **agent:** proxy (because of his role in arranging the marriage of Margaret and Henry)

119. **Ascanius:** son of Aeneas in Virgil's Latin epic poem the *Aeneid*

120. **madding:** frenzied (in this case, with love); **Dido:** queen of Carthage, where Aeneas lands at the beginning of the epic (See longer note, page 257, and picture, page 138.) **unfold:** disclose, i.e., tell

121. **burning Troy:** See note to 1.4.19, above.

(continued)

With tears as salt as sea, through thy unkindness.
The splitting rocks cow'red in the sinking sands 100
And would not dash me with their ragged sides
Because thy flinty heart, more hard than they,
Might in thy palace perish ⌈Margaret.⌉
As far as I could ken thy chalky cliffs,
When from thy shore the tempest beat us back, 105
I stood upon the hatches in the storm,
And when the dusky sky began to rob
My earnest-gaping sight of thy land's view,
I took a costly jewel from my neck—
A heart it was, bound in with diamonds— 110
And threw it towards thy land. The sea received it,
And so I wished thy body might my heart.
And even with this I lost fair England's view,
And bid mine eyes be packing with my heart,
And called them blind and dusky spectacles 115
For losing ken of Albion's wishèd coast.
How often have I tempted Suffolk's tongue,
The agent of thy foul inconstancy,
To sit and watch me, as Ascanius did
When he to madding Dido would unfold 120
His father's acts commenced in burning Troy!
Am I not witched like her, or thou not false like
  him?
Ay me, I can no more. Die, ⌈Margaret,⌉
For Henry weeps that thou dost live so long. 125

Noise within. Enter Warwick ⌈and Salisbury,⌉
and many Commons.

WARWICK
It is reported, mighty sovereign,
That good Duke Humphrey traitorously is murdered
By Suffolk and the Cardinal Beaufort's means.
The Commons, like an angry hive of bees
That want their leader, scatter up and down 130

122. **witched like her:** charmed as Dido was by love

122–23. **false like him:** inconstant as Aeneas was when he sailed away from Dido to fulfill his destiny

124. **I . . . more:** i.e., my strength fails me

130. **want:** lack

131. **his revenge:** i.e., **revenge** of his death

132. **spleenful:** angry; **mutiny:** rebellion

133. **order:** i.e., circumstances

139. **rude:** ignorant, barbarous; **multitude:** crowd

140. **O Thou . . . things:** See Genesis 18.25: "the judge of **all** the world." **stay:** check, restrain

143. **suspect:** suspicion

145. **Fain:** gladly; **chafe:** warm; **paly:** pale

146. **drain:** let fall

148. **trunk:** corpse

150. **mean:** i.e., unworthy, insignificant

151. **his . . . image: his dead** body, now earth or dust

A leper. (3.2.77)
From Guillaume Guéroult, *Figures de la Bible* . . . (1565–70).

And care not who they sting in his revenge.
Myself have calmed their spleenful mutiny,
Until they hear the order of his death.

KING HENRY
That he is dead, good Warwick, 'tis too true;
But how he died God knows, not Henry.   135
Enter his chamber, view his breathless corpse,
And comment then upon his sudden death.

WARWICK
That shall I do, my liege.—Stay, Salisbury,
With the rude multitude till I return.

⌜*Warwick exits through one door; Salisbury and
Commons exit through another.*⌝

KING HENRY
O Thou that judgest all things, stay my thoughts,   140
My thoughts that labor to persuade my soul
Some violent hands were laid on Humphrey's life.
If my suspect be false, forgive me, God,
For judgment only doth belong to Thee.
Fain would I go to chafe his paly lips   145
With twenty thousand kisses, and to drain
Upon his face an ocean of salt tears,
To tell my love unto his dumb deaf trunk
And with my fingers feel his hand unfeeling;
But all in vain are these mean obsequies.   150
And to survey his dead and earthy image,
What were it but to make my sorrow greater?

*Bed put forth, ⌜bearing Gloucester's body.
Enter Warwick.⌝*

WARWICK
Come hither, gracious sovereign. View this body.

KING HENRY
That is to see how deep my grave is made,
For with his soul fled all my worldly solace;   155
For seeing him, I see my life in death.

158. **King:** i.e., Christ

159. **curse:** See Genesis 3.17: "Accursed shall be the ground on your account."

161. **thrice-famèd:** very famous

163. **instance:** proof, evidence

164. **settled:** come to rest

165. **timely-parted ghost:** corpse of someone who died (**parted**) in a natural or **timely** manner

166. **semblance:** appearance; **meager:** thin, emaciated

167. **Being:** i.e., the blood **being**

168. **Who:** i.e., which

169. **the same:** i.e., **the blood** (line 164); **aidance:** assistance

170. **Which:** i.e., **the blood**

175. **full:** very

176. **upreared:** on end

178. **abroad displayed:** spread out

181. **well-proportioned:** well-shaped

181–82. **rough and rugged:** shaggy

183. **corn:** wheat; **lodged:** beaten down

185. **were probable:** i.e., would be sufficient proof (literally, would be worthy of belief)

Dido. (3.2.120)
From [Guillaume Rouillé,] . . . *Promptuarii iconum* . . . (1553).

WARWICK
  As surely as my soul intends to live
  With that dread King that took our state upon Him
  To free us from His Father's wrathful curse,
  I do believe that violent hands were laid   160
  Upon the life of this thrice-famèd duke.

SUFFOLK
  A dreadful oath, sworn with a solemn tongue!
  What instance gives Lord Warwick for his vow?

WARWICK
  See how the blood is settled in his face.
  Oft have I seen a timely-parted ghost,   165
  Of ashy semblance, meager, pale, and bloodless,
  Being all descended to the laboring heart,
  Who, in the conflict that it holds with death,
  Attracts the same for aidance 'gainst the enemy,
  Which with the heart there cools and ne'er   170
    returneth
  To blush and beautify the cheek again.
  But see, his face is black and full of blood;
  His eyeballs further out than when he lived,
  Staring full ghastly, like a strangled man;   175
  His hair upreared, his nostrils stretched with
    struggling;
  His hands abroad displayed, as one that grasped
  And tugged for life and was by strength subdued.
  Look, on the sheets his hair, you see, is sticking;   180
  His well-proportioned beard made rough and
    rugged,
  Like to the summer's corn by tempest lodged.
  It cannot be but he was murdered here.
  The least of all these signs were probable.   185
                      ⌈*The bed is removed.*⌉

SUFFOLK
  Why, Warwick, who should do the Duke to death?

191. **keep:** hold in custody
192. **like:** likely
194. **belike:** perhaps, possibly
195. **timeless:** untimely
197. **fast:** close
199. **puttock's:** kite's, vulture's (See line 201, and picture, below.)
202. **tragedy:** fatal event
203. **Are . . . knife:** See picture, page 184.
206. **ease:** i.e., lack of use
207. **scoured:** cleansed
208. **badge:** distinctive sign
210. **faulty:** to blame
212. **contumelious:** insolent, overbearing
213. **controller:** one who reproves or censures

A kite. (3.1.251; 3.2.204; 5.2.11)
From Konrad Gesner, . . . *Historiae animalium* . . . (1585–1604).

Myself and Beaufort had him in protection,
And we, I hope, sir, are no murderers.

WARWICK
But both of you were vowed Duke Humphrey's foes,
⌜To Cardinal.⌝ And you, forsooth, had the good duke 190
    to keep.
'Tis like you would not feast him like a friend,
And 'tis well seen he found an enemy.

QUEEN MARGARET
Then you, belike, suspect these noblemen
As guilty of Duke Humphrey's timeless death. 195

WARWICK
Who finds the heifer dead and bleeding fresh,
And sees fast by a butcher with an ax,
But will suspect 'twas he that made the slaughter?
Who finds the partridge in the puttock's nest
But may imagine how the bird was dead, 200
Although the kite soar with unbloodied beak?
Even so suspicious is this tragedy.

QUEEN MARGARET
Are you the butcher, Suffolk? Where's your knife?
Is Beaufort termed a kite? Where are his talons?

SUFFOLK
I wear no knife to slaughter sleeping men, 205
But here's a vengeful sword, rusted with ease,
That shall be scoured in his rancorous heart
That slanders me with murder's crimson badge.—
Say, if thou dar'st, proud lord of Warwickshire,
That I am faulty in Duke Humphrey's death. 210

WARWICK
What dares not Warwick, if false Suffolk dare him?

QUEEN MARGARET
He dares not calm his contumelious spirit
Nor cease to be an arrogant controller,
Though Suffolk dare him twenty thousand times.

215. **still:** quiet

220. **blameful:** guilty

221. **stern:** grim, merciless; **untutored:** uneducated, boorish; **churl:** peasant; **stock:** i.e., family tree

222. **graft with:** i.e., grafted to (See picture, page 144.) **crab-tree:** wild-apple tree; **slip:** shoot

223. **race:** family

224. **bucklers:** shields

225. **deathsman:** executioner

226. **Quitting:** freeing, clearing

227. **mild:** not easily provoked

229. **thy passèd speech:** what you just said

232. **fearful homage:** timorous reverence (the kneeling to apologize)

233. **Give thee thy hire: give** you your reward; i.e., kill you (proverbial)

234. **Pernicious:** dangerous

236. **this presence:** i.e., the **presence** of the king

238. **cope:** fight

240. **What . . . untainted:** See Ephesians 6.14: "the **breastplate** of righteousness."

242. **locked up in steel:** i.e., enclosed in armor

WARWICK
    Madam, be still—with reverence may I say—   215
    For every word you speak in his behalf
    Is slander to your royal dignity.

SUFFOLK
    Blunt-witted lord, ignoble in demeanor!
    If ever lady wronged her lord so much,
    Thy mother took into her blameful bed   220
    Some stern untutored churl, and noble stock
    Was graft with crab-tree slip, whose fruit thou art
    And never of the Nevilles' noble race.

WARWICK
    But that the guilt of murder bucklers thee
    And I should rob the deathsman of his fee,   225
    Quitting thee thereby of ten thousand shames,
    And that my sovereign's presence makes me mild,
    I would, false murd'rous coward, on thy knee
    Make thee beg pardon for thy passèd speech
    And say it was thy mother that thou meant'st,   230
    That thou thyself wast born in bastardy;
    And after all this fearful homage done,
    Give thee thy hire and send thy soul to hell,
    Pernicious bloodsucker of sleeping men!

SUFFOLK
    Thou shalt be waking while I shed thy blood,   235
    If from this presence thou dar'st go with me.

WARWICK
    Away even now, or I will drag thee hence!
    Unworthy though thou art, I'll cope with thee
    And do some service to Duke Humphrey's ghost.
                      ⌜*Warwick and Suffolk*⌝ *exit.*

KING HENRY
    What stronger breastplate than a heart untainted?   240
    Thrice is he armed that hath his quarrel just,
    And he but naked, though locked up in steel,
    Whose conscience with injustice is corrupted.

243 SD. **within:** offstage

247. **in our presence:** It was treason to have a weapon **drawn in** the **presence** of the monarch.

249. **men of Bury:** townsmen **of Bury** St. Edmunds

250. **Set all upon me: all** attacked **me**

253. **straight:** straightaway, immediately

259. **mere:** pure

260. **opposite:** hostile, antagonistic

261. **As being:** i.e., which might be

262. **forward in:** i.e., eager for

265. **charge:** order

266. **In pain:** on penalty; **dislike:** displeasure

267. **strait:** strict

271. **being suffered:** i.e., you **being** allowed to remain; **harmful:** a transferred epithet (because it is the snake and not the **slumber** that is **harmful**)

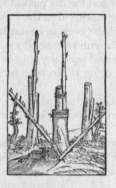

Grafting. (3.2.222)
From Marco Bussato, *Giardino di agricoltura* . . . (1599).

A noise within.

QUEEN MARGARET   What noise is this?

Enter Suffolk and Warwick, with their weapons drawn.

KING HENRY
Why, how now, lords? Your wrathful weapons   245
  drawn
Here in our presence? Dare you be so bold?
Why, what tumultuous clamor have we here?

SUFFOLK
The trait'rous Warwick, with the men of Bury,
Set all upon me, mighty sovereign.   250

Enter Salisbury.

SALISBURY, ⌈*to the offstage Commons*⌉
Sirs, stand apart. The King shall know your mind.—
Dread lord, the Commons send you word by me,
Unless Lord Suffolk straight be done to death
Or banishèd fair England's territories,
They will by violence tear him from your palace   255
And torture him with grievous ling'ring death.
They say, by him the good duke Humphrey died;
They say, in him they fear your Highness' death;
And mere instinct of love and loyalty,
Free from a stubborn opposite intent,   260
As being thought to contradict your liking,
Makes them thus forward in his banishment.
They say, in care of your most royal person,
That if your Highness should intend to sleep,
And charge that no man should disturb your rest,   265
In pain of your dislike or pain of death,
Yet, notwithstanding such a strait edict,
Were there a serpent seen with forkèd tongue
That slyly glided towards your Majesty,
It were but necessary you were waked,   270
Lest, being suffered in that harmful slumber,

272. **mortal:** deadly; **worm:** snake
274. **whe'er:** whether
275. **fell:** deadly
276. **sting:** i.e., bite
278. **bereft:** deprived
280. **like:** i.e., likely that; **rude:** uneducated; **unpolished:** unrefined; **hinds:** boors
284. **quaint:** clever, affected
287. **sort:** band; **tinkers:** menders of metal household utensils, but also a term for vagrants and suspected thieves
291. **cited:** summoned, aroused
292. **did I purpose:** I resolved (to act)
293. **sure:** surely, certainly
294. **Mischance:** calamity; **state:** government
296. **far:** very
297. **infection in:** i.e., **infection** into
299. **gentle:** noble
300. **Ungentle:** discourteous, unmannerly

A weeping crocodile. (3.1.228–29)
From Jacob Typot, *Symbola diuina* . . . (1652).

The mortal worm might make the sleep eternal.
And therefore do they cry, though you forbid,
That they will guard you, whe'er you will or no,
From such fell serpents as false Suffolk is,   275
With whose envenomèd and fatal sting
Your loving uncle, twenty times his worth,
They say, is shamefully bereft of life.

COMMONS, *within*
An answer from the King, my lord of Salisbury!

SUFFOLK
'Tis like the Commons, rude unpolished hinds,   280
Could send such message to their sovereign!
⌜*To Salisbury.*⌝ But you, my lord, were glad to be
employed,
To show how quaint an orator you are.
But all the honor Salisbury hath won   285
Is that he was the lord ambassador
Sent from a sort of tinkers to the King.

⌜COMMONS,⌝ *within*
An answer from the King, or we will all break in.

KING HENRY
Go, Salisbury, and tell them all from me,
I thank them for their tender loving care;   290
And, had I not been cited so by them,
Yet did I purpose as they do entreat.
For, sure, my thoughts do hourly prophesy
Mischance unto my state by Suffolk's means.
And therefore, by His Majesty I swear,   295
Whose far unworthy deputy I am,
He shall not breathe infection in this air
But three days longer, on the pain of death.
                                              ⌜*Salisbury exits.*⌝

QUEEN MARGARET
O Henry, let me plead for gentle Suffolk!

KING HENRY
Ungentle queen to call him gentle Suffolk!   300

313. **playfellows:** companions in amusement

314. **the devil . . . third:** let **the devil make a third** (Proverbial: "There cannot lightly come a worse except **the devil** come himself.")

315. **tend upon:** accompany

317. **heavy:** sorrowful

320. **Wherefore:** why

322. **mandrake's groan:** According to superstition, the mandragora plant, when uprooted, gave a shriek that caused its hearers to run mad or die. See *Romeo and Juliet* 4.3.48–49.

323. **invent:** find; **searching:** probing, piercing

324. **curst:** malignant

325. **fixèd:** perhaps, clenched or gritted

326. **full:** entirely

327. **lean-faced Envy:** In Ovid's *Metamorphoses*, Envy's home is a hideous, filthy **cave.** She is **lean-faced** because "she pines away" at "the sight of men's successes, she gnaws and is gnawed, herself her own punishment" (book 2, lines 760–805, esp. lines 779–82). See picture, page 152.

329. **flint:** stone from which sparks are struck

330. **distract:** distracted, driven mad

No more, I say. If thou dost plead for him,
Thou wilt but add increase unto my wrath.
Had I but said, I would have kept my word;
But when I swear, it is irrevocable.
⌐*To Suffolk.*⌐ If, after three days' space, thou here   305
  be'st found
On any ground that I am ruler of,
The world shall not be ransom for thy life.—
Come, Warwick, come, good Warwick, go with me.
I have great matters to impart to thee.   310
                    ⌐*All but the Queen and Suffolk*⌐ *exit.*
QUEEN MARGARET, ⌐*calling after King Henry and*
    Warwick⌐
Mischance and sorrow go along with you!
Heart's discontent and sour affliction
Be playfellows to keep you company!
There's two of you; the devil make a third,
And threefold vengeance tend upon your steps!   315
SUFFOLK
Cease, gentle queen, these execrations,
And let thy Suffolk take his heavy leave.
QUEEN MARGARET
Fie, coward woman and soft-hearted wretch!
Hast thou not spirit to curse thine ⌐*enemies*⌐?
SUFFOLK
A plague upon them! Wherefore should I curse   320
  them?
⌐*Could*⌐ curses kill, as doth the mandrake's groan,
I would invent as bitter searching terms,
As curst, as harsh, and horrible to hear,
Delivered strongly through my fixèd teeth,   325
With full as many signs of deadly hate,
As lean-faced Envy in her loathsome cave.
My tongue should stumble in mine earnest words;
Mine eyes should sparkle like the beaten flint;
Mine hair be fixed on end, as one distract;   330

331. **ban:** call down damnation

334. **Gall:** bile; **daintiest:** most delicate thing

335. **grove . . . trees:** associated with graveyards

336. **prospect:** view; **basilisks:** legendary reptiles whose glance can kill (see line 54 above); or, large cannons

337. **smart:** painful; **lizards' stings:** Lizards were thought to have **stings** and, according to Pliny's *Natural History* (c. 80 C.E.), they were poisonous.

339. **boding:** foreboding, ominous; **consort:** company of musicians

340. **dark-seated:** situated in darkness

342. **sun 'gainst glass:** i.e., sun's rays dazzlingly reflected by a mirror (**glass**)

343. **over-chargèd:** overloaded

345. **leave:** stop

350. **sport:** diversion

352. **dew . . . tears:** proverbial

354. **woeful monuments:** commemorations of grief (i.e., **tears**)

355. **printed:** i.e., imprinted as if in wax

356. **these:** i.e., her lips; **seal:** device (e.g., heraldic design) imprinted in wax on a document (here the imprint of her lips on his **hand**)

357. **whom:** i.e., which (her lips)

359. **know:** be familiar with by experience

360. **surmised:** imagined

361. **surfeits:** overeats; **want:** lack (i.e., of food)

362. **repeal thee:** recall you from exile; **be well assured:** assure yourself; trust me

Ay, every joint should seem to curse and ban;
And even now my burdened heart would break
Should I not curse them. Poison be their drink!
Gall, worse than gall, the daintiest that they taste;
Their sweetest shade, a grove of cypress trees; 335
Their chiefest prospect, murd'ring basilisks;
Their softest touch, as smart as lizards' stings!
Their music, frightful as the serpent's hiss,
And boding screech owls make the consort full!
All the foul terrors in dark-seated hell— 340

QUEEN MARGARET
Enough, sweet Suffolk, thou torment'st thyself,
And these dread curses, like the sun 'gainst glass,
Or like an over-chargèd gun, recoil
And ⌜turn⌝ the force of them upon thyself.

SUFFOLK
You bade me ban, and will you bid me leave? 345
Now, by the ground that I am banished from,
Well could I curse away a winter's night,
Though standing naked on a mountain top
Where biting cold would never let grass grow,
And think it but a minute spent in sport. 350

QUEEN MARGARET
O, let me entreat thee cease! Give me thy hand,
That I may dew it with my mournful tears;
Nor let the rain of heaven wet this place
To wash away my woeful monuments.
                              ⌜*She kisses his hand.*⌝
O, could this kiss be printed in thy hand, 355
That thou mightst think upon these by the seal,
Through whom a thousand sighs are breathed for
    thee!
So, get thee gone, that I may know my grief;
'Tis but surmised whiles thou art standing by, 360
As one that surfeits thinking on a want.
I will repeal thee, or, be well assured,

363. **Adventure:** venture, dare

373. **wilderness:** uninhabited region

374. **So:** provided that

376. **several:** particular, individual

378. **I . . . more:** i.e., my strength fails; **joy:** enjoy

379. **no . . . naught:** i.e., will **joy in** nothing (double negative for emphasis)

381. **signify:** announce

384. **catch:** grasp, seize

388. **as to him:** i.e., **as if to the King** (line 387)

389. **overchargèd:** overburdened

392. **heavy:** sorrowful, grievous

". . . lean-faced Envy in her loathsome cave." (3.2.327)
From Gabriele Simeoni, *La vita . . .* (1559).

Adventure to be banishèd myself;
And banishèd I am, if but from thee.
Go, speak not to me. Even now be gone! 365
O, go not yet! Even thus two friends condemned
Embrace and kiss and take ten thousand leaves,
Loather a hundred times to part than die.
⌜*They embrace.*⌝
Yet now farewell, and farewell life with thee.

SUFFOLK
Thus is poor Suffolk ten times banishèd, 370
Once by the King, and three times thrice by thee.
'Tis not the land I care for, wert thou thence.
A wilderness is populous enough,
So Suffolk had thy heavenly company;
For where thou art, there is the world itself, 375
With every several pleasure in the world;
And where thou art not, desolation.
I can no more. Live thou to joy thy life;
Myself no joy in naught but that thou liv'st.

Enter Vaux.

QUEEN MARGARET
Whither goes Vaux so fast? What news, I prithee? 380
VAUX   To signify unto his Majesty,
That Cardinal Beaufort is at point of death;
For suddenly a grievous sickness took him
That makes him gasp and stare and catch the air,
Blaspheming God and cursing men on earth. 385
Sometimes he talks as if Duke Humphrey's ghost
Were by his side; sometimes he calls the King
And whispers to his pillow, as to him,
The secrets of his overchargèd soul.
And I am sent to tell his Majesty 390
That even now he cries aloud for him.
QUEEN MARGARET
Go, tell this heavy message to the King. ⌜*Vaux*⌝ *exits.*

393. **What is this world:** Proverbial: **"What** a **world is this!"**

394. **an hour's poor loss:** i.e., the (Cardinal's) **loss** of an hour (of his aged life)

395. **Omitting:** leaving disregarded

397. **southern clouds:** i.e., the source of much rain; **contend:** compete

398. **increase:** crops

402. **by me:** i.e., in my company; **thou art but dead:** i.e., you are sure to die

408. **dug:** nipple

409. **Where:** whereas; **from:** i.e., out of

411. **stop:** block up

412. **turn:** send back

414. **Elysium:** classical paradise for those favored by the gods

415. **by thee:** in your company

416. **From:** away **from**

417. **befall . . . befall:** i.e., whatever happens (proverbial)

418. **a fretful corrosive:** a caustic (a substance used medicinally to burn away flesh)

419. **deathful:** mortal

422. **Iris:** i.e., messenger (In mythology, **Iris,** the rainbow, is Juno's messenger. See picture, page 52.)

425. **cask:** casket, small box for jewels

Ay me! What is this world? What news are these!
But wherefore grieve I at an hour's poor loss,
Omitting Suffolk's exile, my soul's treasure?   395
Why only, Suffolk, mourn I not for thee,
And with the southern clouds contend in tears—
Theirs for the earth's increase, mine for my
    sorrows'?
Now get thee hence. The King, thou know'st, is   400
    coming;
If thou be found by me, thou art but dead.

SUFFOLK
If I depart from thee, I cannot live;
And in thy sight to die, what were it else
But like a pleasant slumber in thy lap?   405
Here could I breathe my soul into the air,
As mild and gentle as the cradle babe
Dying with mother's dug between its lips;
Where, from thy sight, I should be raging mad
And cry out for thee to close up mine eyes,   410
To have thee with thy lips to stop my mouth.
So shouldst thou either turn my flying soul,
Or I should breathe it so into thy body,
And then it lived in sweet Elysium.
To die by thee were but to die in jest;   415
From thee to die were torture more than death.
O, let me stay, befall what may befall!

QUEEN MARGARET
Away! Though parting be a fretful corrosive,
It is applièd to a deathful wound.
To France, sweet Suffolk. Let me hear from thee,   420
For wheresoe'er thou art in this world's globe,
I'll have an Iris that shall find thee out.

SUFFOLK   I go.
QUEEN MARGARET   And take my heart with thee.
SUFFOLK
A jewel locked into the woefull'st cask   425

427. **splitted bark:** ship split in two; **sunder we:** are we torn apart

3.3   The Cardinal dies.

———————

4. **So:** provided that
9. **he:** i.e., Gloucester; **Where should he die:** i.e., **where** else would you think **he** would **die**
10. **whe'er:** whether
14. **dust:** i.e., that to which all things are reduced in death
16. **lime-twigs:** i.e., twigs smeared with birdlime to trap birds
18. **of him:** i.e., from him

An apothecary. (3.3.17)
From Ambroise Paré, *The workes of . . .* (1634).

That ever did contain a thing of worth!
Even as a splitted bark, so sunder we.
This way fall I to death.

QUEEN MARGARET   This way for me.
They exit ⌐through different doors.⌐

⌐Scene 3⌐

*Enter King ⌐Henry,⌐ Salisbury and Warwick, to the
Cardinal in bed, ⌐raving and staring.⌐*

KING HENRY
How fares my lord? Speak, Beaufort, to thy sovereign.

CARDINAL
If thou be'st Death, I'll give thee England's treasure,
Enough to purchase such another island,
So thou wilt let me live and feel no pain.

KING HENRY
Ah, what a sign it is of evil life,   5
Where Death's approach is seen so terrible!

WARWICK
Beaufort, it is thy sovereign speaks to thee.

CARDINAL
Bring me unto my trial when you will.
Died he not in his bed? Where should he die?
Can I make men live, whe'er they will or no?   10
O, torture me no more! I will confess.
Alive again? Then show me where he is.
I'll give a thousand pound to look upon him.
He hath no eyes! The dust hath blinded them.
Comb down his hair. Look, look. It stands upright,   15
Like lime-twigs set to catch my wingèd soul.
Give me some drink, and bid the apothecary
Bring the strong poison that I bought of him.

KING HENRY
O, Thou eternal mover of the heavens,

24. **grin:** bare his teeth
25. **pass:** die
26. **if . . . be:** i.e., if God so pleases
30. **argues:** indicates
31. **Forbear to judge:** See Matthew 7.1: "**Judge** not, that you be not judged." **we . . . all:** See Matthew 3.23: "**all** have sinned."
32. **curtain:** bed **curtain; close:** shut

Being tortured on the rack. (3.1.381)
From Girolamo Maggi, . . . *De tintinnabulis liber postumus . . . Accedit . . . De equuleo liber . . .* (1689).

Look with a gentle eye upon this wretch!   20
O, beat away the busy meddling fiend
That lays strong siege unto this wretch's soul,
And from his bosom purge this black despair!

WARWICK
See how the pangs of death do make him grin!

SALISBURY
Disturb him not. Let him pass peaceably.   25

KING HENRY
Peace to his soul, if God's good pleasure be!—
Lord Card'nal, if thou think'st on heaven's bliss,
Hold up thy hand; make signal of thy hope.
                          ⌜*The Cardinal dies.*⌝
He dies and makes no sign. O, God forgive him!

WARWICK
So bad a death argues a monstrous life.   30

KING HENRY
Forbear to judge, for we are sinners all.
Close up his eyes, and draw the curtain close,
And let us all to meditation.
                 ⌜*After the curtains are closed around
        the bed,*⌝ *they exit.* ⌜*The bed is removed.*⌝

HENRY VI
Part 2

ACT 4

4.1 Attempting to sail to France, Suffolk is captured by shipmen and brutally assassinated.

---

0 SD. **Ordnance:** cannon; **Master:** officer, ranking just below the lieutenant, responsible for navigation on a warship; **Master's Mate:** officer subordinate to but working with the **Master**

1. **gaudy:** showy; **blabbing:** secret-revealing; **remorseful:** compassionate

3. **jades:** worn-out horses (imagined to **drag** Night's wagon across the sky) See longer note, page 257.

5. **flagging:** drooping, failing

6. **Clip:** embrace

8. **of our prize:** i.e., from the ship we have captured

9. **pinnace:** small, light vessel; **the Downs:** the sea just off the east coast of Kent

10. **make their ransom:** pay a sum to procure their freedom

11. **discolored:** stained (i.e., with **their blood** after they are slain—an example of prolepsis)

13. **boot:** profit; **this:** i.e., **this** second **prisoner** (line 12)

⌜ACT 4⌝

⌜Scene 1⌝

*Alarum. ⌜Offstage⌝ fight at sea. Ordnance goes off.
Enter Lieutenant, Suffolk, ⌜captive and in disguise,⌝
and Others, ⌜including a Master, a Master's Mate,
Walter Whitmore, and Prisoners.⌝*

LIEUTENANT
The gaudy, blabbing, and remorseful day
Is crept into the bosom of the sea,
And now loud-howling wolves arouse the jades
That drag the tragic melancholy night,
Who, with their drowsy, slow, and flagging wings   5
Clip dead men's graves, and from their misty jaws
Breathe foul contagious darkness in the air.
Therefore bring forth the soldiers of our prize;
For, whilst our pinnace anchors in the Downs,
Here shall they make their ransom on the sand,   10
Or with their blood stain this discolored shore.—
Master, this prisoner freely give I thee.—
And, thou that art his mate, make boot of this.—
The other, Walter Whitmore, is thy share.
            ⌜*Three gentlemen prisoners, including Suffolk,
                                are handed over.*⌝

FIRST GENTLEMAN
What is my ransom, master? Let me know.   15

163

16. **crowns:** coins worth five shillings

18. **think you much:** i.e., do **you think** it too **much**

19. **port:** social position

22. **counterpoised:** counterbalanced

24. **straight:** straightaway, immediately

25. **laying the prize aboard:** running **our pinnace** (line 9) alongside **the prize** in order to board it

29. **George:** jewel that forms part of the insignia of the Order of the Knights of the Garter (See picture, page 206.)

30. **Rate . . . wilt:** i.e., estimate my value however you wish

31. **Walter:** Suffolk's response to this name indicates its Elizabethan pronunciation, in which the *l* is not sounded, making **Walter** sound like **water.** (See 1.4.35 and lines 35–36 below.)

35. **cunning man:** fortune-teller; **birth:** fortune as influenced by the aspect of the planets at the moment of birth

36. **by water:** See note to line 31, above.

37. **bloody-minded:** cruel, bloodthirsty

38. **Gualtier:** the French equivalent of *Walter;* **sounded:** pronounced

MASTER
  A thousand crowns, or else lay down your head.
MATE, ⌜*to the Second Gentleman*⌝
  And so much shall you give, or off goes yours.
LIEUTENANT
  What, think you much to pay two thousand crowns,
  And bear the name and port of gentlemen?—
  Cut both the villains' throats—for die you shall;   20
  The lives of those which we have lost in fight
  Be counterpoised with such a petty sum!
FIRST GENTLEMAN
  I'll give it, sir, and therefore spare my life.
SECOND GENTLEMAN
  And so will I, and write home for it straight.
WHITMORE, ⌜*to Suffolk*⌝
  I lost mine eye in laying the prize aboard,   25
  And therefore to revenge it shalt thou die;
  And so should these, if I might have my will.
LIEUTENANT
  Be not so rash. Take ransom; let him live.
SUFFOLK
  Look on my George; I am a gentleman.
  Rate me at what thou wilt, thou shalt be paid.   30
WHITMORE
  And so am I. My name is Walter Whitmore.
                  ⌜*Suffolk starts.*⌝
  How now, why starts thou? What, doth death
    affright?
SUFFOLK
  Thy name affrights me, in whose sound is death.
  A cunning man did calculate my birth   35
  And told me that by water I should die.
  Yet let not this make thee be bloody-minded;
  Thy name is Gualtier, being rightly sounded.
WHITMORE
  Gualtier or Walter, which it is, I care not.

40. **blur:** defile, blot

42. **sell revenge:** i.e., accept ransom rather than take **revenge**

43. **Broke:** i.e., broken; **arms:** coat of **arms; defaced:** obliterated

45. **Stay:** stop, pause

49. **Jove . . . disguised:** For a catalogue of the god Jove's disguises in the pursuit of women, see Ovid's *Metamorphoses* 6.103–14.

51. **lousy:** vile; **swain:** man of low social status; **King Henry's blood:** i.e., Suffolk's **blood** (an exaggerated claim of consanguinity)

52. **blood of Lancaster:** descendants of John of Gaunt, Duke of **Lancaster** (See genealogical chart, page 2.)

53. **jaded groom:** i.e., contemptible fellow

54. **kissed thy hand:** paid your respects (See longer note, page 257.) **held my stirrup:** helped me to mount, as a sign of reverence to me

55. **Bareheaded:** with head uncovered as a sign of respect; **footcloth mule: mule** bearing or covered in a **footcloth,** a large ornamented cloth

56. **happy:** fortunate; **shook my head:** i.e., nodded to you

57. **waited at my cup:** i.e., kept my goblet full

58. **Fed from my trencher:** i.e., eaten my food **trencher:** platter; **kneeled . . . board:** perhaps, served at table **board:** table for serving food

60. **crestfall'n:** humbled

61. **abortive pride:** i.e., **pride** that can come to nothing

(continued)

Never yet did base dishonor blur our name 40
But with our sword we wiped away the blot.
Therefore, when merchantlike I sell revenge,
Broke be my sword, my arms torn and defaced,
And I proclaimed a coward through the world!

SUFFOLK
Stay, Whitmore, for thy prisoner is a prince, 45
The Duke of Suffolk, William de la Pole.

WHITMORE
The Duke of Suffolk muffled up in rags?

SUFFOLK
Ay, but these rags are no part of the Duke.
⌐Jove sometimes went disguised, and why not I?⌐

LIEUTENANT
But Jove was never slain, as thou shalt be. 50

⌐SUFFOLK⌐
Obscure and lousy swain, King Henry's blood,
The honorable blood of Lancaster,
Must not be shed by such a jaded groom.
Hast thou not kissed thy hand and held my stirrup?
Bareheaded plodded by my footcloth mule, 55
And thought thee happy when I shook my head?
How often hast thou waited at my cup,
Fed from my trencher, kneeled down at the board,
When I have feasted with Queen Margaret?
Remember it, and let it make thee crestfall'n, 60
Ay, and allay this thy abortive pride.
How in our voiding lobby hast thou stood
And duly waited for my coming forth?
This hand of mine hath writ in thy behalf,
And therefore shall it charm thy riotous tongue. 65

WHITMORE
Speak, captain, shall I stab the forlorn swain?

LIEUTENANT
First let my words stab him as he hath me.

62. **our voiding lobby:** corridor or passageway by which we departed

64. **writ in thy behalf:** i.e., written in defense of or in favor of you

65. **charm:** silence; **riotous:** noisy, unrestrained

66. **forlorn swain:** trite poetic term for an unrequited lover (literally, forsaken sweetheart)

68. **slave:** rascal (term of contempt); **blunt:** without point or edge

69. **our longboat's side:** the **side** of the largest boat belonging to our ship

71. **for thy own:** i.e., **for** fear of losing your **own**

72. **Pole:** i.e., de la **Pole,** Suffolk's surname (with possible wordplay on *poll* or head, on the *pole* on which heads were fixed after beheading, on *Sir Pol* or parrot in line 74, and on *pool* in lines 75–76)

75. **kennel:** gutter; **sink:** cesspool

76. **Troubles:** muddies

77. **yawning:** gaping, eager to devour

78. **For:** i.e., to prevent its

83. **Against:** exposed to; **senseless:** unfeeling; **grin:** bare the teeth (in a death grimace)

84. **Who:** i.e., which (**the winds** [line 83]); **again:** in response

85. **hags of hell:** i.e., Furies, mythological semi-divine avengers

86. **affy:** marry (as a proxy); **lord:** i.e., Henry VI

87. **worthless king:** i.e., Reignier

88. **Having:** i.e., who has; **diadem:** crown

89. **policy:** political cunning

90. **Sylla:** Lucius Cornelius Sulla, Roman general whose time as dictator (82–80 B.C.E.), was notorious for the butchery of citizens; **overgorged:** crammed

(continued)

SUFFOLK
  Base slave, thy words are blunt, and so art thou.
LIEUTENANT
  Convey him hence, and on our longboat's side,
  Strike off his head.   70
SUFFOLK   Thou dar'st not for thy own.
⌜LIEUTENANT
  Yes, Pole.
SUFFOLK   Pole!⌝
LIEUTENANT   Pole! Sir Pole! Lord!
  Ay, kennel, puddle, sink, whose filth and dirt   75
  Troubles the silver spring where England drinks!
  Now will I dam up this thy yawning mouth
  For swallowing the treasure of the realm.
  Thy lips that kissed the Queen shall sweep the
      ground,   80
  And thou that smiledst at good Duke Humphrey's
      death
  Against the senseless winds shall grin in vain,
  Who in contempt shall hiss at thee again.
  And wedded be thou to the hags of hell   85
  For daring to affy a mighty lord
  Unto the daughter of a worthless king,
  Having neither subject, wealth, nor diadem.
  By devilish policy art thou grown great,
  And, like ambitious Sylla, overgorged   90
  With gobbets of thy ⌜mother's⌝ bleeding heart.
  By thee Anjou and Maine were sold to France.
  The false revolting Normans thorough thee
  Disdain to call us lord, and Picardy
  Hath slain their governors, surprised our forts,   95
  And sent the ragged soldiers wounded home.
  The princely Warwick, and the Nevilles all,
  Whose dreadful swords were never drawn in vain,
  As hating thee, ⌜are⌝ rising up in arms.
  And now the house of York, thrust from the crown   100

91. **gobbets:** pieces of raw flesh; **thy mother's:** i.e., England's (The implication is that **Sylla** gorged on his **mother's** [Rome's] **bleeding heart.**)

93. **false:** treacherous; **revolting:** rebelling; **thorough:** on account of

95. **surprised:** captured without warning

98. **dreadful:** dreaded, terrible

99. **As hating thee:** i.e., because they hate you

101. **a guiltless king:** i.e., Richard II (See 2.2.19–30, above.)

102. **lofty:** haughty

103. **hopeful colors:** i.e., battle standards raised in the hope of winning the crown

104. **Advance:** raise; **half-faced sun:** presumably alluding to the sunburst device associated with King Edward III and Richard II

105. **writ:** i.e., written; **Invitis nubibus:** despite the clouds (Latin)

107. **reproach:** disgrace; **beggary:** poverty

109. **by thee:** i.e., because of you

110. **god:** probably Jupiter, the Roman **god** called the **thunder-**darter, or wielder of thunderbolts

111. **servile:** slavish

115. **Bargulus . . . pirate:** In *De officiis* (44 B.C.E.), a work widely read in Elizabethan schools, Cicero mentions this **pirate** from the Adriatic seacoast.

116. **Drones . . . beehives:** According to folklore, drone beetles creep under the wings of eagles and suck their veins dry, and drone bees eat up the honey from hives.

118. **By:** i.e., by the hand of; **vassal:** slave

(continued)

By shameful murder of a guiltless king
And lofty, proud, encroaching tyranny,
Burns with revenging fire, whose hopeful colors
Advance our half-faced sun, striving to shine,
Under the which is writ *"Invitis nubibus."*   105
The commons here in Kent are up in arms,
And, to conclude, reproach and beggary
Is crept into the palace of our king,
And all by thee.—Away! Convey him hence.

SUFFOLK
O, that I were a god, to shoot forth thunder   110
Upon these paltry, servile, abject drudges!
Small things make base men proud. This villain
  here,
Being captain of a pinnace, threatens more
Than Bargulus, the strong Illyrian pirate.   115
Drones suck not eagles' blood, but rob beehives.
It is impossible that I should die
By such a lowly vassal as thyself.
Thy words move rage and not remorse in me.
I go of message from the Queen to France.   120
I charge thee waft me safely cross the Channel.

LIEUTENANT ⌜Walter.⌝

WHITMORE
Come, Suffolk, I must waft thee to thy death.

SUFFOLK
Paene gelidus timor occupat artus.
It is thee I fear.   125

WHITMORE
Thou shalt have cause to fear before I leave thee.
What, are you daunted now? Now will you stoop?

FIRST GENTLEMAN
My gracious lord, entreat him; speak him fair.

SUFFOLK
Suffolk's imperial tongue is stern and rough,
Used to command, untaught to plead for favor.   130

119. **remorse:** repentance
120. **go of message:** i.e., carry communication
121. **charge:** order; **waft:** convey
124. **Paene . . . artus:** "Cold fear almost entirely seizes my limbs" (Latin; an echo of Lucan, *Civil War* 1.246).
127. **stoop:** bow to superior power
128. **entreat:** implore; **speak him fair:** address him courteously
129. **imperial:** commanding, majestic
131. **Far be it:** i.e., God forbid; **we:** the royal "we"
132. **suit:** petition
133. **Stoop:** bend; **block:** executioner's **block**
135. **pole:** See note to line 72 above.
136. **uncovered:** See note to line 55 above. **vulgar:** common
139. **Hale:** haul
142. **bezonians:** knaves, beggars (from the Italian *bisogno*, meaning "need, want")
143. **sworder:** gladiator; **banditto:** outlaw
144. **sweet:** gracious; **Tully:** Marcus Tullius Cicero (106–43 B.C.E.), famous Roman orator, politician, and philosopher, actually killed by a centurion and a tribune
144–45. **Brutus' . . . Caesar:** See Shakespeare's *Julius Caesar* 3.1. (Brutus's mother became Caesar's mistress after the death of her husband.)
145–46. **savage . . . Great:** i.e., **savage islanders** killed **Pompey the Great,** Pompeius Magnus (106–48 B.C.E.), Roman general and rival to Caesar (actually killed by his own former centurions)

Far be it we should honor such as these
With humble suit. No, rather let my head
Stoop to the block than these knees bow to any
Save to the God of heaven and to my king;
And sooner dance upon a bloody pole   135
Than stand uncovered to the vulgar groom.
True nobility is exempt from fear.—
More can I bear than you dare execute.

LIEUTENANT
Hale him away, and let him talk no more.

⌈SUFFOLK⌉
Come, soldiers, show what cruelty you can,   140
That this my death may never be forgot!
Great men oft die by vile bezonians:
A Roman sworder and banditto slave
Murdered sweet Tully; Brutus' bastard hand
Stabbed Julius Caesar; savage islanders   145
Pompey the Great, and Suffolk dies by pirates.
                    ⌈*Walter Whitmore*⌉ *exits with*
                        Suffolk ⌈*and Others.*⌉

LIEUTENANT
And as for these whose ransom we have set,
It is our pleasure one of them depart.
⌈*To Second Gentleman.*⌉ Therefore come you with us,
     and let him go.   *Lieutenant and the rest exit.* 150
                        The First Gentleman remains.

           Enter Walter ⌈*Whitmore*⌉ *with the body*
               ⌈*and severed head of Suffolk.*⌉

WHITMORE
There let his head and lifeless body lie,
Until the Queen his mistress bury it.
                        Walter ⌈*Whitmore*⌉ *exits.*

FIRST GENTLEMAN
O, barbarous and bloody spectacle!
His body will I bear unto the King.

4.2 In a plot instigated by York, Jack Cade leads a rebellion against King Henry. The Staffords seek to put it down.

———————————

0 SD. **Bevis:** See longer note, page 257. **John Holland:** The text in the First Folio gives this character the name of a known Elizabethan actor.

2. **lath:** thin wood (Swords **of lath** were used by the Vice character in medieval morality plays.) **up:** in rebellion (Line 3 plays on **up** as "awake.")

4. **clothier:** maker of woolen cloth

4–6. **dress . . . upon it:** Cade is described as treating **the commonwealth** as if it were a piece of cloth, which he will finish, **turn** inside out, and give **a new** surface or **nap.**

9. **came up: came** into fashion; rose in rank

11. **handicraftsmen:** artisans

12–13. **think . . . aprons:** i.e., scorn to work as artisans or laborers

16–17. **Labor . . . vocation:** proverbial (See also *Homily against Idleness* and 1 Corinthians 7.20.)

17–18. **magistrates:** rulers

20. **hit it:** i.e., **hit** the mark, correctly conjectured

21. **brave:** fine; **hard:** hardened, calloused

22–23. **Best's son . . . tanner:** i.e., the **son** of Best, **the tanner**

23. **Wingham:** village east of Canterbury

25. **dog's leather:** dogskin, used in making gloves

If he revenge it not, yet will his friends.   155
So will the Queen, that living held him dear.
⌐*He exits with the head and body.*⌐

⌐Scene 2⌐

Enter Bevis and John Holland ⌐*with staves.*⌐

BEVIS Come, and get thee a sword, though made of a
     lath. They have been up these two days.
HOLLAND They have the more need to sleep now, then.
BEVIS I tell thee, Jack Cade the clothier means to dress
     the commonwealth, and turn it, and set a new nap   5
     upon it.
HOLLAND So he had need, for 'tis threadbare. Well, I
     say, it was never merry world in England since
     gentlemen came up.
BEVIS O miserable age! Virtue is not regarded in   10
     handicraftsmen.
HOLLAND The nobility think scorn to go in leather
     aprons.
BEVIS Nay, more, the King's Council are no good
     workmen.   15
HOLLAND True, and yet it is said "Labor in thy voca-
     tion," which is as much to say as "Let the magis-
     trates be laboring men." And therefore should we
     be magistrates.
BEVIS Thou hast hit it, for there's no better sign of a   20
     brave mind than a hard hand.
HOLLAND I see them, I see them! There's Best's son, the
     tanner of Wingham—
BEVIS He shall have the skins of our enemies to make
     dog's leather of.   25
HOLLAND And Dick the butcher—
BEVIS Then is sin struck down like an ox, and iniq-
     uity's throat cut like a calf.

30. **Argo:** i.e., ergo (therefore); **thread . . . spun:** wordplay on weaving and on one's **thread of life, spun,** measured, and cut by the Fates (See picture, page 240.)

31. **fall in with:** join

31 SD. **Sawyer:** one who saws lumber; **infinite numbers:** i.e., a large number of nonspeaking actors dressed as artisans

32. **We:** the royal "we"; **termed of our:** named after my

34. **of:** as a consequence **of; cade:** barrel

35. **enemies . . . us:** See Leviticus 26.8: "and your **enemies shall fall before** you upon the sword"

36. **putting down:** crushing, overcoming

39. **Mortimer:** See 3.1.364.

42. **Plantagenet:** name attached to the royal family of England since the time of King Henry II and revived by Richard, Duke of York as his family name (See *Henry VI, Part 1*, 2.4.)

44. **Lacys:** family name of the earls of Lincoln

47. **of late:** recently

48. **furred pack:** animal-skin knapsack; **bucks:** loads of washing (There may be obscene wordplay here on **furred pack** as female genitalia and **bucks** as young men.)

52. **cage:** prison for petty criminals

54. **must needs:** i.e., **must** be (**valiant**); **beggary is valiant:** "Valiant beggar" referred to one denied alms because he was strong enough to work.

57. **whipped:** the usual punishment for vagabonds (See 2.1.171.) **market-days:** fixed days for holding markets; **together:** without intermission

(continued)

HOLLAND And Smith the weaver.
BEVIS Argo, their thread of life is spun.   30
HOLLAND Come, come, let's fall in with them.

> *Drum. Enter Cade, Dick ⌈the⌉ butcher, Smith the*
> *weaver, and a Sawyer, with infinite numbers,*
> *⌈all with staves.⌉*

CADE We, John Cade, so termed of our supposed
  father—
DICK, ⌈*aside*⌉ Or rather of stealing a cade of herrings.
CADE For our enemies shall ⌈fall⌉ before us, inspired   35
  with the spirit of putting down kings and princes—
  command silence.
DICK Silence!
CADE My father was a Mortimer—
DICK, ⌈*aside*⌉ He was an honest man and a good brick- 40
  layer.
CADE My mother a Plantagenet—
DICK, ⌈*aside*⌉ I knew her well; she was a midwife.
CADE My wife descended of the Lacys.
DICK, ⌈*aside*⌉ She was indeed a peddler's daughter, and 45
  sold many laces.
SMITH, ⌈*aside*⌉ But now of late, not able to travel with
  her furred pack, she washes bucks here at home.
CADE Therefore am I of an honorable house.
DICK, ⌈*aside*⌉ Ay, by my faith, the field is honorable;   50
  and there was he born, under a hedge, for his
  father had never a house but the cage.
CADE Valiant I am—
SMITH, ⌈*aside*⌉ He must needs, for beggary is valiant.
CADE I am able to endure much—   55
DICK, ⌈*aside*⌉ No question of that; for I have seen him
  whipped three market-days together.
CADE I fear neither sword nor fire.
SMITH, ⌈*aside*⌉ He need not fear the sword, for his coat
  is of proof.   60

60. **of proof:** impenetrable (perhaps because caked with mud, or covered with pitch)

62. **burnt:** branded

65–66. **three-hooped pot:** the wooden quart **pot** for the sale of beer (The number of hoops, or equidistant bands, around the **pot** indicated the quantity of liquor the **pot** contained.)

67. **felony:** serious crime; **small beer:** weak **beer**

67–68. **in common:** possessed equally by all

68. **Cheapside:** chief commercial district in London (which Cade imagines as transformed into a pasture on which he will graze his horse)

72. **score:** account

74. **worship:** honor, treat with respect

78. **parchment:** used for legal documents

79. **undo:** destroy

80. **beeswax:** used for the seals on legal documents

80–81. **seal ... thing:** i.e., become surety for someone

81. **mine own man:** i.e., a free **man**

83. **Chartham:** village in Kent

84. **cast account:** cipher, use arithmetic

86. **setting of boys' copies:** writing specimens of handwriting to be copied by pupils

88. **red letters:** used to indicate saints' days and church festivals, and in school primers for capital letters

90. **obligations:** written contracts

90–91. **court hand:** style of handwriting used in law courts

92. **proper:** respectable, worthy; **of:** i.e., on

DICK, ⌜*aside*⌝ But methinks he should stand in fear of
    fire, being burnt i' th' hand for stealing of sheep.

CADE Be brave, then, for your captain is brave and
    vows reformation. There shall be in England seven
    halfpenny loaves sold for a penny. The three-   65
    hooped pot shall have ten hoops, and I will make it
    felony to drink small beer. All the realm shall be in
    common, and in Cheapside shall my palfrey go to
    grass. And when I am king, as king I will be—

ALL God save your Majesty!   70

CADE I thank you, good people.—There shall be no
    money; all shall eat and drink on my score; and I
    will apparel them all in one livery, that they may
    agree like brothers and worship me their lord.

DICK The first thing we do, let's kill all the lawyers.   75

CADE Nay, that I mean to do. Is not this a lamentable
    thing, that of the skin of an innocent lamb should
    be made parchment? That parchment, being scrib-
    bled o'er, should undo a man? Some say the bee
    stings, but I say, 'tis the beeswax; for I did but seal   80
    once to a thing, and I was never mine own man
    since. How now? Who's there?

Enter a Clerk ⌜*of Chartham, under guard.*⌝

SMITH The clerk of Chartham. He can write and read
    and cast account.

CADE O, monstrous!   85

SMITH We took him setting of boys' copies.

CADE Here's a villain!

SMITH H'as a book in his pocket with red letters in 't.

CADE Nay, then, he is a conjurer.

DICK Nay, he can make obligations and write court   90
    hand.

CADE I am sorry for 't. The man is a proper man, of
    mine honor. Unless I find him guilty, he shall not

94. **sirrah:** term of address to male social inferior

97. **it:** the word **Emmanuel** (Hebrew), which may be translated as "God with us" (a pious formula)

98. **go hard:** fare badly

99. **Let me alone:** i.e., don't interfere

100. **mark:** a character, made with a pen, used by the illiterate in place of a signature

107. **inkhorn:** a small portable vessel for holding ink

109. **particular:** individual, special (playing on **general** [line 108] as communal, common)

111. **hard by:** nearby

112. **Stand:** stop

115. **No:** i.e., no more

117. **presently:** immediately; **Sir John Mortimer:** See note to 3.1.364, above.

118. **have at him:** i.e., let me **at him**

119. **hinds:** boors

120. **Marked:** destined

121. **groom:** fellow (contemptuous)

122. **revolt:** return to your allegiance

die.—Come hither, sirrah; I must examine thee.
What is thy name?   95

CLERK Emmanuel.

DICK They use to write it on the top of letters.—'Twill
go hard with you.

CADE Let me alone.—Dost thou use to write thy
name? Or hast thou a mark to thyself, like ⌈an⌉   100
honest, plain-dealing man?

CLERK Sir, I thank God, I have been so well brought
up that I can write my name.

ALL He hath confessed. Away with him! He's a villain
and a traitor.   105

CADE Away with him, I say! Hang him with his pen
and inkhorn about his neck.

> *One exits with the Clerk.*

> *Enter Michael.*

MICHAEL Where's our general?

CADE Here I am, thou particular fellow.

MICHAEL Fly, fly, fly! Sir Humphrey Stafford and his   110
brother are hard by, with the King's forces.

CADE Stand, villain, stand, or I'll fell thee down. He
shall be encountered with a man as good as himself. He is but a knight, is he?

MICHAEL No.   115

CADE To equal him I will make myself a knight
presently. ⌈*He kneels.*⌉ Rise up Sir John Mortimer.
⌈*He rises.*⌉ Now have at him!

> *Enter Sir Humphrey Stafford and his Brother, with*
> ⌈*a Herald,*⌉ *Drum, and Soldiers.*

STAFFORD
Rebellious hinds, the filth and scum of Kent,
Marked for the gallows, lay your weapons down!   120
Home to your cottages; forsake this groom.
The King is merciful, if you revolt.

123. **blood:** bloodshed

125. **silken-coated:** By law only those of the rank of gentleman and above could wear silk. **slaves:** a term of contempt; **pass:** care

130. **shearman:** one who shears the superfluous nap from woolen cloth

131. **Adam . . . gardener:** Proverbial: "When **Adam** delved and Eve span, / Who was then the gentleman?"

133. **Marry:** indeed

138. **question:** problem, uncertainty

139. **put to nurse:** committed to the care of a wet nurse

146. **testify:** i.e., **testify** to

148. **credit:** believe

A bricklayer. (3.2.203; 4.2.26; 4.3.3–5)
From Jan Luiken, *Spiegal . . .* (1704).

BROTHER
  But angry, wrathful, and inclined to blood,
  If you go forward. Therefore yield, or die.
CADE
  As for these silken-coated slaves, I pass not.   125
  It is to you, good people, that I speak,
  Over whom, in time to come, I hope to reign,
  For I am rightful heir unto the crown.
STAFFORD
  Villain, thy father was a plasterer,
  And thou thyself a shearman, art thou not?   130
CADE
  And Adam was a gardener.
BROTHER   And what of that?
CADE
  Marry, this: Edmund Mortimer, Earl of March,
  Married the Duke of Clarence' daughter, did he not?
STAFFORD   Ay, sir.   135
CADE
  By her he had two children at one birth.
BROTHER   That's false.
CADE
  Ay, there's the question. But I say 'tis true.
  The elder of them, being put to nurse,
  Was by a beggar-woman stol'n away,   140
  And, ignorant of his birth and parentage,
  Became a bricklayer when he came to age.
  His son am I. Deny it if you can.
DICK
  Nay, 'tis too true. Therefore he shall be king.
SMITH   Sir, he made a chimney in my father's house,   145
    and the bricks are alive at this day to testify it.
    Therefore deny it not.
STAFFORD
  And will you credit this base drudge's words,
  That speaks he knows not what?

152. **Go to:** an expression of remonstrance

154–55. **boys . . . crowns:** i.e., **boys** won **French** kingdoms playing such games as **span-counter** (the goal of which is to throw one's counters so close to one's opponent's that the distance between them is a mere handspan) **French crowns:** diadems of **French** rulers, with wordplay on (1) **French** coins; (2) bald heads of those suffering from the **French** disease, syphilis

159. **mained:** maimed

160. **fain to go:** obliged to walk; **puissance:** power

162. **gelded:** castrated

165. **miserable:** despicable

166. **answer:** rebut this

168. **tongue:** (1) language; (2) organ of speech

174. **up:** risen in rebellion

A butcher. (3.2.203; 4.2.26; 4.3.3–5)
From Jan Luiken, *Spiegal* . . . (1704).

ALL
  Ay, marry, will we. Therefore get you gone.   150
BROTHER
  Jack Cade, the Duke of York hath taught you this.
CADE He lies, ⌜*aside*⌝ for I invented it myself.—Go to,
    sirrah. Tell the King from me that, for his father's
    sake, Henry the Fifth, in whose time boys went to
    span-counter for French crowns, I am content he   155
    shall reign, but I'll be Protector over him.
DICK And, furthermore, we'll have the Lord Saye's
    head for selling the dukedom of Maine.
CADE And good reason: for thereby is England mained
    and fain to go with a staff, but that my puissance   160
    holds it up. Fellow kings, I tell you that that Lord
    Saye hath gelded the commonwealth and made it
    an eunuch; and, more than that, he can speak
    French, and therefore he is a traitor.
STAFFORD
  O, gross and miserable ignorance!   165
CADE Nay, answer if you can. The Frenchmen are our
    enemies. Go to, then, I ask but this: can he that
    speaks with the tongue of an enemy be a good
    counselor, or no?
ALL No, no, and therefore we'll have his head!   170
BROTHER, ⌜*to Stafford*⌝
  Well, seeing gentle words will not prevail,
  Assail them with the army of the King.
STAFFORD
  Herald, away, and throughout every town
  Proclaim them traitors that are up with Cade,
  That those which fly before the battle ends   175
  May, even in their wives' and children's sight
  Be hanged up for example at their doors.—
  And you that be the King's friends, follow me.
                    ⌜*The Staffords, Soldiers, and Herald*⌝ *exit.*

182. **clouted shoon:** hobnailed boots, or patched shoes

183. **thrifty:** respectable, worthy

184. **take our parts:** join us

185. **They . . . order:** i.e., the king's forces are drawn up **in** battle **order**

186. **in order:** in normal condition

186–87. **out of order:** in disorder, in violation of recognized **order**

4.3 Cade defeats and kills the Staffords and marches on London.

———————————

0 SD. **Alarums:** calls to arms

6. **as long again:** i.e., twice **as long**

7. **license to kill:** Slaughter and sale of **sheep and oxen** (line 3) was forbidden in **Lent** except by special **license**

7–8. **for a hundred lacking one:** The usual lease was for 99 years. Here, the number may refer to years or to the number of animals or customers.

11. **monument:** token

18. **Fear:** doubt

CADE
    And you that love the Commons, follow me.
    Now show yourselves men. 'Tis for liberty!   180
    We will not leave one lord, one gentleman;
    Spare none but such as go in clouted shoon,
    For they are thrifty, honest men and such
    As would, but that they dare not, take our parts.

DICK   They are all in order and march toward us.   185

CADE   But then are we in order when we are most out
    of order. Come, march forward.

                             ⌐*They exit.*¬

⌐Scene 3¬

Alarums to the fight, wherein both the Staffords are
slain. Enter Cade and the rest.

CADE   Where's Dick, the butcher of Ashford?

DICK   Here, sir.

CADE   They fell before thee like sheep and oxen, and
    thou behaved'st thyself as if thou hadst been in
    thine own slaughterhouse. Therefore, thus will I   5
    reward thee: the Lent shall be as long again as it is,
    and thou shalt have a license to kill for a hundred
    lacking one.

DICK   I desire no more.

CADE   And to speak truth, thou deserv'st no less. This   10
    monument of the victory will I bear. ⌐*He puts on*
    Sir Humphrey Stafford's armor and helmet, or sal-
    let.¬ And the bodies shall be dragged at my horse
    heels till I do come to London, where we will have
    the Mayor's sword borne before us.   15

DICK   If we mean to thrive and do good, break open
    the jails and let out the prisoners.

CADE   Fear not that, I warrant thee. Come, let's march
    towards London.

              They exit ⌐*with the bodies of the Staffords.*¬

4.4   King Henry flees London and Queen Margaret mourns Suffolk's death. Lord Saye, whom the rebels hate, decides to hide in London.

---

0 SD. **supplication:** written petition

2. **fearful:** full of fears, apprehensive

9. **entreat:** enter into negotiations; or, persuade by pleading

10. **simple:** innocent

11. **perish by the sword:** See Matthew 26.52: "All that take the sword shall **perish** with **the sword.**"

12. **cut them short:** See 3.1.82 and note.

13. **parley:** speak

14. **stay:** wait

16. **Ruled . . . me:** In astrology, the **planet** under which one is born can exercise a fateful influence over one. **wandering:** orbiting in an irregular manner, as in Ptolemaic astronomy the planets were thought to do in circling the earth (See picture, page xxxviii.)

18. **That:** i.e., who

23. **fear me:** i.e., **fear** (the ethical dative)

A porcupine. (3.1.368)
From Edward Topsell, *The historie of foure-footed beastes . . .* (1607).

⌜Scene 4⌝

*Enter King ⌜Henry,⌝ with a supplication, and
Queen ⌜Margaret⌝ with Suffolk's head, the Duke
of Buckingham, and the Lord Saye.*

QUEEN MARGARET, ⌜*aside*⌝
  Oft have I heard that grief softens the mind
  And makes it fearful and degenerate.
  Think therefore on revenge, and cease to weep.
  But who can cease to weep and look on this?
  Here may his head lie on my throbbing breast,   5
  But where's the body that I should embrace?
BUCKINGHAM, ⌜*to King Henry*⌝
  What answer makes your Grace to the rebels'
    supplication?
KING HENRY
  I'll send some holy bishop to entreat,
  For God forbid so many simple souls   10
  Should perish by the sword! And I myself,
  Rather than bloody war shall cut them short,
  Will parley with Jack Cade, their general.
  But stay, I'll read it over once again.   ⌜*He reads.*⌝
QUEEN MARGARET, ⌜*aside*⌝
  Ah, barbarous villains! Hath this lovely face   15
  Ruled, like a wandering planet, over me,
  And could it not enforce them to relent
  That were unworthy to behold the same?
KING HENRY
  Lord Saye, Jack Cade hath sworn to have thy head.
SAYE
  Ay, but I hope your Highness shall have his.   20
KING HENRY   How now, madam?
  Still lamenting and mourning for Suffolk's death?
  I fear me, love, if that I had been dead,
  Thou wouldst not have mourned so much for me.

28. **Southwark:** district just south of the Thames, with access to London across London Bridge

34. **hinds:** rustics, servants; **rude:** uncivilized, violent

38. **false:** treacherous; **caterpillars:** extortionists, those who prey on society (Proverbial: "The **caterpillars** of the commonwealth.")

39. **graceless men:** i.e., **men** lacking divine grace; **they . . . do:** See Luke 23.34: "Father, forgive them, for **they know not what they do.**"

40. **Killingworth:** Kenilworth, near Warwick

41. **power:** army

43. **appeased:** pacified, quieted

44. **hateth:** i.e., hate

46. **So:** then

49. **secret:** hidden

A scholar, or "learnèd" clerk. (4.4.37; 4.7.71)
From Geoffrey Whitney, *A choice of emblemes . . .* (1586).

QUEEN MARGARET
No, my love, I should not mourn, but die for thee. 25

Enter a Messenger.

KING HENRY
How now, what news? Why com'st thou in such
  haste?
MESSENGER
The rebels are in Southwark. Fly, my lord!
Jack Cade proclaims himself Lord Mortimer,
Descended from the Duke of Clarence' house, 30
And calls your Grace usurper, openly,
And vows to crown himself in Westminster.
His army is a ragged multitude
Of hinds and peasants, rude and merciless.
Sir Humphrey Stafford and his brother's death 35
Hath given them heart and courage to proceed.
All scholars, lawyers, courtiers, gentlemen
They call false caterpillars and intend their death.
KING HENRY
O, graceless men, they know not what they do!
BUCKINGHAM
My gracious lord, retire to Killingworth 40
Until a power be raised to put them down.
QUEEN MARGARET
Ah, were the Duke of Suffolk now alive,
These Kentish rebels would be soon appeased!
KING HENRY Lord Saye, the traitors hateth thee;
Therefore away with us to Killingworth. 45
SAYE
So might your Grace's person be in danger.
The sight of me is odious in their eyes;
And therefore in this city will I stay
And live alone as secret as I may.

Enter another Messenger.

52. **rascal people:** rabble
54. **spoil:** sack, pillage
56. **succor:** help
60–61. **The trust . . . resolute:** Proverbial: **"Innocence is bold."**

4.5 Citizens of London plead for military aid from Lord Scales, who commands forces at the Tower. He sends Matthew Gough, a famous warrior.

———————

0 SD. **Tower: the Tower** of London, a fortress and armory (See picture, below.)
1. **How now:** i.e., **how** is it **now**
3. **they:** i.e., the rebels; **the Bridge:** i.e., London **Bridge** (See picture, page 204.)
4. **craves aid of:** begs **aid** from
9. **essayed:** tried

The Tower of London. (4.5.0 SD; 4.6.15)
From John Seller, *A book of the prospects of the remarkable places in . . . London . . .* [c. 1700?].

⌜SECOND⌝ MESSENGER
    Jack Cade hath gotten London Bridge.   50
    The citizens fly and forsake their houses.
    The rascal people, thirsting after prey,
    Join with the traitor, and they jointly swear
    To spoil the city and your royal court.

BUCKINGHAM
    Then linger not, my lord. Away! Take horse!   55

KING HENRY
    Come, Margaret. God, our hope, will succor us.

QUEEN MARGARET
    My hope is gone, now Suffolk is deceased.

KING HENRY, ⌜to Saye⌝
    Farewell, my lord. Trust not the Kentish rebels.

BUCKINGHAM
    Trust nobody, for fear you ⌜be⌝ betrayed.

SAYE
    The trust I have is in mine innocence,   60
    And therefore am I bold and resolute.

                   They exit.

⌜Scene 5⌝

Enter Lord Scales upon the Tower, walking. Then enters
two or three Citizens below.

SCALES   How now? Is Jack Cade slain?

FIRST CITIZEN   No, my lord, nor likely to be slain; for
    they have won the Bridge, killing all those that
    withstand them. The Lord Mayor craves aid of
    your Honor from the Tower to defend the city   5
    from the rebels.

SCALES
    Such aid as I can spare you shall command;
    But I am troubled here with them myself:
    The rebels have essayed to win the Tower.

10. **Smithfield:** open space beyond London's walls; **gather head:** raise an army

11. **Matthew Gough:** a renowned English military leader, who fought in Normandy

4.6 Cade enters London.

———————

0 SD. **London Stone:** the central milestone of Roman London (See picture, below.)

2. **charge:** order

3. **of:** i.e., at; **Pissing Conduit:** popular name for a Cheapside water supply in a channel that ran with a small stream **Pissing:** paltry

4. **claret wine:** wine of yellowish or light red color (The day a newly crowned monarch entered London, the Cheapside conduit would run with wine.)

6. **other:** i.e., anything **other**

9. **If . . . wise:** Proverbial: "He is **wise** that is ware in time."

LONDON STONE.

"London Stone." (4.6.0 SD)
An anonymous eighteenth-century rendering.
From the Folger Library Collection.

But get you to Smithfield and gather head,   10
And thither I will send you Matthew Gough.
Fight for your king, your country, and your lives.
And so farewell, for I must hence again.

                                              They exit.

⌜Scene 6⌝

*Enter Jack Cade and the rest, and strikes his staff on
London Stone.*

CADE   Now is Mortimer lord of this city. And here, sitting upon London Stone, I charge and command
that, of the city's cost, the Pissing Conduit run
nothing but claret wine this first year of our reign.
And now henceforward it shall be treason for any   5
that calls me other than Lord Mortimer.

                    Enter a Soldier running.

SOLDIER   Jack Cade, Jack Cade!
CADE   Knock him down there.   *They kill him.*
DICK   If this fellow be wise, he'll never call you Jack
Cade more. I think he hath a very fair warning.   10
              ⌜*Takes a paper from the dead Soldier and
                            reads the message.*⌝
My lord, there's an army gathered together in
Smithfield.
CADE   Come, then, let's go fight with them. But first, go
and set London Bridge on fire, and, if you can,
burn down the Tower too. Come, let's away.   15
                                              All exit.

4.7 Cade defeats and kills Gough. Lord Saye is captured and killed.

———————

1. **the Savoy:** the London home of the duke of Lancaster (actually destroyed the previous century)
2. **Inns of Court:** the London law schools and property of the legal societies
3. **suit:** petition
4. **lordship:** title and land of a lord
7. **Mass:** i.e., by the Roman Catholic **Mass** (a strong oath); **sore:** severe (with the obvious pun)
9. **whole:** healed
15. **biting:** bitter, painful (with the obvious pun)
17–18. **be in common:** possessed equally by all
19. **prize:** captive of war
21. **one-and-twenty fifteens:** a tax of 140% (See note to 1.1.139.)
21–22. **one shilling to the pound:** a tax of 5%
22. **the last subsidy:** i.e., **the last** time Parliament granted the king financial aid for special needs
24. **thou say, . . . serge, . . . buckram lord:** Cade plays with the fact that Lord Saye's name sounds the same as **say,** a fine-textured, partly silk fabric; he then reduces him to a **serge** (woolen) **lord,** and then to a **lord** made of **buckram** (cloth stiffened with gum or paste).
25. **point-blank:** direct aim
27. **Basimecu:** vulgarization of the French *baise mon cul* (kiss my ass)

(continued)

⌜Scene 7⌝

Alarums. Matthew Gough is slain, and all the rest.
Then enter Jack Cade with his company.

CADE So, sirs. Now go some and pull down the Savoy;
others to th' Inns of Court. Down with them all!
DICK I have a suit unto your Lordship.
CADE Be it a lordship, thou shalt have it for that word.
DICK Only that the laws of England may come out of   5
your mouth.
HOLLAND, ⌜*aside*⌝ Mass, 'twill be sore law, then, for he
was thrust in the mouth with a spear, and 'tis not
whole yet.
SMITH, ⌜*aside*⌝ Nay, John, it will be stinking law, for   10
his breath stinks with eating toasted cheese.
CADE I have thought upon it; it shall be so. Away!
Burn all the records of the realm. My mouth shall
be the Parliament of England.
HOLLAND, ⌜*aside*⌝ Then we are like to have biting   15
statutes—unless his teeth be pulled out.
CADE And henceforward all things shall be in common.

Enter a Messenger.

MESSENGER My lord, a prize, a prize! Here's the Lord
Saye, which sold the towns in France, he that   20
made us pay one-and-twenty fifteens, and one
shilling to the pound, the last subsidy.

Enter George with the Lord Saye.

CADE Well, he shall be beheaded for it ten times.—Ah,
thou say, thou serge, nay, thou buckram lord, now
art thou within point-blank of our jurisdiction   25
regal. What canst thou answer to my Majesty for
giving up of Normandy unto Monsieur Basimecu,
the Dauphin of France? Be it known unto thee by

28–30. **by these . . . Mortimer:** a blending of (1) the Latin legal formula "by these present documents" (*per has literas presentes*) and (2) "in this presence," i.e., in **the presence of** a person of superior rank, **Lord Mortimer**

30. **besom:** broom

33. **grammar school:** the kind of **school** established by sixteenth-century Humanists for the study of rhetoric (an anachronism in this play set in the fifteenth century, as is the mention of **printing** [line 35] and the **paper mill** [line 37], both of which postdate the events dramatized here)

35. **score:** notch cut in a stick of wood called **the tally** in order to keep accounts without writing

36–37. **contrary to . . . dignity:** a legal formula **King his:** i.e., king's

38–39. **usually:** ordinarily

39. **abominable:** offensive

43. **answer:** make defense against

44. **could not read:** i.e., **could not** claim benefit of clergy to escape capital punishment

45. **that cause:** i.e., their illiteracy

47. **a footcloth:** i.e., a horse wearing a **footcloth,** large richly ornamented cloth

51. **hose and doublets:** breeches and tight-fitting jackets (See picture, page 46.)

56. **bona terra, mala gens:** good land, bad people (Latin, proverbial)

60. **the . . . writ:** Julius Caesar's *De bello gallico* (*Concerning the Gallic War*)

61. **civil'st:** most civilized

63. **liberal:** generous

these presence, even the presence of Lord Mortimer, that I am the besom that must sweep the 30
court clean of such filth as thou art. Thou hast
most traitorously corrupted the youth of the realm
in erecting a grammar school; and whereas,
before, our forefathers had no other books but the
score and the tally, thou hast caused printing to be 35
used, and, contrary to the King his crown and dignity, thou hast built a paper mill. It will be proved
to thy face that thou hast men about thee that usually talk of a noun and a verb and such abominable
words as no Christian ear can endure to hear. 40
Thou hast appointed justices of peace to call poor
men before them about matters they were not able
to answer. Moreover, thou hast put them in prison;
and, because they could not read, thou hast
hanged them, when indeed only for that cause 45
they have been most worthy to live. Thou dost ride
⌜on⌝ a footcloth, dost thou not?

SAYE What of that?

CADE Marry, thou oughtst not to let thy horse wear a
cloak when honester men than thou go in their 50
hose and doublets.

DICK And work in their shirt too—as myself, for example, that am a butcher.

SAYE You men of Kent—

DICK What say you of Kent? 55

SAYE Nothing but this: 'tis *bona terra, mala gens.*

CADE Away with him, away with him! He speaks
Latin.

SAYE

Hear me but speak, and bear me where you will.
Kent, in the commentaries Caesar writ, 60
Is termed the civil'st place of all this isle.
Sweet is the country, because full of riches;
The people liberal, valiant, active, wealthy;

64. **void of:** lacking

67. **favor:** goodwill, mitigation of punishment

69. **aught:** anything; **exacted:** required (but also "required by force" or "extorted")

71. **learnèd clerks:** scholars (See picture, page 190.)

72. **book:** learning; **preferred me:** won me preferment or advancement to the king's service

76. **cannot but:** i.e., must; **forbear to murder:** refrain from murdering

78. **behoof:** benefit, advantage

79. **field:** battlefield

80. **reaching hands: hands** able to reach far (Proverbial: "Kings have long arms.")

84. **watching:** staying awake at night

87. **sitting:** i.e., as a judge; **determine:** settle; **causes:** suits, subjects of litigation

89. **hempen caudle:** i.e., hangman's rope **caudle:** a drink given to the sick (a thin warm gruel, mixed with wine or ale, sweetened or spiced)

90. **help:** remedy, cure; **hatchet:** i.e., executioner's ax

92. **palsy:** tremulous paralysis in the aged

93. **as who should:** i.e., **as** one **who** would

Which makes me hope you are not void of pity.
I sold not Maine; I lost not Normandy;   65
Yet to recover them would lose my life.
Justice with favor have I always done;
Prayers and tears have moved me; gifts could never.
When have I aught exacted at your hands
Kent to maintain, the King, the realm, and you?   70
Large gifts have I bestowed on learnèd clerks,
Because my book preferred me to the King.
And seeing ignorance is the curse of God,
Knowledge the wing wherewith we fly to heaven,
Unless you be possessed with devilish spirits,   75
You cannot but forbear to murder me.
This tongue hath parleyed unto foreign kings
For your behoof—

CADE   Tut, when struck'st thou one blow in the field?

SAYE
Great men have reaching hands. Oft have I struck   80
Those that I never saw, and struck them dead.

GEORGE   O monstrous coward! What, to come behind
folks?

SAYE
These cheeks are pale for watching for your good.

CADE   Give him a box o' th' ear, and that will make 'em   85
red again.

SAYE
Long sitting to determine poor men's causes
Hath made me full of sickness and diseases.

CADE   You shall have a hempen ⌈caudle,⌉ then, and
the help of hatchet.   90

DICK   Why dost thou quiver, man?

SAYE   The palsy, and not fear, provokes me.

CADE   Nay, he nods at us, as who should say "I'll be
even with you." I'll see if his head will stand stead-
ier on a pole, or no. Take him away, and behead   95
him.

98. **affected:** sought to obtain

102. **guiltless blood-shedding:** shedding the blood of the guiltless

105. **remorse:** compassion

106. **an it be but:** i.e., if only

107. **familiar:** demon who serves him

110. **presently:** immediately

119. **peer:** noble

121–22. **There ... it:** a reference to the *droit de seigneur,* a feudal lord's right to the first night with his vassal's bride

123. **hold of me:** possess land from me; **in capite:** directly (This Latin legal phrase applied to land held directly from the Crown.) **charge:** order

124. **free:** unrestrained

124–25. **as heart can wish ... tell:** proverbial

126–27. **take up ... bills:** wordplay on "pick up goods with our weapons" and "buy goods on credit" **bills:** (1) long-handled bladed weapons; (2) notes of charges for goods

129. **brave:** splendid

SAYE

  Tell me, wherein have I offended most?

  Have I affected wealth or honor? Speak.

  Are my chests filled up with extorted gold?

  Is my apparel sumptuous to behold?   100

  Whom have I injured, that you seek my death?

  These hands are free from guiltless blood-shedding,

  This breast from harboring foul deceitful thoughts.

  O, let me live!

CADE   I feel remorse in myself with his words, but I'll 105
    bridle it. He shall die, an it be but for pleading so
    well for his life. Away with him! He has a familiar
    under his tongue; he speaks not i' God's name. Go,
    take him away, I say, and strike off his head
    presently; and then break into his son-in-law's 110
    house, Sir James Cromer, and strike off his head;
    and bring them both upon two poles hither.

ALL   It shall be done.

SAYE

  Ah, countrymen, if when you make your prayers,

  God should be so obdurate as yourselves,   115

  How would it fare with your departed souls?

  And therefore yet relent, and save my life.

CADE   Away with him, and do as I command you.

                   ⌈*Some exit with Lord Saye.*⌉

    The proudest peer in the realm shall not wear a
    head on his shoulders unless he pay me tribute. 120
    There shall not a maid be married but she shall
    pay to me her maidenhead ere they have it. Men
    shall hold of me *in capite;* and we charge and com-
    mand that their wives be as free as heart can wish
    or tongue can tell.   125

DICK   My lord, when shall we go to Cheapside and take
    up commodities upon our bills?

CADE   Marry, presently.

ALL   O, brave!

134. **spoil:** sack, pillage
136. **maces:** staffs of office **borne before,** or carried by, certain officials

4.8 Lord Clifford and Buckingham persuade Cade's followers to return to King Henry. Cade flees.

---

0 SD. **retreat:** a trumpet signal to withdraw; **rabblement:** rabble, mob
1. **Fish Street:** a street near London Bridge; **Saint Magnus' Corner:** the location of **Saint Magnus'** church at the lower end of **Fish Street**
2 SD. **parley:** trumpet signal calling for negotiations between the contending forces
9. **pronounce:** proclaim officially
11. **relent:** give way

London Bridge. (4.5.3, 50; 4.6.14)
From Claes Jansz Visscher, *Londinum florentissima Britanniae urbs* . . . [c. 1625].

Enter one with the heads ⌜of Lord Saye and Sir James
Cromer on poles.⌝

CADE   But is not this braver? Let them kiss one anoth-   130
er, for they loved well when they were alive. ⌜*The*
heads are brought together.⌝ Now part them again,
lest they consult about the giving up of some more
towns in France. Soldiers, defer the spoil of the
city until night, for, with these borne before us   135
instead of maces, will we ride through the streets
and at every corner have them kiss. Away!
                                        He exits ⌜with his company.⌝

⌜**Scene 8**⌝

Alarum, and retreat. Enter again Cade and
all his rabblement.

CADE   Up Fish Street! Down Saint Magnus' Corner!
Kill and knock down! Throw them into Thames!
                                        Sound a parley.
What noise is this I hear? Dare any be so bold to
sound retreat or parley when I command them
kill?   5

Enter Buckingham and old Clifford ⌜with Attendants.⌝

BUCKINGHAM
Ay, here they be that dare and will disturb thee.
Know, Cade, we come ambassadors from the King
Unto the Commons, whom thou hast misled,
And here pronounce free pardon to them all
That will forsake thee and go home in peace.   10
CLIFFORD
What say you, countrymen? Will you relent
And yield to mercy whil'st 'tis offered you,
Or let a rabble lead you to your deaths?

14. **Who:** i.e., whoever; **embrace:** accept
21. **brave:** daring
22. **Will you needs:** must you
25. **the White Hart:** an inn, Cade's headquarters
26. **given out:** i.e., surrendered
28. **recreants:** deserters; **dastards:** despicable cowards
30. **over:** from **over**
32. **I will . . . one:** i.e., **I will** secure myself (Proverbial: "I'll shift for myself.")
33. **light:** descend
38. **meanest:** lowliest born
40. **the spoil:** pillage
42. **at jar:** in discord
43. **fearful:** frightened; terrible
44. **start:** sudden invasion
45. **Methinks:** it seems to me; **broil:** turmoil
47. **Villiago:** coward (Italian)
48. **miscarry:** be destroyed

A George. (4.1.29)
From Elias Ashmole, *The institution, laws & ceremonies of the . . . Order of the Garter . . .* (1672).

Who loves the King and will embrace his pardon,
Fling up his cap and say "God save his Majesty!"   15
Who hateth him and honors not his father,
Henry the Fifth, that made all France to quake,
Shake he his weapon at us and pass by.
ALL   God save the King! God save the King!
              ⌜*They fling their caps in the air.*⌝
CADE   What, Buckingham and Clifford, are you so   20
     brave?—And, you base peasants, do you believe
     him? Will you needs be hanged with your pardons
     about your necks? Hath my sword therefore broke
     through London gates, that you should leave me at
     the White Hart in Southwark? I thought you   25
     would never have given out these arms till you had
     recovered your ancient freedom. But you are all
     recreants and dastards, and delight to live in slav-
     ery to the nobility. Let them break your backs with
     burdens, take your houses over your heads, ravish   30
     your wives and daughters before your faces. For
     me, I will make shift for one, and so God's curse
     light upon you all!
ALL   We'll follow Cade! We'll follow Cade!
CLIFFORD   Is Cade the son of Henry the Fifth,   35
     That thus you do exclaim you'll go with him?
     Will he conduct you through the heart of France
     And make the meanest of you earls and dukes?
     Alas, he hath no home, no place to fly to,
     Nor knows he how to live but by the spoil,   40
     Unless by robbing of your friends and us.
     Were 't not a shame that, whilst you live at jar,
     The fearful French, whom you late vanquishèd,
     Should make a start o'er seas and vanquish you?
     Methinks already in this civil broil   45
     I see them lording it in London streets,
     Crying "*Villiago!*" unto all they meet.
     Better ten thousand baseborn Cades miscarry

51. **coast:** country
53. **God:** i.e., with **God**
54. **À Clifford:** a rallying cry "to **Clifford**" **À:** to (French)
56–57. **Was . . . fro:** Proverbial: "As light as a **feather**" and "As wavering as a **feather** in the wind."
58. **hales:** draws; **mischiefs:** evils, calamities
59. **desolate:** alone
59–60. **lay . . . together:** conspire (proverbial)
60. **surprise:** capture
61. **despite:** spite
62. **have through:** a threat to attack
63. **want:** lack
65. **betake me:** take
69. **crowns:** gold coins worth five shillings or a quarter of a pound

4.9 As King Henry rejoices at Cade's defeat, a messenger announces York's approach with an Irish army ostensibly seeking Somerset's arrest for treason. Buckingham is sent to tell York that Somerset has been imprisoned in the Tower.

———————————

0 SD. **on the terrace, aloft:** i.e., in the gallery above and behind the stage
1. **Was ever:** i.e., **was** there **ever** a; **joyed:** enjoyed
2. **content:** satisfaction, pleasure

Than you should stoop unto a Frenchman's mercy.
To France, to France, and get what you have lost! 50
Spare England, for it is your native coast.
Henry hath money; you are strong and manly.
God on our side, doubt not of victory.

ALL
À Clifford! À Clifford! We'll follow the King and
Clifford! 55

CADE, ⌈*aside*⌉ Was ever feather so lightly blown to and
fro as this multitude? The name of Henry the Fifth
hales them to an hundred mischiefs and makes
them leave me desolate. I see them lay their heads
together to surprise me. My sword make way for 60
me, for here is no staying!—In despite of the devils
and hell, have through the very middest of you!
And heavens and honor be witness that no want of
resolution in me, but only my followers' base and
ignominious treasons, makes me betake me to my 65
heels. *He exits, ⌈running.⌉*

BUCKINGHAM
What, is he fled? Go, some, and follow him;
And he that brings his head unto the King
Shall have a thousand crowns for his reward.
Some of them exit.
Follow me, soldiers. We'll devise a means 70
To reconcile you all unto the King.
All exit.

⌈Scene 9⌉

Sound trumpets. Enter King ⌈Henry,⌉ Queen ⌈Margaret,⌉
and Somerset on the terrace, ⌈aloft.⌉

KING HENRY
Was ever king that joyed an earthly throne
And could command no more content than I?

7. **tidings:** news
8. **surprised:** captured
9. **is he but retired:** i.e., has he only retreated;
him: i.e., himself
10. **powers:** forces
12. **Expect:** wait for; **doom:** judgment
14. **entertain:** receive, accept
15. **Soldiers:** i.e., Cade's **soldiers**
18. **still:** always
19. **infortunate:** unlucky
20. **unkind:** cruel
22. **several countries:** various regions
24. **advertisèd:** informed, warned
25. **newly:** recently
26. **puissant:** potent, strong; **power:** army

Henry VI.
From John Taylor, *All the workes of . . .* (1630).

No sooner was I crept out of my cradle
But I was made a king at nine months old.
Was never subject longed to be a king   5
As I do long and wish to be a subject!

Enter Buckingham and ⌜old⌝ Clifford.

BUCKINGHAM
Health and glad tidings to your Majesty!
KING HENRY
Why, Buckingham, is the traitor Cade surprised,
Or is he but retired to make him strong?

Enter ⌜below⌝ multitudes with halters about their necks.

CLIFFORD
He is fled, my lord, and all his powers do yield   10
And, humbly thus, with halters on their necks,
Expect your Highness' doom of life or death.
KING HENRY
Then, heaven, set ope thy everlasting gates
To entertain my vows of thanks and praise!
Soldiers, this day have you redeemed your lives   15
And showed how well you love your prince and
   country.
Continue still in this so good a mind,
And Henry, though he be infortunate,
Assure yourselves, will never be unkind.   20
And so with thanks and pardon to you all,
I do dismiss you to your several countries.
ALL   God save the King! God save the King!
                              ⌜*The multitudes exit.*⌝

Enter a Messenger.

MESSENGER
Please it your Grace to be advertisèd
The Duke of York is newly come from Ireland   25
And, with a puissant and a mighty power

27. **gallowglasses:** heavily armed and well-trained Irish soldiers; **stout:** fierce; brave; **kerns:** lightly armed Irish foot soldiers (See picture, page 122.)

28. **proud:** valiant; **array:** martial order

29. **still:** i.e., repeatedly

32. **state:** government; condition; **'twixt:** between

35. **straightway:** immediately; **calmed:** becalmed, delayed by absence of wind; **with:** i.e., by

36. **But:** just

37. **second him:** take his place, succeed him

39. **of:** i.e., for

40. **Duke Edmund: Edmund** Beaufort, **duke** of Somerset

46. **rough:** harsh; **terms:** i.e., the conditions or stipulations you propose

47. **brook:** endure; **hard:** severe

48. **deal:** negotiate

51. **yet:** i.e., as **yet,** till now

An hautboy. (1.1.0 SD)
From Balthasar Küchler, *Repraesentatio der fürstlichen Auffzug* . . . [1611].

Of gallowglasses and stout kerns,
Is marching hitherward in proud array,
And still proclaimeth, as he comes along,
His arms are only to remove from thee   30
The Duke of Somerset, whom he terms a traitor.

KING HENRY
Thus stands my state, 'twixt Cade and York
      distressed,
Like to a ship that, having scaped a tempest,
Is straightway ⌐calmed⌐ and boarded with a pirate.   35
But now is Cade driven back, his men dispersed,
And now is York in arms to second him.
I pray thee, Buckingham, go and meet him,
And ask him what's the reason of these arms.
Tell him I'll send Duke Edmund to the Tower.—   40
And, Somerset, we will commit thee thither
Until his army be dismissed from him.

SOMERSET   My lord,
I'll yield myself to prison willingly,
Or unto death, to do my country good.   45

KING HENRY, ⌐to Buckingham⌐
In any case, be not too rough in terms,
For he is fierce and cannot brook hard language.

BUCKINGHAM
I will, my lord, and doubt not so to deal
As all things shall redound unto your good.

KING HENRY
Come, wife, let's in, and learn to govern better,   50
For yet may England curse my wretched reign.
                              Flourish. They exit.

4.10 A starving Cade is killed in a fight with the Kentish gentleman Alexander Iden, in whose garden Cade looked for food.

---

1. **Fie:** an exclamation of reproach
3. **hid me:** i.e., **hid; durst:** dared
4. **laid:** i.e., on the watch
5–6. **if . . . years:** i.e., even if **I** were guaranteed **I** would live **a thousand years** (Proverbial: "No man has **a lease of** his **life.**")
6. **stay:** wait
7. **Wherefore:** for which reason
8. **sallet:** salad (In line 12, the word means "helmet.")
9. **another while:** yet again
12. **brainpan:** skull
13. **brown bill:** long-handled axe used by both soldiers and constables **brown:** varnished or painted; **dry:** thirsty
17. **turmoilèd:** in agitation or commotion
18. **And may:** i.e., when he might
21. **wax:** grow
22. **I care not with what:** i.e., without regard for; **envy:** malice
23. **Sufficeth that I:** i.e., it suffices **that** what **I; state:** condition
24. **well pleasèd:** i.e., with alms
26. **stray:** i.e., stray animal; **fee-simple:** land belonging to the owner and heirs forever
27–28. **get . . . of:** receive **a thousand crowns** from
29. **eat iron . . . ostrich:** See picture, page 218.

⌜Scene 10⌝

Enter Cade.

CADE Fie on ambitions! Fie on myself, that have a
sword and yet am ready to famish! These five days
have I hid me in these woods and durst not peep
out, for all the country is laid for me. But now am
I so hungry that, if I might have a lease of my life   5
for a thousand years, I could stay no longer.
Wherefore, ⌜o'er⌝ a brick wall have I climbed into
this garden, to see if I can eat grass, or pick a sallet
another while, which is not amiss to cool a man's
stomach this hot weather. And I think this word   10
sallet was born to do me good; for many a time,
but for a sallet, my brainpan had been cleft with a
brown bill; and many a time, when I have been dry
and bravely marching, it hath served me instead of
a quart pot to drink in; and now the word *sallet*   15
must serve me to feed on.

Enter Iden ⌜*and his Men.*⌝

IDEN
Lord, who would live turmoilèd in the court
And may enjoy such quiet walks as these?
This small inheritance my father left me
Contenteth me, and worth a monarchy.   20
I seek not to wax great by others' ⌜waning,⌝
Or gather wealth, I care not with what envy.
Sufficeth that I have maintains my state
And sends the poor well pleasèd from my gate.
CADE, ⌜*aside*⌝ Here's the lord of the soil come to seize   25
me for a stray, for entering his fee-simple without
leave.—Ah, villain, thou wilt betray me and get a
thousand crowns of the King by carrying my head
to him; but I'll make thee eat iron like an ostrich

32. **rude:** violent, harsh; uncivilized; **companion:** fellow

37. **brave:** challenge, defy; **saucy:** insolent

38–39. **by . . . broached:** an oath on Jesus' **blood broached:** set running, as if it were liquor from a cask that has been pierced

39. **beard:** openly oppose, affront

40. **eat:** i.e., eaten; **meat:** food

42. **dead as a doornail:** proverbial

45. **esquire:** the higher order of the gentry, just below a knight

46. **odds:** advantage (i.e., the help of his **five men**)

48. **outface me:** stare or face me down

49. **Set:** compare

50. **a finger to:** i.e., a finger's width in comparison to

51. **truncheon:** short thick staff (i.e., Iden's **leg**)

53. **heavèd:** raised

55. **answers:** i.e., can do no more than merely answer

56. **report:** account for; **forbears:** refrains from

57. **complete:** accomplished; **champion:** fighting man

58. **turn:** blunt

59. **burly-boned:** corpulent; **clown:** country boor; **chines:** joints

  and swallow my sword like a great pin, ere thou   30
  and I part.   ⌜*He draws his sword.*⌝
IDEN
  Why, rude companion, whatsoe'er thou be,
  I know thee not. Why, then, should I betray thee?
  Is 't not enough to break into my garden
  And, like a thief, to come to rob my grounds,   35
  Climbing my walls in spite of me the owner,
  But thou wilt brave me with these saucy terms?
CADE   Brave thee? Ay, by the best blood that ever was
  broached, and beard thee too. Look on me well: I
  have eat no meat these five days, yet come thou   40
  and thy five men, and if I do not leave you all as
  dead as a doornail, I pray God I may never eat
  grass more.
IDEN
  Nay, it shall ne'er be said, while England stands,
  That Alexander Iden, an esquire of Kent,   45
  Took odds to combat a poor famished man.
  Oppose thy steadfast gazing eyes to mine;
  See if thou canst outface me with thy looks.
  Set limb to limb, and thou art far the lesser;
  Thy hand is but a finger to my fist,   50
  Thy leg a stick comparèd with this truncheon.
  My foot shall fight with all the strength thou hast;
  And if mine arm be heavèd in the air,
  Thy grave is digged already in the earth.
  As for words, whose greatness answers words,   55
  Let this my sword report what speech forbears.
                    ⌜*He draws his sword.*⌝
CADE   By my valor, the most complete champion that
  ever I heard! Steel, if thou turn the edge or cut not
  out the burly-boned clown in chines of beef ere
  thou sleep in thy sheath, I beseech ⌜God⌝ on my   60
  knees thou mayst be turned to hobnails.
                    (*Here they fight,* ⌜*and Cade falls.*⌝)

62. **Famine:** starvation (here personified); **no other:** no one else

68. **monstrous:** unnatural

69. **hallow thee:** treat you with reverence

72. **herald's coat:** Heralds wore red coats.

73. **emblaze:** make resplendent; set forth by means of heraldic devices

80. **as:** i.e., just **as,** in the same way that; **thrust ... sword:** i.e., **thrust my sword** into your **body**

82. **headlong:** head downmost

84. **ungracious:** graceless, wicked

An ostrich eating a nail. (4.10.29)
From Gabriele Simeoni, *Le sententiose imprese . . .* (1560).

O, I am slain! Famine, and no other, hath slain me.
Let ten thousand devils come against me, and give
me but the ten meals I have lost, and I'd defy them
all. Wither, garden, and be henceforth a burying　65
place to all that do dwell in this house, because the
unconquered soul of Cade is fled.

IDEN
Is 't Cade that I have slain, that monstrous traitor?
Sword, I will hallow thee for this thy deed,
And hang thee o'er my tomb when I am dead.　70
Ne'er shall this blood be wipèd from thy point,
But thou shalt wear it as a herald's coat
To emblaze the honor that thy master got.

CADE　Iden, farewell, and be proud of thy victory. Tell
Kent from me she hath lost her best man, and　75
exhort all the world to be cowards; for I, that never
feared any, am vanquished by famine, not by valor.
　　　　　　　　　　　　　　　　　　Dies.

IDEN
How much thou wrong'st me, heaven be my judge!
Die, damnèd wretch, the curse of her that bare thee!
And as I thrust thy body in with my sword,　80
So wish I, I might thrust thy soul to hell.
Hence will I drag thee headlong by the heels
Unto a dunghill, which shall be thy grave,
And there cut off thy most ungracious head,
Which I will bear in triumph to the King,　85
Leaving thy trunk for crows to feed upon.
　　　He exits ⌈with his Men, dragging Cade's body.⌉

HENRY VI
Part 2

ACT 5

5.1 Buckingham seemingly placates York, and King Henry rewards Iden. York, seeing Somerset at liberty, announces his claim to the throne, and his supporters openly oppose those of King Henry.

---

0 SD. **Colors:** battle standards or flags

1. **right:** i.e., **right** to the throne

4. **entertain:** hospitably receive

5. **sancta maiestas:** holy majesty (Latin); **dear:** at great cost

6. **Let . . . knows:** i.e., **let** those **obey** who know

7. **naught:** nothing; **gold:** i.e., regalia, the emblems and symbols of monarchy

8. **due:** rightful, proper, fitting

9. **Except:** unless; **sword: sword** of state; **balance it:** counterpoise my **action**

10. **have I:** i.e., as **I have**

11. **fleur-de-luce:** France's royal insignia is the heraldic lily called the fleur-de-lis or **fleur-de-luce.**

14. **sure:** surely

17. **of pleasure:** i.e., because you wish to

A screech owl. (3.2.339)
From Konrad Gesner, *Icones animalium quadrupedum* . . . (1560).

⌜ACT 5⌝

⌜Scene 1⌝

Enter York, ⌜wearing the white rose,⌝ and his army of
Irish, with ⌜Attendants,⌝ Drum and Colors.

YORK
From Ireland thus comes York to claim his right
And pluck the crown from feeble Henry's head.
Ring, bells, aloud! Burn, bonfires, clear and bright
To entertain great England's lawful king!
Ah, *sancta maiestas*, who would not buy thee dear?   5
Let them obey that knows not how to rule.
This hand was made to handle naught but gold.
I cannot give due action to my words
Except a sword or scepter balance it.
A scepter shall it have, have I a soul,   10
On which I'll toss the fleur-de-luce of France.

  Enter Buckingham, ⌜wearing the red rose.⌝

⌜*Aside.*⌝ Whom have we here? Buckingham, to
  disturb me?
The King hath sent him, sure. I must dissemble.
BUCKINGHAM
York, if thou meanest well, I greet thee well.   15
YORK
Humphrey of Buckingham, I accept thy greeting.
Art thou a messenger, or come of pleasure?

223

18. **dread liege:** revered superior, to whom we owe allegiance and service

19. **reason of:** i.e., **reason** for

22. **power:** army

24. **Scarce:** i.e., scarcely; **choler:** anger

26. **abject:** despicable

27. **Ajax Telamonius:** son of Telamon and hero of the Trojan War, who, when he lost the contest for possession of the dead Achilles' armor, went insane and killed a flock of **sheep** (under the delusion that they were his enemies) before committing suicide

28. **spend:** expend

29. **am far better born:** i.e., by birth have a **better** claim to the throne

31. **make fair weather:** i.e., be conciliatory

40. **to . . . end:** i.e., for **no other** purpose

Foxes preying on sheep. (3.1.259–60)
From *Le microcosme* (n.d.).

BUCKINGHAM
 A messenger from Henry, our dread liege,
 To know the reason of these arms in peace;
 Or why thou, being a subject as I am,   20
 Against thy oath and true allegiance sworn,
 Should raise so great a power without his leave,
 Or dare to bring thy force so near the court.

YORK, ⌜*aside*⌝
 Scarce can I speak, my choler is so great.
 O, I could hew up rocks and fight with flint, 25
 I am so angry at these abject terms!
 And now, like Ajax Telamonius,
 On sheep or oxen could I spend my fury.
 I am far better born than is the King,
 More like a king, more kingly in my thoughts. 30
 But I must make fair weather yet awhile,
 Till Henry be more weak and I more strong.—
 Buckingham, I prithee, pardon me,
 That I have given no answer all this while.
 My mind was troubled with deep melancholy. 35
 The cause why I have brought this army hither
 Is to remove proud Somerset from the King,
 Seditious to his Grace and to the state.

BUCKINGHAM
 That is too much presumption on thy part.
 But if thy arms be to no other end,   40
 The King hath yielded unto thy demand:
 The Duke of Somerset is in the Tower.

YORK
 Upon thine honor, is he prisoner?

BUCKINGHAM
 Upon mine honor, he is prisoner.

YORK
 Then, Buckingham, I do dismiss my powers.— 45
 Soldiers, I thank you all. Disperse yourselves.

47. **Saint George's field:** an open space between Southwark and Lambeth, across the Thames from London

50. **Command:** order (that I give)

51. **pledges:** guarantees; **fealty:** fidelity

52. **willing:** i.e., willingly

54. **so:** provided that

61. **intends:** i.e., signify, mean

63. **monstrous:** unnatural

64. **since:** subsequently; **to be discomfited:** was defeated

65. **rude:** unrefined; **mean condition:** low rank

A garden with a brick wall. (4.10.7–8)
From [Thomas Hill,] *The gardeners labyrinth* . . . (1577).

Meet me tomorrow in Saint George's field;
You shall have pay and everything you wish.
⌐*Soldiers exit.*⌐

And let my sovereign, virtuous Henry,
Command my eldest son, nay, all my sons,   50
As pledges of my fealty and love;
I'll send them all as willing as I live.
Lands, goods, horse, armor, anything I have
Is his to use, so Somerset may die.

BUCKINGHAM
York, I commend this kind submission.   55
We twain will go into his Highness' tent.
⌐*They walk arm in arm.*⌐

Enter King ⌐*Henry*⌐ *and Attendants.*

KING HENRY
Buckingham, doth York intend no harm to us
That thus he marcheth with thee arm in arm?

YORK
In all submission and humility
York doth present himself unto your Highness.   60

KING HENRY
Then what intends these forces thou dost bring?

YORK
To heave the traitor Somerset from hence
And fight against that monstrous rebel Cade,
Who since I heard to be discomfited.

Enter Iden, with Cade's head.

IDEN
If one so rude and of so mean condition   65
May pass into the presence of a king,
Lo, I present your Grace a traitor's head,
The head of Cade, whom I in combat slew.

KING HENRY
The head of Cade? Great God, how just art Thou!

73. **an 't like:** if it please
74. **degree:** rank
80. **marks:** coins worth two-thirds of a pound (far more than the **thousand crowns** of 4.8.69 and 4.10.28)
81. **will:** order; **attend on us:** serve me (as an attendant)
83. **true:** faithful
86. **For thousand:** i.e., were it **for a thousand**
87. **front:** oppose
88. **How now:** i.e., **how** is it **now**
90. **be equal with:** be of the same (royal) rank as; or, **be** as courageous as

The Tower

The Tower of London.
From Claes Jansz Visscher, *Londinum florentissima Britanniae urbs* . . . [c. 1625].

O, let me view his visage, being dead,   70
That living wrought me such exceeding trouble.
Tell me, my friend, art thou the man that slew him?

IDEN   I was, an 't like your Majesty.

KING HENRY
How art thou called? And what is thy degree?

IDEN
Alexander Iden, that's my name,   75
A poor esquire of Kent that loves his king.

BUCKINGHAM
So please it you, my lord, 'twere not amiss
He were created knight for his good service.

KING HENRY
Iden, kneel down. ⌜*He kneels.*⌝ Rise up a knight. ⌜*He
rises.*⌝
We give thee for reward a thousand marks,   80
And will that thou henceforth attend on us.

IDEN
May Iden live to merit such a bounty,
And never live but true unto his liege!

Enter Queen ⌜*Margaret*⌝ *and Somerset,*
⌜*wearing the red rose.*⌝

KING HENRY, ⌜*aside to Buckingham*⌝
See, Buckingham, Somerset comes with th' Queen.
Go bid her hide him quickly from the Duke.   85
⌜*Buckingham whispers to the Queen.*⌝

QUEEN MARGARET
For thousand Yorks he shall not hide his head,
But boldly stand and front him to his face.

YORK, ⌜*aside*⌝
How now? Is Somerset at liberty?
Then, York, unloose thy long-imprisoned thoughts,
And let thy tongue be equal with thy heart.   90
Shall I endure the sight of Somerset?—
False king, why hast thou broken faith with me,

93. **how hardly:** i.e., with what difficulty; **brook:** tolerate; **abuse:** deceit

96. **Which:** i.e., who

97. **doth not become:** i.e., is **not** suitable for; is **not** congruous with

98. **palmer's:** pilgrim's (See picture, page 236.)

99. **awful:** awe-inspiring

100. **gold:** i.e., crown; **round engirt:** encircle

101. **Achilles' spear:** in mythology, this **spear** could both wound and heal (See longer note, page 258.)

102. **the change:** i.e., from **frown** to **smile**

104. **act:** make; **controlling:** powerful

108. **Of capital treason:** i.e., for **treason** punishable by death

110. **these:** i.e., York's attendants

111. **brook:** i.e., tolerate that; **bow:** bend; **man:** anyone

113. **bail:** persons who procure the release of a prisoner from custody (here, not by offering themselves up as pledges, but rather by offering to fight for his release)

114. **ward:** prison

115. **pawn their swords:** i.e., fight   **pawn:** pledge; **enfranchisement:** release from prison

116. **amain:** at once

119. **Neapolitan:** as daughter to Reignier, king of **Naples** (line 120)

120. **Outcast:** homeless vagabond (with reference to her failure to provide a dowry); **England's bloody scourge:** bloodthirsty and blood-covered instrument of divine punishment of England

122. **bane:** destruction

Knowing how hardly I can brook abuse?
"King" did I call thee? No, thou art not king,
Not fit to govern and rule multitudes,   95
Which dar'st not—no, nor canst not—rule a traitor.
That head of thine doth not become a crown;
Thy hand is made to grasp a palmer's staff,
And not to grace an awful princely scepter.
That gold must round engirt these brows of mine,   100
Whose smile and frown, like to Achilles' spear,
Is able with the change to kill and cure.
Here is a hand to hold a scepter up
And with the same to act controlling laws.
Give place. By heaven, thou shalt rule no more   105
O'er him whom heaven created for thy ruler.

SOMERSET
O monstrous traitor! I arrest thee, York,
Of capital treason 'gainst the King and crown.
Obey, audacious traitor. Kneel for grace.

YORK
Wouldst have me kneel? First let me ask of ⌈these⌉   110
If they can brook I bow a knee to man.
⌈*To an Attendant.*⌉ Sirrah, call in my ⌈sons⌉ to be my
    bail.   ⌈*Attendant exits.*⌉
I know, ere they will have me go to ward,
They'll pawn their swords ⌈for⌉ my enfranchisement. 115

QUEEN MARGARET, ⌈*to Buckingham*⌉
Call hither Clifford; bid him come amain,
To say if that the bastard boys of York
Shall be the surety for their traitor father.
                                          ⌈*Buckingham exits.*⌉

YORK, ⌈*to Queen Margaret*⌉
O, blood-bespotted Neapolitan,
Outcast of Naples, England's bloody scourge!   120
The sons of York, thy betters in their birth,
Shall be their father's bail, and bane to those
That for my surety will refuse the boys.

124. **warrant:** predict as certain

124–25. **make it good:** i.e., (1) pay my **bail,** or (2) succeed in being your **bane** (line 122)

129. **us:** the royal plural

133. **mistakes me:** have the wrong view of me

134. **Bedlam:** St. Mary of Bethlehem Hospital for the insane in London

135. **bedlam:** mad, insane; **humor:** inclination; mood; whim

137. **Let him:** i.e., **let him** be sent; **Tower:** See picture, page 228.

138. **factious:** seditious; **pate:** head

Bearbaiting. (5.1.147–54)
From William Lily, *Antibossicon* . . . (1521).

Enter ⌜York's sons⌝ Edward and Richard,
⌜wearing the white rose.⌝

See where they come; I'll warrant they'll make it
　good.   125

Enter ⌜old⌝ Clifford ⌜and his Son, wearing the red rose.⌝

QUEEN MARGARET
　And here comes Clifford to deny their bail.
CLIFFORD, *⌜kneeling before King Henry⌝*
　Health and all happiness to my lord the King.
　　　　　　　　　　　　　　　　　⌜He rises.⌝
YORK
　I thank thee, Clifford. Say, what news with thee?
　Nay, do not fright us with an angry look.
　We are thy sovereign, Clifford; kneel again.   130
　For thy mistaking so, we pardon thee.
CLIFFORD
　This is my king, York; I do not mistake,
　But thou mistakes me much to think I do.—
　To Bedlam with him! Is the man grown mad?
KING HENRY
　Ay, Clifford, a bedlam and ambitious humor   135
　Makes him oppose himself against his king.
CLIFFORD
　He is a traitor. Let him to the Tower,
　And chop away that factious pate of his.
QUEEN MARGARET
　He is arrested, but will not obey.
　His sons, he says, shall give their words for him. 140
YORK   Will you not, sons?
EDWARD
　Ay, noble father, if our words will serve.
RICHARD
　And if words will not, then our weapons shall.
CLIFFORD
　Why, what a brood of traitors have we here!

145. **glass:** looking **glass,** mirror; **image:** reflection

146. **false-heart:** false-hearted, treacherous

147. **stake:** the first of a number of allusions to the blood sport of bearbaiting, in which a bear or **bears** were chained to a **stake** and attacked by dogs; **bears:** See lines 206–7, below, for Warwick's allusion to the crest of the rampant bear; and see pictures, pages 232 and 238.

149. **astonish:** terrify; **fell-lurking curs:** savage dogs waiting to attack

152. **bait:** set on the dogs to attack

153. **bearherd:** bearward, bear keeper (i.e., York)

155. **hot:** eager, angry; **o'erweening:** presumptuous

156. **Run ... withheld:** i.e., turn around and (1) **bite** at the leash that restrains it; or, (2) **bite** the master who restrains him (Proverbial: A man may cause his own dog to **bite** him.)

157. **Who:** i.e., which; **suffered with:** injured by; **fell:** deadly

158. **cried:** yelped

160. **match:** fight

161. **heap:** alluding to the hump on Richard's back (the first of many references to Richard as a hunchback, the deformity attributed to him in Shakespeare's historical sources); **indigested:** shapeless

163. **anon:** soon

165. **bow:** bend (in submission to King Henry)

169. **spectacles:** eyeglasses (associated with old age)

YORK
  Look in a glass, and call thy image so.   145
  I am thy king and thou a false-heart traitor.
  Call hither to the stake my two brave bears,
  That, with the very shaking of their chains,
  They may astonish these fell-lurking curs.
  ⌐*To an Attendant.*⌐ Bid Salisbury and Warwick come   150
    to me.   ⌐*Attendant exits.*⌐

Enter the Earls of Warwick and Salisbury, ⌐*wearing the
                white rose.*⌐

CLIFFORD
  Are these thy bears? We'll bait thy bears to death
  And manacle the bearherd in their chains,
  If thou dar'st bring them to the baiting place.

RICHARD
  Oft have I seen a hot o'erweening cur   155
  Run back and bite because he was withheld,
  Who, being suffered with the bear's fell paw,
  Hath clapped his tail between his legs and cried;
  And such a piece of service will you do
  If you oppose yourselves to match Lord Warwick.   160

CLIFFORD
  Hence, heap of wrath, foul indigested lump,
  As crooked in thy manners as thy shape!

YORK
  Nay, we shall heat you thoroughly anon.

CLIFFORD
  Take heed, lest by your heat you burn yourselves.

KING HENRY
  Why, Warwick, hath thy knee forgot to bow?—   165
  Old Salisbury, shame to thy silver hair,
  Thou mad misleader of thy brainsick son!
  What, wilt thou on thy deathbed play the ruffian
  And seek for sorrow with thy spectacles?
  O, where is faith? O, where is loyalty?   170

171. **frosty:** i.e., white-haired
172. **harbor:** refuge
173. **Wilt . . . war:** The meaning of this line is uncertain.
175. **want'st:** lack; **experience:** i.e., judgment
176. **wherefore:** why; **abuse:** misuse
178. **That:** i.e., you who stoop; **mickle:** much
181. **repute:** consider
185. **dispense with heaven for:** get a dispensation from God to break
190. **force:** violate
191. **reave:** rob
192. **customed:** customary
195. **sophister:** specious reasoner
198. **resolved for:** determined on; **dignity:** high rank (i.e., monarchy)

A palmer with his staff. (5.1.98)
From Henry Peacham, *Minerua Britanna . . .* [1612].

If it be banished from the frosty head,
Where shall it find a harbor in the earth?
Wilt thou go dig a grave to find out war,
And shame thine honorable age with blood?
Why art thou old and want'st experience?　　175
Or wherefore dost abuse it, if thou hast it?
For shame! In duty bend thy knee to me
That bows unto the grave with mickle age.

SALISBURY
My lord, I have considered with myself
The title of this most renownèd duke,　　180
And in my conscience do repute his Grace
The rightful heir to England's royal seat.

KING HENRY
Hast thou not sworn allegiance unto me?

SALISBURY　I have.

KING HENRY
Canst thou dispense with heaven for such an oath?　　185

SALISBURY
It is great sin to swear unto a sin,
But greater sin to keep a sinful oath.
Who can be bound by any solemn vow
To do a murd'rous deed, to rob a man,
To force a spotless virgin's chastity,　　190
To reave the orphan of his patrimony,
To wring the widow from her customed right,
And have no other reason for this wrong
But that he was bound by a solemn oath?

QUEEN MARGARET
A subtle traitor needs no sophister.　　195

KING HENRY, ⌜*to an Attendant*⌝
Call Buckingham, and bid him arm himself.
⌜*Attendant exits.*⌝

YORK, ⌜*to King Henry*⌝
Call Buckingham and all the friends thou hast,
I am resolved for death ⌜or⌝ dignity.

201. **field:** battlefield

202. **bear:** endure

204. **burgonet:** helmet with a visor

205. **badge:** distinctive emblem

206. **father's:** i.e., father-in-law's; **crest:** ornament borne above a knight's helmet

207. **rampant:** rearing, standing with forepaws in the air (See picture, below.) **ragged:** with protruding lumps or knobs

209. **cedar:** associated with royalty; **shows:** is seen

211. **affright:** terrify; **view:** sight

216. **complices:** associates

219. **stigmatic:** physically deformed person (accent on first syllable)

A rampant bear, being baited.
From Giacomo Franco, *Habiti* . . . [1609?].

CLIFFORD
  The first, I warrant thee, if dreams prove true.

WARWICK
  You were best to go to bed and dream again,   200
  To keep thee from the tempest of the field.

CLIFFORD
  I am resolved to bear a greater storm
  Than any thou canst conjure up today;
  And that I'll write upon thy burgonet,
  Might I but know thee by thy ⌈house's⌉ badge.   205

WARWICK
  Now, by my father's badge, old Neville's crest,
  The rampant bear chained to the ragged staff,
  This day I'll wear aloft my burgonet—
  As on a mountaintop the cedar shows
  That keeps his leaves in spite of any storm—   210
  Even to affright thee with the view thereof.

CLIFFORD
  And from thy burgonet I'll rend thy bear
  And tread it under foot with all contempt,
  Despite the bearherd that protects the bear.

YOUNG CLIFFORD
  And so to arms, victorious father,   215
  To quell the rebels and their complices.

RICHARD
  Fie! Charity, for shame! Speak not in spite,
  For you shall sup with Jesu Christ tonight.

YOUNG CLIFFORD
  Foul stigmatic, that's more than thou canst tell!

RICHARD
  If not in heaven, you'll surely sup in hell.   220
                    ⌈*They exit separately.*⌉

5.2 York kills Lord Clifford, and York's son Richard kills the Duke of Somerset. Defeated in battle, King Henry flees to London.

———————————

2. **An if:** i.e., if; **bear:** See 5.1.206–14.
3. **alarum:** the call to arms
4. **dead:** i.e., dying
8. **afoot:** on foot (rather than on horseback)
9. **deadly-handed:** murderous
10. **match to match:** enemy to enemy
11. **carrion:** i.e., carrion-eating (See picture, page 140.)
12. **bonny:** fine
13. **Of . . . come:** Proverbial: "One dies when his hour comes."
14. **Hold:** stop; **some other chase:** something else to **hunt**
21. **fast:** firmly, fixedly

The Fates and the thread of life. (4.2.30)
From Vincenzo Cartari, *Imagines deorum . . .* (1581).

⌜Scene 2⌝

⌜*The sign of the Castle Inn is displayed. Alarms.*⌝
Enter Warwick, ⌜*wearing the white rose.*⌝

WARWICK
 Clifford of Cumberland, 'tis Warwick calls!
 An if thou dost not hide thee from the bear,
 Now, when the angry trumpet sounds alarum
 And dead men's cries do fill the empty air,
 Clifford, I say, come forth and fight with me; 5
 Proud northern lord, Clifford of Cumberland,
 Warwick is hoarse with calling thee to arms.

  Enter York, ⌜*wearing the white rose.*⌝

 How now, my noble lord? What, all afoot?
YORK
 The deadly-handed Clifford slew my steed,
 But match to match I have encountered him 10
 And made a prey for carrion kites and crows
 Even of the bonny beast he loved so well.

  Enter ⌜*old*⌝ *Clifford,* ⌜*wearing the red rose.*⌝

WARWICK
 Of one or both of us the time is come.
YORK
 Hold, Warwick! Seek thee out some other chase,
 For I myself must hunt this deer to death. 15
WARWICK
 Then, nobly, York! 'Tis for a crown thou fight'st.—
 As I intend, Clifford, to thrive today,
 It grieves my soul to leave thee unassailed.
          Warwick exits.
CLIFFORD
 What seest thou in me, York? Why dost thou pause?
YORK
 With thy brave bearing should I be in love, 20
 But that thou art so fast mine enemy.

22. **want:** lack

23. **But that: but** for the fact **that**

25. **true right:** legitimate claim (i.e., to the throne)

26. **My soul:** i.e., I bet **my soul**

27. **dreadful lay:** formidable wager; **Address thee:** prepare yourself

28. **La fin . . . oeuvres:** The end crowns the works (French proverb).

29. **still:** quiet; motionless

31. **confusion:** overthrow, destruction; **All . . . rout:** i.e., the whole army is in disorderly retreat

32. **frames:** causes, produces

34. **minister:** agent (in punishing evil humanity)

35. **part:** party, side

36. **fly:** flee

37. **that:** i.e., who; **dedicate:** dedicated

39. **essentially:** in his essential nature; **by circumstance:** only in external conditions

42. **premised . . . day:** i.e., preordained **flames** of Doomsday **premised:** literally, "sent before the time," but here used proleptically to mean "preordained" (See longer note, page 258.)

44. **general trumpet:** i.e., **trumpet** proclaiming Doomsday to all; **his:** its

45. **Particularities:** individual matters

46. **ordained:** destined

CLIFFORD
 Nor should thy prowess want praise and esteem,
  But that 'tis shown ignobly and in treason.

YORK
  So let it help me now against thy sword
  As I in justice and true right express it!   25

CLIFFORD
  My soul and body on the action both!

YORK
  A dreadful lay! Address thee instantly.
                      ⌜*They fight and Clifford falls.*⌝

CLIFFORD
  La fin courrone les oeuvres.   ⌜*He dies.*⌝

YORK
  Thus war hath given thee peace, for thou art still.
  Peace with his soul, heaven, if it be thy will!   30
                                      ⌜*He exits.*⌝

      Enter young Clifford, ⌜*wearing the red rose.*⌝

YOUNG CLIFFORD
  Shame and confusion! All is on the rout.
  Fear frames disorder, and disorder wounds
  Where it should guard. O war, thou son of hell,
  Whom angry heavens do make their minister,
  Throw in the frozen bosoms of our part   35
  Hot coals of vengeance! Let no soldier fly.
  He that is truly dedicate to war
  Hath no self-love; nor he that loves himself
  Hath not essentially, but by circumstance,
  The name of valor. ⌜*He sees his father, lying dead.*⌝ O,   40
    let the vile world end
  And the premised flames of the last day
  Knit earth and heaven together!
  Now let the general trumpet blow his blast,
  Particularities and petty sounds   45
  To cease! Wast thou ordained, dear father,

47. **lose:** waste

48. **silver livery:** i.e., gray hair; **advisèd:** wary, cautious

49. **thy reverence ... chair-days:** i.e., your revered old age

52. **stony:** unfeeling

55. **the tyrant oft reclaims:** often restrains **the tyrant**

56. **oil and flax:** Proverbial: "Put not fire to **flax**" and "To add **oil** to the fire."

59. **gobbets:** pieces of raw flesh

60. **Medea ... Absyrtis:** In mythology, **Medea,** fleeing by boat with her lover Jason, killed her brother **Absyrtis** and strewed pieces of his body in the ocean to slow her father's pursuit of her.

63. **Aeneas ... bear:** In Virgil's *Aeneid,* book 2, the Trojan **Aeneas** carries his father **Anchises** on his back out of burning Troy, thereby becoming a figure of filial piety. (See picture, page 248.)

65. **bare:** bore

68. **For underneath:** i.e., **for** by dying **underneath**

70. **the wizard:** Roger Bolingbroke (See 1.4.36–40.)

71. **hold:** maintain; **temper:** hardness and resiliency (with possible wordplay on "mental balance, composure") **still:** always

72 SD. **Excursions:** sorties, sallies

To lose thy youth in peace, and to achieve
The silver livery of advisèd age,
And, in thy reverence and thy chair-days, thus
To die in ruffian battle? Even at this sight   50
My heart is turned to stone, and while 'tis mine,
It shall be stony. York not our old men spares;
No more will I their babes. Tears virginal
Shall be to me even as the dew to fire;
And beauty, that the tyrant oft reclaims,   55
Shall to my flaming wrath be oil and flax.
Henceforth I will not have to do with pity.
Meet I an infant of the house of York,
Into as many gobbets will I cut it
As wild Medea young Absyrtis did.   60
In cruelty will I seek out my fame.
⌐*He takes his father's body onto his back.*⌐
Come, thou new ruin of old Clifford's house;
As did Aeneas old Anchises bear,
So bear I thee upon my manly shoulders.
But then Aeneas bare a living load,   65
Nothing so heavy as these woes of mine. ⌐*He exits.*⌐

Enter Richard, ⌐*wearing the white rose,*⌐ *and Somerset,*
⌐*wearing the red rose,*⌐ *to fight.*
⌐*Richard kills Somerset under the sign of Castle Inn.*⌐

RICHARD So lie thou there.
For underneath an alehouse' paltry sign,
The Castle in Saint Albans, Somerset
Hath made the wizard famous in his death.   70
Sword, hold thy temper! Heart, be wrathful still!
Priests pray for enemies, but princes kill. ⌐*He exits.*⌐

Fight. Excursions. Enter King ⌐*Henry,*⌐ *Queen*
⌐*Margaret, both wearing the red rose,*⌐ *and Others.*

QUEEN MARGARET
Away, my lord! You are slow. For shame, away!

74. **the heavens:** i.e., divine wrath; **stay:** stop
75. **nor fight:** i.e., neither **fight**
77. **give the enemy way:** retreat from **the enemy; us:** ourselves
78. **By what:** i.e., in whatever way; **which:** who
79. **ta'en:** taken, captured; **bottom:** lowest point
80. **haply:** by chance; **scape:** escape
81. **if ... neglect:** i.e., unless your indifference prevents it
85. **But:** except; **mischief:** trouble
87. **Uncurable discomfit:** irreversible defeat
88. **present parts:** perhaps, remaining forces
89. **relief:** deliverance
90. **see their day:** i.e., experience victory; **them our fortune give:** i.e., **give them our** misfortune

5.3 Victorious, York and his followers set out for London.

---

2. **winter:** i.e., aged
3. **brush of:** i.e., hostile encounter with
4. **gallant:** fine fellow; **in the brow of youth:** i.e., with an unwrinkled forehead

KING HENRY
  Can we outrun the heavens? Good Margaret, stay!

QUEEN MARGARET
  What are you made of? You'll nor fight nor fly.   75
  Now is it manhood, wisdom, and defense
  To give the enemy way, and to secure us
  By what we can, which can no more but fly.
                          Alarum afar off.
  If you be ta'en, we then should see the bottom
  Of all our fortunes; but if we haply scape,   80
  As well we may—if not through your neglect—
  We shall to London get, where you are loved
  And where this breach now in our fortunes made
  May readily be stopped.

     Enter ⌜Young⌝ Clifford, ⌜wearing the red rose.⌝

YOUNG CLIFFORD
  But that my heart's on future mischief set,   85
  I would speak blasphemy ere bid you fly;
  But fly you must. Uncurable discomfit
  Reigns in the hearts of all our present parts.
  Away, for your relief! And we will live
  To see their day and them our fortune give.   90
  Away, my lord, away!
                         They exit.

⌜Scene 3⌝

Alarum. Retreat. Enter York, ⌜Edward,⌝ Richard,
Warwick, and Soldiers, ⌜all wearing the white rose,⌝
with Drum and Colors.

YORK
  Of Salisbury, who can report of him,
  That winter lion, who in rage forgets
  Agèd contusions and all brush of time,
  And, like a gallant in the brow of youth,

5. **Repairs him:** restores himself; **occasion:** opportunity (i.e., to fight); **happy:** fortunate

9. **holp:** helped

10. **bestrid him:** i.e., stood over him to protect him when he was down

12. **But still:** but continuously; **still there:** always **there**

13. **hangings:** wall tapestries; **homely:** humble

21. **have not got:** i.e., do **not** (securely) possess; **that which we have:** i.e., what **we have** obtained

23. **opposites:** enemies; **repairing nature:** i.e., ability to flee; ability to restore themselves

24. **safety:** means of **safety**

26. **present:** immediate

27. **writs:** summonses (to attend **Parliament**)

32. **eternized:** made eternal; immortalized; **age:** i.e., ages

34. **befall:** belong

Aeneas carrying his father, "old Anchises." (5.2.63)
From Geoffrey Whitney, *A choice of emblemes . . .* (1586).

Repairs him with occasion? This happy day 5
Is not itself, nor have we won one foot,
If Salisbury be lost.

RICHARD   My noble father,
Three times today I holp him to his horse,
Three times bestrid him. Thrice I led him off, 10
Persuaded him from any further act;
But still, where danger was, still there I met him,
And, like rich hangings in a homely house,
So was his will in his old feeble body.
But, noble as he is, look where he comes. 15

       Enter Salisbury, ⌜*wearing the white rose.*⌝
Now, by my sword, well hast thou fought today!

SALISBURY
By th' Mass, so did we all. I thank you, Richard.
God knows how long it is I have to live,
And it hath pleased Him that three times today
You have defended me from imminent death. 20
Well, lords, we have not got that which we have;
'Tis not enough our foes are this time fled,
Being opposites of such repairing nature.

YORK
I know our safety is to follow them;
For, as I hear, the King is fled to London 25
To call a present court of Parliament.
Let us pursue him ere the writs go forth.—
What says Lord Warwick? Shall we after them?

WARWICK
After them? Nay, before them, if we can.
Now, by my hand, lords, 'twas a glorious day. 30
Saint Albans battle won by famous York
Shall be eternized in all age to come.—
Sound drum and trumpets, and to London all;
And more such days as these to us befall!

                 ⌜*Flourish.*⌝ *They exit.*

Longer Notes

1.1.1. imperial: The word **imperial** was used to describe England after its break with the Roman Catholic Church in the early sixteenth century to indicate that the king and the country were subject to no outside sovereign. Its use in this play may be anachronistic. Or it may, instead, refer to the fact that Henry VI was king not just of England but also, from the English perspective, of France and of Ireland, and was thus, in a way, an emperor.

1.1.4. To marry . . . Grace: In the last scene of *Henry VI, Part 1* (5.5), Suffolk persuades Henry to marry Reignier's daughter Margaret, over the protests of Gloucester, the Protector and thus effectively the ruler of England. At Gloucester's urging, Henry had already promised to marry the daughter of the earl of Armagnac. After hearing Suffolk's praise of Margaret, Henry ignores his previous betrothal and orders Suffolk to return to France as Henry's agent in acquiring Margaret as Henry's bride:

> Take therefore shipping; post, my lord, to France;
> Agree to any covenants, and procure
> That Lady Margaret do vouchsafe to come
> To cross the seas to England and be crowned
> King Henry's faithful and anointed queen.
>
> (5.5.87–91)

In the opening scene of *Henry VI, Part 2*, Suffolk's humble public submission to Henry VI is in line with his

251

public speeches to Henry in the final scene of *Henry VI, Part 1*, but it stands in marked contrast to his soliloquy that concludes that play: "Margaret shall now be queen, and rule the King, / But I will rule both her, the King, and realm" (107–8).

1.1.7–8. Orleance, Calaber, Britaigne, Alanson: The names of some French towns and regions are given anglicized spellings in the Folio text of this play. While it is customary for editors to replace these spellings with the appropriate French spellings (so that **Orleance** appears as Orléans and **Alanson** as Alençon), such a practice introduces French pronunciations of the words and thus disrupts the meter. In this play, in which the iambic pentameter rhythm is so strongly emphasized, such disruption is particularly disturbing. Retaining the anglicized spellings grants the reader or actor the flexibility to place the stress as the line demands, with **Orleance** pronounced with the stress on the first (instead of the final) syllable and **Alanson** pronounced with the stress on the first syllable (as AL-anson). We retain the Folio spelling of **Britaigne** (BRIT-ane) because both modern spellings of this region (the English "Brittany" and the French "Bretagne") add an extra syllable to the word, again disrupting the meter.

When the word "Dauphin" appears later in the play, we use the French spelling because the anglicized Folio version, "Dolphin," though the standard English spelling at the time, seems distractingly comic. It is important, however, to accent *Dauphin* on the first syllable (DAW-fin), as the Folio "DOL-phin" indicates.

1.1.60. read on: There are discrepancies between Gloucester's reading of the **peace** between the English and French and the Cardinal's reading of it, even though they are apparently reading the same document. For example, Gloucester reads *"Item, that the duchy of Anjou and the county of Maine shall be released and delivered to the King her father,"* whereas the Cardinal reads *"Item,* **it is further agreed between them** *that the* **duchies** *of Anjou and* [**omission**] *Maine shall be released and delivered to the King her father."* These discrepancies have troubled some editors, who have emended the play's text so as to make Gloucester's and the Cardinal's readings identical; other editors, refusing to emend, have attempted to explain the discrepancies in realistic terms by suggesting that the Cardinal merely skims over, rather than reading word for word, what Gloucester has already read. Probably there is no need for either emendation or resort to realism, since early modern dramatists show little concern for exact repetition in cases such as this.

1.1.87. true inheritance: The English traced Henry VI's right to the throne of France to (1) his descent from Edward II, who had married Isabel, daughter of the French King Philip IV, and (2) to the Treaty of Troyes (1420), according to which Henry V or his heir (Henry VI) would inherit the French crown upon the death of the French king Charles VI. By this point in history both Henry V and Charles VI are dead, and, for the English, Henry VI is king of France. See "England's Claim to France," page xviii.

1.1.245–46. As . . . Calydon: When, in mythology, Meleager, **prince of Calydon,** was born, the Fates prophesied that he would live only as long as a **brand** (piece of wood) then on the hearth remained unburned. His mother, **Althaea,** took the brand from the fire and kept it safe until Meleager killed her two brothers in a fight. She then threw it back on the fire. (See Ovid's *Metamorphoses*, book 8.)

1.2.77. cunning witch: This phrase combines words used at the time to describe two different kinds of persons who purportedly engaged in supernatural practices. **Cunning** men or **cunning** women were sought out for their ability to find lost objects, to provide love potions, and otherwise to help out the troubled. **Witches**—whether male or female—reputedly dealt with evil spirits, and through them put curses on enemies, found out the future, and caused impotence and death. It is clear from the action in this scene that Margery Jourdain (a historical figure) is to be seen as a practicing **witch** rather than a **cunning** woman.

1.3.175. Last time: In *Henry VI, Part 1*, 4.3, York accuses Somerset of having delayed York's "promisèd supply / Of horsemen that were levied for this siege"—referring to Talbot's siege of Bordeaux in 1453. Because York specifically mentions Paris, here in *Part 2*—"Last time I danced attendance on [Somerset's] will / Till *Paris* was besieged, famished, and lost"—it is also possible that the reference is rather to the siege of Paris recorded for 1437 in Hall's *Union of the two noble and illustre famelies of Lancastre & Yorke*: "the duke of Somerset . . . by all waies and meanes possible . . . bothe hindered and detracted [York], . . . causying hym to linger in Englande, without dispatche, till Paris and the floure of Fraunce, were gotten by the Frenche kyng."

1.4.24 SD. **circle:** When Christopher Marlowe has Doctor Faustus conjure, Faustus describes the **circle:**

Within this circle is Jehovah's name,
Forward and backward anagrammatized*,   *made
                                      into anagrams
The breviated* names of holy saints,   *abbreviated
Figures of every adjunct to the heavens,
And characters of signs and erring stars,
By which the spirits are enforced to rise.
                        (*Doctor Faustus* [1604] 1.3.8–13,
                              ed. Bevington and Rasmussen)

"Figures . . . stars" refers to "charts of every heavenly body fixed in the firmament and astrological symbols or diagrams of the constellations of the Zodiac and the planets." According to Reginald Scot (*The Discovery of Witchcraft*), the conjurer "must make a circle . . . when that he has made, go into the circle, and close again the place, there where thou wentest in." The circle was thought not only to force the spirit(s) to appear, as Faustus says, but also to protect, as **a hallowed verge,** the conjurer against the risen spirit(s).

2.1.103. **lame:** For the association of **lame** with **blind** (line 83) and **the North** (line 91), see Jeremiah 31.8: "Behold I will bring them from **the North** country, and gather them from the coasts of the world, with the **blind** and the **lame** among them."

2.2.42–45. **This Edmund . . . died:** In Shakespeare's *Henry IV, Part 1*, Edmund is captured by Glendower, but then becomes his ally and marries his daughter. Like his historical sources, Shakespeare may here confuse Edmund Mortimer, the fifth earl of March, with

Sir Edmund Mortimer, brother to the fourth earl, Glendower's captive. For the same probable confusion, see Shakespeare's *Henry VI, Part 1*, 2.5.

2.3.96 SD. They fight, and Peter strikes him down: It would be easy for the modern reader to dismiss the trial by combat between Thump and Horner as a bit of clowning in a very dark play—as comic relief, that is. However, there is reason to question such a reading of a very complex scene. As the deadly outcome of the combat indicates, fighting with flails was a serious matter. The flail may seem a silly thing when it is described by the Folio as a **"staff with a sandbag fastened to it"** (line 60 SD). Yet when more properly described as a "staff with a long thin leather bag of sand attached to the end of it," the flail seems, as it indeed looks in contemporary portrayals, as elegant as it is deadly. It was also used by infantry in war. In many ways, then, the look of the fight between Horner and Thump would not have been comic, despite Horner's drunkenness and Thump's terror.

The scene's complexity is increased by a certain amount of irony. King Henry, as usual, maintains a pious and conventional view throughout. Before the trial begins he exclaims "God defend the right!" (line 57), expressing the belief that the combat offers God the chance to intervene in the world to determine the outcome by favoring the just combatant against the treacherous one. When Thump prevails, Henry declares that "God in justice hath revealed to us / The truth and innocence of this poor fellow [Thump]," while of Horner he declares "by his death we do perceive his guilt" (lines 103–5). However, this pious response is set off against York's comment to the victorious Thump: "Fellow, thank God and the good wine in thy master's way" (lines 98–99), an explanation of

Thump's victory that clouds the likelihood of divine intervention. To a certain extent, then, the Thump-Horner fight can be seen as a mockery of Henry's staunchly religious view of trial by combat.

3.2.120. Dido: As editors observe, these lines fail accurately to represent Virgil's *Aeneid*, where it is Aeneas himself, at the beginning of book 2, who tells Dido his story. Ascanius seems to make an appearance earlier, in book 1, though the figure of Ascanius is actually a disguised Cupid, sent by Aeneas's mother, Venus, to give gifts to Dido and thereby inflame her with love for Aeneas.

4.1.3. jades: Some editors refer to other Shakespeare plays to argue that these **jades** are dragons, not horses. See *A Midsummer Night's Dream* 3.2.400, "night's swift dragons," and *Cymbeline* 2.2.52, "Swift, swift, you dragons of the night."

4.1.54. kissed thy hand: This and the following lines (55–65) seem at first to suggest that Suffolk recognizes the Lieutenant as a former servant of his, who performed many duties for him. However, it seems more likely that Suffolk is merely characterizing the Lieutenant as belonging to the same social rank as the people who once served the duke in the ways now described. If so, the duke's words would be insulting because they would indicate that, as far as he is concerned, members of that social rank are all the same, not worthy of having any distinctions made among them.

4.2.0 SD. Bevis: Most editors name this character "George Bevis"; they equate him with the character named "George" in 4.7, and argue that, like John Hol-

land, George Bevis was the name of an actor. While the
name "J. Holland" appears in a playhouse document
from around 1590, the name "George Bevis" cannot be
demonstrated to be that of an actor. Proponents of this
reading point to a phrase in a version of this play published in 1594 as *The First part of the Contention
betwixt the two famous Houses of Yorke and Lancaster*,
a version that differs widely from *Henry VI, Part 2* as
published in the First Folio in 1623. The phrase in the
Contention (here printed in italics) concludes Horner's
line at 2.3.94, which, in the *Contention*, reads "haue at
you Peter with downright blowes, *as Beuys of South-
hampton fell vpon Askapart*." The name *Beuys* is a contemporary spelling of our *Bevis* and alludes to a
legendary English hero. The editorial argument is that
this phrase in *Contention* was added by an actor as
wordplay on his own name—*Bevis*. While this supposi-
tion is not impossible—actors' names were often added
to playhouse manuscripts by theatrical personnel—it is
by no means certain. Our decision is thus not to combine "Bevis" in 4.2 with "George" in 4.7. In the theater,
a director may well choose to combine "George" with
"Bevis." Like "John Holland," "George" and "Bevis" are
minor characters whose parts, on the Elizabethan
stage, could easily have been assigned to whichever
actors were available for doubling.

5.1.101. **Achilles' spear:** During the Trojan War,
Telephus was wounded, while defending Troy, by the
spear of the greatest of the Greek attackers, Achilles.
Telephus's wound was subsequently healed by the
application of the rust that had fallen from the spear.
The incident became proverbial.

5.2.42. **premised flames of the last day:** See 2 Peter
3.7–12: "But the heavens and **the earth** . . . are

reserved unto fire against the **day** of judgment. . . . But the **day** of the Lord will come as a thief in the night, in the which . . . the heavens being on fire shall be dissolved, and the elements shall melt with heat."

Textual Notes

The reading of the present text appears to the left of the square bracket. Unless otherwise noted, the reading to the left of the bracket is from **F,** the First Folio text (upon which this edition is based). The earliest sources of readings not in F are indicated as follows: **Q** is the first quarto of 1594; **F2** is the Second Folio of 1632; **F3** is the Third Folio of 1663–64; **F4** is the Fourth Folio of 1685; **Ed.** is an earlier editor of Shakespeare, beginning with Rowe in 1709. No sources are given for emendations of punctuation or for corrections of obvious typographical errors, like turned letters that produce no known word. **SD** means stage direction; **SP** means speech prefix; ~ stands in place of a word already quoted before the square bracket; ∧ indicates the omission of a punctuation mark.

1.1   0. SD *Queen*] Ed.; *The Queene* F;   4. Princess] F (Princes);   19 *and hereafter.* SP KING HENRY] Ed.; *King.* F;   27 *and hereafter.* SP QUEEN MARGARET] Ed.; *Queen.* F;   34. overjoy] F (ouer ioy);   40. Queen] F (Qu.);   46. *Imprimis*] F (Inprimis);   47. *king*] F (K.);   55. *father—*] ~. F;   61. SP CARDINAL] Ed.; *Win.* F;   62. *duchies*] Ed.; *Dutchesse* F;   63. *delivered*] Ed.; *deliuered ouer*;   98. had] Ed.; hath F;   106. Razing] F (Racing);   110. peroration] preroration F;   114. roast] F (rost);   138 *and hereafter in this act.* SP GLOUCESTER] Ed.; *Hum.* F;   149. out.] ~, F;   153. SD *Gloucester exits.*] F (*Exit Humfrey.*);   184. besides] F (beside);   186. Protector] Q; Protectors F;   193. cardinal,] ~. F;   268. in] in in F

1.2   1 *and hereafter.* SP DUCHESS] Ed.; *Elia.* F;   8. Enchased] Inehac'd F;   19. hour] Ed.; thought F;   21.

261

world] worid F;   59. Saint] F (S.);   62. SD *Gloucester exits*] F (*Ex. Hum*) *1 line earlier*;   80. promisèd:] ~∧ F; 89. SD *Duchess exits*.] F (*Exit Elianor.*)

1.3 6. SP FIRST PETITIONER] F4; *Peter*. F;   32. master] Ed.; *Mistresse* F;   43. SD *They exit*.] *Exit*. F;   70. Besides] F (Beside);   103. helm] Ed.; *Helme. Exit.* F;   103. SD *King . . . Cardinall . . . Warwick*] Ed.; *the King . . . Cardinall, Buckingham, Yorke, Salisbury, Warwicke* F;   116. Buckingham] *Buekingham* F;   133. wife's] F (Wiues);   140. SD *Gloucester exits*.] F (*Exit Humfrey.*);   146. I'd] Q; I could F;   151. SD *Eleanor . . . exits*.] F (*Exit Elianor.*);   192 *and hereafter*. SP HORNER] Ed.; *Armorer*. F

1.4 24. SD *etc*.] Ed.; *&c*. F;   26. SP JOURDAIN] Ed.; *Witch*. F;   58. SD *Jourdain . . . aloft*.] F (*Exit*.);   66. *posse*] Ed.; *posso* F;   74. lord] Ed.; Lords F

2.1 0. SD *King*] Ed; *the King* F;   32. Lord] F4; Lords F;   54. SP CARDINAL] Ed.; Cardinall, F;   65. SD *a man from St. Albans*] Ed.; *one* F;   68 *and hereafter*. SP MAN] Ed.; *One*. F;   122. Alban] F2 (*Albon*); *Albones* F;   146. his] Q; it F;   171. them] F (thē);   172. SD *The . . . exit*.] Ed. *Exit*. F

2.2 38 *and hereafter*. Philippa] F (*Phillip*);   49. son] Ed.; *not in* F;   50. son] Ed.; *Sonnes Sonne* F;   67. SP SALISBURY, WARWICK] Ed.; *Both*. F

2.3 0. SD *King*] Ed.; *the King* F;   4. sins] Ed.; sinne F;   54. therefor] F (therefore);   56. I'] F (A)

2.4 5. o'clock] F (a Clock);   43. Sometimes] F (Sometime)

3.1 39. lords] This ed.; Lord F;   212. strains] Ed.; strayes F;   333. SD *All . . . exit*.] Ed.; *Exeunt. Manet Yorke*. F;   336. art∧] ~; F;   340. than] F (thē);   387. Humphrey∧] ~; F

3.2 1 *and hereafter*. SP FIRST MURDERER] Ed.; 1. F; 3. SP SECOND MURDERER] Ed.; 2. F;   14. SD *King Henry, Queen Margaret, Cardinal, Somerset*] Ed.; *the King, the*

Queene, Cardinall, Suffolke, Somerset F; 26. Meg] Ed.;
Nell F; 33. SD *swoons*] F (*sounds*); 81, 103, 124.
Margaret] Ed.; *Elianor* F; 138. Salisbury] Salsburie F;
152. SD *Bed . . . forth*] F, *2 lines earlier;* 186, 189.
Duke] F (D.); 274. whe'er] F (where); 310. SD *All . . .
exit.*] Ed.; *Exit.* F; 319. enemies] Q; enemy F; 322.
Could] Q; Would F; 330. on] F (an); 344. turn] Ed.;
turnes F; 345. bade] F (bad); 363. Adventure]
Aduenrure F; 380. Whither] F (Whether); 386, 387.
Sometimes] F (Sometime); 419. It] Ir F

3.3 8. SP CARDINAL] Ed.; *Beau.* F; 10. whe'er] F
(where)

4.1 6. Clip] F (Cleape); 10. their] theit F; 49.
Jove . . . I] Q *only; not in* F; 49. sometimes] Q (sometime); 51. SP SUFFOLK] Q *only* (*Suf.*); *not in* F; 51.
blood,] ~. F; 52. The] Q; *Suf.* The F; 72–73. SP LIEUTENANT . . . Pole!] Q (*Cap.* Yes Poull. | *Suffolke.* Poull.);
not in F; 91. mother's bleeding] Ed.; Mother-bleeding
F; 99. are] Ed.; and F; 122. Walter] Ed.; Water F;
123. SP WHITMORE] Ed.; W. F; 124. *Paene*] Ed.; *Pine* F;
126 *and hereafter.* SP WHITMORE] Ed.; *Wal.* F; 140. SP
SUFFOLK] Ed.; *not in* F; 140. can,] ~. F; 141. That]
Ed.; *Suf.* That F; 144. Brutus'] *Brutsn* F; 146. SD
Walter Whitmore] Ed.; *Water* F

4.2 34 *and hereafter until 4.7.52.* SP DICK] Ed.; *But.*
F; 35. fall] F4; faile F; 47 *and hereafter until 4.7.10.*
SP SMITH] Ed.; *Weauer.* F; 88. H'as] F (Ha's); 100.
an] F2; a F; 133. this:] ~⌃ F; 151. Duke] F (D.);
178. SD *The . . . exit.*] Ed.; *Exit.* F

4.4 0. SD *King . . . Queen*] Ed.; *the King . . . the
Queene* F; 19. have] huae F; 28. Southwark] Southwatke F; 50. SP SECOND MESSENGER] *Mess.* F; 59. be
betrayed] F2; betraid F

4.5 4. Lord] F (L.)

4.6 11. My] Ed.; *Dicke.* My F

4.7 3. SP DICK] *Rut.* F; 7 *and hereafter.* SP HOL-

LAND] Ed.; *Iohn*. F;   47. on] Q; in F;   59. where] F
(wher'e);   89. caudle] F4; Candle F;   108. i'] F (a)

4.8 27. freedom] Fteedome F;   70. means] F
(meane)

4.9 35. calmed] F4; calme F

4.10 7. o'er] Ed.; on F;   21. waning] Ed.; warning
F;   27. Ah] F (A);   60. God] Q; Ioue F

5.1 0. SD *with*] *wi*t*h* F;   47. Saint] F (S.);   74.
thou] rhou F;   110. these] Ed.; thee F;   112. sons] Q;
sonne F;   115. for] F2; of F;   139. arrested] atrested F;
150, 166. Salisbury] Salsbury F;   177. shame!] ~∧ F;
198. or] Ed.; and F;   199, 202, 212. SP CLIFFORD] Ed.;
Old Clif. F;   205. house's] F2; housed F;   211. to] io F

5.2 8. How] Ed.; *War*. How F;   18. thee] theee
F;   18. SD *Warwick*] F (*War*.);   28. oeuvres] F2;
eumenes F;   29. thou] F (у̏);   31 *and hereafter.* SP
YOUNG CLIFFORD] Q; *Clif*. F;   69. Saint] F (S.)

5.3 1, 7. Salisbury] Salsbury F;   16. Now] Ed.; *Sal*.
Now F;   17. SP SALISBURY] Ed.; *not in* F

Appendices

Authorship of *Henry VI, Part 2*

Henry VI, Part 2 was first published in 1623, together with thirty-five other plays, in the first collection of Shakespeare's plays to be issued in a single volume—the book we now call the Shakespeare First Folio. Until Lewis Theobald in 1734, no one suggested that any of the play was the work of someone else besides Shakespeare. After Theobald expressed skepticism about Shakespeare's sole authorship, a great many editors and scholars have echoed his doubts, most influentially the renowned Shakespeare editor Edmond Malone in 1787. Others have contested Theobald's doubts, including the respected Samuel Johnson. Beginning with Jane Lee in 1876, a number of investigators using different methods have attempted to discriminate between those parts of the play to be credited to Shakespeare and those parts to be attributed to other named playwrights of the period, including Robert Greene, Thomas Nashe, and Christopher Marlowe. These scholars have arrived at no consensus about exactly who wrote which parts.

We do not think it impossible or even improbable that other hands may be represented in the play. It is conservatively estimated that at least half the plays from the public theater of Shakespeare's time were collaborative efforts. We respect the labor expended and skill exhibited by attribution scholars, and, at the same time, we take seriously the limitations that they acknowledge necessarily attend their efforts. On this basis we simply set aside the question of whether Greene, Nashe, or Marlowe wrote some of *Henry VI*,

Part 2 and contest neither those who have argued for collaboration nor those who have claimed the play for Shakespeare.

We treat the play in the same way as the others published in the Shakespeare First Folio, referring to it for convenience as a Shakespeare play. In doing so, we fully recognize that the theater is always the location of collaborative creation, not just among named dramatists but also among members of acting companies and their employees and associates. We are aware of documentary evidence of other hands reaching into dramatic manuscripts in the course of their annotation or transcription, and we suspect that Shakespeare's words could not possibly have commanded in their own time the same reverence they have been accorded in later times. Such circumstances attach to all the Shakespeare printed plays that come down to us. In calling *Henry VI, Part 2* Shakespeare's, we are simply acknowledging its inclusion in the 1623 First Folio.

Shakespeare's Two Tetralogies

When Shakespeare's plays were collected and published in 1623, the volume included eight plays that together dramatize the "Wars of the Roses." This name has been given to a period in English history that, while shown as flaring into actual warfare at the end of *Henry VI, Part 2*, arguably stems from the death of Edward the Black Prince in 1376 and ends when Henry Tudor is proclaimed King Henry VII in 1485. Edward, the oldest son of King Edward III, was a valiant warrior and skilled diplomat who held out the promise of continuing his father's rule over England and much of France. When, however, the Black Prince predeceased his father, his infant son Richard became heir to the throne, and, on Edward III's death, was proclaimed King Richard II. His royal uncles began to compete for power, and Richard was deposed in 1399 by his cousin Henry, son of the duke of Lancaster. In the following years, the descendants of Edward III divided themselves into two factions—those who sympathized with the deposed and murdered Richard II and his Yorkist supporters, and those who followed the Lancastrians. The factions battled each other for the nation's throne with increasing ferocity, with first one faction then the other in the ascendancy. In 1485, Richard III, the last of the Yorkist kings, was killed at the Battle of Bosworth Field. His opponent, Henry Tudor, a descendant of the Lancastrians, married Elizabeth York and thereby brought together the two battling family lines and brought an end to the Wars of the Roses.

The four plays that dramatize the period between 1422 (the death of Henry V) and 1485 (the death of Richard III and the proclamation of Henry VII as king) were written in the late 1580s or early 1590s. Three of them cover the tumultuous reign of Henry VI, who, like Richard II, was named king when yet a child. During the years covered by the three *Henry VI* plays, England was caught up not only in the struggles between the Yorks and the Lancasters but also in an ongoing war to hold on to, or to regain, lands in France. The fourth of these plays, *Richard III*, shows Richard's violent climb to the throne and his equally violent ejection and death. All four plays were published as Shakespeare's in the First Folio, though there is ongoing debate about how much of *Henry VI, Part 1*, in particular, was actually written by Shakespeare, and though there are many scholars who argue for other authorial hands in *Parts 2* and *3* as well.

The four plays that dramatize the earlier period in this saga, which begins in 1398 near the close of

Richard II's reign and ends in 1421 with Henry V in triumph, were written in the late 1590s, and three of
them—*Richard II, Henry IV, Part 1,* and *Henry IV, Part
2*—were printed numerous times in individual quarto
editions beginning in 1597, 1598, and 1600. (*Henry V*
did not receive a full printing until it appeared in the
First Folio.) These four plays are generally accepted as
not only written by Shakespeare but as being the very
best of his history plays. They have a complex and confusing relationship to the plays written earlier, to
which they provide a kind of prequel, as is acknowl-
edged in the Chorus that closes *Henry V:*

> Small time, but in that small most greatly lived
> This star of England. Fortune made his sword,
> By which the world's best garden he achieved
> And of it left his son imperial lord.
> Henry the Sixth, in infant bands crowned King
> Of France and England, did this king succeed,
> Whose state so many had the managing
> That they lost France and made his England bleed,
> *Which oft our stage hath shown.*
>   *Henry V,* Epilogue, 5–13 (emphasis added)

Part of the complexity of the relationship between
the two tetralogies arises from the fact that because
the plays covering the later portion of the period were
written first, editors from the mid–twentieth century
onward began calling them "The First Tetralogy" (i.e.,
the first-written tetralogy). These editors began placing
the First Tetralogy in collected editions before the four
plays that depict the earlier years, rather than putting
all eight plays in the order in which their historical
figures lived, as did the First Folio of 1623. Thus
"The Second Tetralogy" refers to the set of plays written as a kind of prequel to what we now know as "The

First Tetralogy." As a consequence, few readers today, trained to read the plays in the order in which they were written, would ever encounter the eight plays by beginning with *Richard II* and reading through to the end of the saga with Richard III's death and the proclamation of the reign of Henry VII. Thus the full story of this turbulent period of English history as depicted in these eight plays—the fall of Richard II, the rise of Henry IV, and the subsequent violence between Edward III's royal descendants—is rarely experienced with its full narrative force.

Henry VI, Part 2:
A Modern Perspective

Nina Levine

Henry VI, Part 2 presents a medieval past utterly devoid of nostalgia. There are no battlefield heroics, no patriotic rallying cries, no famous victories or imperial conquests. What the play offers instead is a chilling documentary of a nation's descent into civil war. The action opens with aristocratic rancor over the king's marriage to Margaret of Anjou and closes with armed conflict at St. Albans between the rival houses of York and Lancaster, marking the start of the Wars of the Roses. In the space between, Shakespeare probes the causes and consequences of civil dissension along a trajectory that extends from seditious rhetoric and political intrigue in the first half to open rebellion and civil warfare in the second. At the play's center, and prologue to the butchery to follow, is the arrest and murder of the "good Duke Humphrey," England's lord protector. The sorrowful king likens Humphrey's arrest to an animal's being led "to the bloody slaughterhouse" (3.1.213), and for once Henry gets it right, invoking with grim accuracy the bloodbath of murder, revolt, and war to follow. With mangled corpses and decapitated heads to rival *Titus Andronicus*, *2 Henry VI* is unusually brutal. Medieval England is not so far from ancient Rome, it seems, and political history not so far from popular revenge tragedy.

The capacity for sadistic violence and civil butchery is not limited to ambitious nobles or aspiring churchmen, however. What most unsettles modern audiences and critics is the play's insistence on making women and commoners instrumental to the carnage. Queen

271

Margaret is the first to threaten outright violence when
she accuses Gloucester of crimes that, "If they were
known, . . . Would make thee quickly hop without thy
head" (1.3.139–40); and she again takes the lead at his
arraignment, insisting that "This Gloucester should be
quickly rid the world" (3.1.235). Eleanor, duchess of
Gloucester, adopts a similarly bloody rhetoric as she
imagines her path to the throne with a violence worthy
of Lady Macbeth: "Were I a man, a duke, and next of
blood, / I would remove these tedious stumbling blocks
/ And smooth my way upon their headless necks"
(1.2.65–67). It is Jack Cade's uprising, though, that
unleashes the play's most horrific scenes of mayhem.
The land now runs with blood, a point of pride for
Cade, who delights in the gruesome craft of his artisan
rebels. "They fell before thee like sheep and oxen, and
thou behaved'st thyself as if thou hadst been in thine
own slaughterhouse" (4.3.3–5), Cade says of Dick the
butcher's handiwork. For Elizabethans, these rebellious artisans and unruly wives would have recalled
popular emblems of disorder, signs of the causes and
consequences of civil chaos. But stereotypes resist
familiar political and moral formulations in *2 Henry
VI*. Pawns *and* players in the proliferating power struggles, women and commoners assume unusual prominence here, contributing to a new and complex
political history that far exceeds predictable patterns
or traditional expectations—for Elizabethans and perhaps for us.

One could argue, of course, that the story was in
some sense ready-made, popularized by the Tudor
chronicles of Edward Hall (1548) and Raphael Holinshed (1577, 1587). And it was in these well-known
sources that Shakespeare found the portrait of the virtuous but weak king overruled by powerful barons and
a "manly" queen. The young playwright would also

have found a starting point in the royal marriage, which, according to Hall, "semed to many, bothe infortunate, and unprofitable to the realme of England."[1] Shakespeare goes beyond his sources, however, in portraying these costs in explicitly gendered terms, setting up an equation between the loss of empire and a loss of valor and manhood that cuts to the heart of English patriarchy. Just as the royal marriage renders the king fond and foolish—Margaret's presence makes Henry "from wond'ring fall to weeping joys" (1.1.37)—so too does it emasculate the realm, as Gloucester sternly warns the court:

> O peers of England, shameful is this league,
> Fatal this marriage, cancelling your fame,
> Blotting your names from books of memory,
> Razing the characters of your renown,
> Defacing monuments of conquered France,
> Undoing all, as all had never been!
>
> (1.1.103–8)

The shameful terms of Henry's marriage soon become the play's common refrain, on the tongues of commons and nobles alike, shorthand for England's loss of territory, national unity, and manhood. As Cade bluntly puts it in Act 4, the losses have "gelded the commonwealth and made it an eunuch" (4.2.162–63).

For the play's audiences, then and now, Gloucester's rhetoric registers more than outrage over Suffolk's sale of Maine and Anjou to France. It also defines the nation's past as a patriotic story of glorious conquest and reminds us of history's role as a model for present and future generations. Writing in 1592, in a passage scholars believe makes reference to Shakespeare's *Henry VI* plays, Thomas Nashe made similar claims about history plays. Celebrating "our forefathers

valiant acts," these plays offered a "rare exercise of
virtue," Nashe declared, and sharp "reproofe to these
degenerate effeminate dayes of ours."[2] For Nashe, English history is a decidedly masculine narrative of
valiant conquest, and his remarks, like those of
Gloucester and Cade, powerfully underscore *2 Henry
VI*'s failure to deliver this narrative on stage. Hardly a
dramatic weakness, this failure is absolutely central to
the play's theme of loss and degeneration. In the wake
of England's defeat in France, the heroic exists only in
the collective memory, in the national mythology
invoked by the name of Henry V. Gloucester himself
sounds these plangent notes at the start of his peroration—"Did he so often lodge in open field, / In winter's
cold and summer's parching heat, / To conquer France,
his true inheritance?" (1.1.85–87)—memorializing the
former king as the apotheosis of the chivalric warrior
and a spur to England's peers to unite in the recovery
of the nation's former glory.

If Shakespeare's audiences looked to the past for lessons about the present, as Nashe and Gloucester suggest, what instruction would they have taken from this
brutal story of conspiracy, treason, murder, and revolt?
Or, as viewers today might ask, what are the play's politics? Not surprisingly, the question has prompted
much critical debate between those who see *2 Henry VI*
as a conservative staging of English history, designed
to solidify the power and legitimacy of the Tudor state,
and those who argue for a more radical position that
questions as much as it affirms political orthodoxies.
In replaying the horrors of civil dissension, the play
certainly recalls official Tudor exhortations against dis-
obedience and rebellion, printed in homilies and pronounced from church pulpits. Over the course of her
reign, Queen Elizabeth had herself been forced to con-
front aristocratic revolts, assassination attempts, and

numerous conspiracies, and fears of unrest troubled audiences in the early 1590s, when *2 Henry VI* was first performed. So too did the threat of artisan disturbances, which sporadically erupted in Elizabethan London, often directed against alien workers. As recently as the summer of 1592, in fact, riots had broken out when clothworkers attempted to break into a Southwark prison, and some critics speculate that Shakespeare's staging of Cade's rebellion targets this protest.

But while the play's call for law and order supports government policy, its lessons apply with equal force to rulers and subjects. The portrait of the "bookish" king who brings ruin to his realm recalls the cautionary tales collected in the popular *Mirror for Magistrates* (1559), whose stories of "the fall of princes" reassured readers that vice would be punished and virtue rewarded, in the hereafter if not the here and now. With the possible exception of Cardinal Beaufort's sudden demise, however, *2 Henry VI* offers no such assurances. Concerned more with historical causation than didactic moralizing, the play eschews traditional providential history for a more radical model of political history.[3] The pious Henry may be fond of invoking the heavens, for example, yet his prayers and prophecies seem powerless and off the mark. The "miracle" of Simpcox, praised by the king as God's work, turns out to be a hoax, and Horner's death by combat remains an ambiguous verdict at best, despite Henry's certainty that "God in justice" (2.3.104) has prevailed. In place of a divinely ordered universe, Shakespeare details a secular world of political complexity reinforced by an episodic dramatic structure whose open-ended conclusion refuses to mete out justice—unless we take Henry's losses at St. Albans as a sign of divine punishment, as he himself seems to. "Can we outrun the heavens?" (5.2.74), the king asks Margaret in the play's final moments, ready to cede the kingdom to the Yorkist rebels. But even this tragedy must wait for its conclusion in another play.

For modern critics, *2 Henry VI* is politically provocative not only because it demystifies royal power and privilege but because it explores an alternative model of governance in the idealized commonwealth represented in the play by Humphrey, duke of Gloucester. Though hardly democratic by our standards, Gloucester's humanist values show a progressive concern for equity and justice that involves commoners as well as elites. Gloucester's trust in the legal system is absolute if not politically naive, so confident is he that an unbiased judiciary will safeguard the innocent. "I must offend before I be attainted" (2.4.60), he assures his wife, even as she is being taken off, under guard, to a life of exile. As his enemies complain, the good duke is much beloved by "the common people" (1.1.165), and it is worth noting that commoners first enter *2 Henry VI* not as a rioting rabble but as "poor" petitioners seeking redress from the lord protector. Like Gloucester, the petitioners hold much faith in the equity of due process, so much so that they seem unafraid to come forward with complaints against their social betters— witness the petition against Suffolk on behalf of the "whole township" for *"enclosing the commons of Melford"* (1.3.26, 23–24). The complaint about enclosures is especially resonant here, not simply because it names Suffolk but because it indicts him as a direct contributor to the abject social conditions that will ignite in open rebellion later in the play.[4] When the inexperienced petitioners deliver their complaints to the wrong man, mistaking Suffolk for the Lord Protector, the calls for redress go unanswered. Indeed, the results are lamentably predictable: all charges are dismissed except the apprentice's complaint against his master's treason, which Margaret and Suffolk will exploit to undermine York's rising power within the court.

For self-serving nobles such as Suffolk and Margaret, as for the upstart Cade, the law represents an expedient means to power, and treason charges are the weapon of choice. The case against Eleanor Cobham establishes the model. As a participant in treasonous necromancy, the ambitious duchess is certainly complicit in her downfall, but she is also a victim of what we might call political entrapment. Suffolk admits as much when he assures the queen that he has "limed a bush for [the Duchess]" (1.3.91), an assurance confirmed by the double-dealing Hume's report that the cardinal and Suffolk, "knowing Dame Eleanor's aspiring humor, / Have hirèd me to undermine the Duchess / And buzz these conjurations in her brain" (1.2.100–102). As York slyly observes, the scene of Eleanor's arrest is a "pretty plot, well chosen to build upon" (1.4.60), and in the end it is the machiavellian York, rather than Suffolk and the cardinal, whose careful plotting will "reap the harvest" (3.1.386).[5] Immediately following Eleanor's sentencing is the equally unsettling scene of Horner's treason trial, and again political ambitions compromise our sense of justice. Fought before a crowd of prentices and neighbors, the lowly combat between the drunken armorer and his fearful apprentice seems a mockery of chivalric justice despite Horner's dying confession and the king's confidence that truth has prevailed. York's more pointed comment—"Fellow, thank God and the good wine in thy master's way" (2.3.98–99)—may be closer to the mark.[6]

The most egregious abuse of judicial process comes with Gloucester's hastily convened treason trial in Act 3 and marks the play's turning point. Led by Suffolk

and Margaret, the scheming nobles operate here under
the pretense of protecting the king from "treason's
secret knife" (3.1.175), but the scene is as much a refer-
endum on Henry's power as it is on Gloucester's. Pre-
dictably, the king abdicates his authority early in the
proceedings, instructing the court to do "what to your
wisdoms seemeth best" (196). Henry excuses his own
failure to act by casting himself as an "unhelpful" victim along with his uncle, claiming that he cannot do
Gloucester "good, / So mighty are his vowèd enemies"
(219, 220–21). Henry then leaves the stage and the
court to its bloody work. Seemingly unconstrained by
law, the nobles agree at once that Gloucester must die,
although the cardinal cynically reminds them that they
lack "a color for his death. / 'Tis meet he be condemned
by course of law" (238–39). They have "but trivial argument" (243), Suffolk admits, but, not to be hindered by
a lack of evidence, the conspirators quickly find their
way to a logic that bypasses legal procedure altogether.
Sanctifying murder as a form of "meritorious" execution, they determine to kill Gloucester not for crimes
he has done but for what he *might* do. "No, let him die
in that he is a fox, / By nature proved an enemy to the
flock" (272, 259–60), Suffolk resolves, as if this argument were legally or morally defensible.

   Justice for Gloucester's murder is unusual in the
world of *2 Henry VI* in that it comes at all. It is also
unusual in that it comes from below, originating with
the commons in collaboration with Warwick and Salisbury. Although the commons initially rise up in anger
at the news of the murder, Warwick restores calm with
an appeal to due process, persuading them to "hear the
order of his death" (3.2.133). The evidence, observed
and reported by Warwick, offers convincing proof of
death by strangulation—protruding eyeballs, dilated
nostrils, hair stuck to sheets, and hands spread wide in

signs of struggle. When the king fails to render judgment, or even to voice convincing outrage, the commons (now offstage) clamor for justice, sending "word" to the king that unless Suffolk is condemned to death or banishment, "They will by violence tear him from your palace / And torture him with grievous ling'ring death" (252, 255–56). It may be argued that the threat of violence qualifies the commons' moral authority, particularly as it anticipates Cade's bloody tactics. Yet the weight of forensic evidence, combined with the request itself, identifies their intentions as just, properly motivated by "love and loyalty" (259) rather than by lawless vengeance. Shakespeare is careful to keep the noisy commons offstage, mediating their words through Salisbury and thus avoiding the spectacle of the populace directly confronting the king. Further affirming the rightness of the common judgment, the king accedes to their demands, confiding that he himself did "purpose as they do entreat" (292). The commons thus provide the moral touchstone in this crucial scene. In the face of weak and corrupt nobles, justice in *2 Henry VI* rests on the commons' participation in due process, and the play seems to endorse their course of action both as judicious and effective *and* as a powerful affirmation of Gloucester's own political ideals.

This endorsement of participatory justice at the play's center does not go uncontested, to be sure. As we have seen, opposing arguments come from the corrupt nobility, whose contempt for equity and justice is matched by their contempt for the so-called lower orders. But another, more troublesome, counterargument comes from the commons themselves, in the form of Cade's revolt in Act 4. At first the rebels' agenda seems cheerfully if not comically utopian, as Cade offers to right aristocratic wrongs through a fantastical program of social and economic leveling: "All the realm shall be in common. . . . There shall be no money; all shall eat . . . on my score; and I will apparel them all in one livery, that they may agree like brothers" (4.2.67–74). Cade's methods, however, make a mockery of his own ideals and the abuses of the ruling elite. His first official act—the ruling that sentences the Clerk of Chartham to hang simply because "he can write and read and cast account" (83–84)—stands as a travesty of English law in line with the play's earlier trials. With the summary trial and execution of Lord Saye, who like Gloucester sought justice for the poor, the rebels become the horrific mirror image of the nobles they set out to reform. Unlike the contentious aristocrats, however, Cade makes no pretense to give a lawful "color" to his rulings but instead directs his radical reformation against judicial process itself, with particular animus against literacy and record keeping: "Burn all the records of the realm. My mouth shall be the Parliament of England" (4.7.13–14), he gleefully proclaims, setting himself up as sole judge and arbiter.

How then to align the Cade episode with the sympathetic presentation of commoners earlier in the play? Does the disturbance demonstrate that the disenfranchised are incapable of sustaining the kind of participatory politics idealized at the play's center and instead need to be governed with a strong hand? Or, as many critics argue, does it rather show the terrible costs of aristocratic misrule and the dangers of excluding the commons from political process? As York's "substitute" (3.1.376), seduced by the duke "to make commotion" (363), the lowly Cade is both a pawn to be sacrificed in the dynastic power play and a clownish burlesque of his social betters. But the play's bold staging of popular revolt is more than a parodic mirror of aristocratic injustices. It is also a provocative *response* to those injustices. Cade's comrades see through his pretensions from the start, mocking his ambitions in pointed asides, yet they willingly fight for his platform and accept him as their spokesman. For though instigated by the ambitious York and led by the maniacal Cade, the uprising appears to gather its force and considerable following from *genuine* injustices and grievances. As critics point out, Cade's articulation of popular grievances derives its authority in part from a tradition of egalitarian complaint extending back to the Peasants' Revolt of 1381. But the immediate power of Cade's complaints may stem from their particularity, from Shakespeare's choice to embed specific contemporary grievances within the utopian appeal to a classless commonwealth. Complaints about enclosures, the causes and conditions of poverty, and the lack of redress for the disenfranchised—indeed, many of the same grievances voiced by the humble petitioners earlier in the play—all had a contemporary currency for Shakespeare's audiences that would have resonated beyond their voicing by their discredited spokesman, and beyond the boundaries of the stage.

In the end, the rebellious commons relent in the face of the king's offer of mercy, abandoning Cade's platform for Clifford's shameless invocation of Henry V and a battlefield camaraderie that might "gentle [their] condition" (*Henry V* 4.3.65). "Is Cade the son of Henry the Fifth," he asks; "Will [Cade] conduct you through the heart of France / And make the meanest of you earls and dukes?" (4.8.35, 37–38). Clifford's burnished rhetoric restores order with the empty promise to return to a heroic past, to recover England's losses and manhood on foreign fields. It also sets the tone for the play's final act, dominated by York's own fondness for heroic discourse and for the widening gulf between rhetoric and reality opened up by the bad faith of civil war. According to plan, York returns with his army

from Ireland "to claim his right / And pluck the crown
from feeble Henry's head" (5.1.1–2). And unlike feeble
Henry, whose hand is suited more to "a palmer's staff"
than to "an awful princely scepter" (98–99), York
comes fully armed, reprising the role of warrior prince
as if he and not Henry VI were the true inheritor to
Henry V. York also dusts off the complaint about the
royal marriage, deftly turning the gendered discourse
of English patriotism against the Lancastrian queen.
"O, blood-bespotted Neapolitan, / Outcast of Naples,
England's bloody scourge!" (5.1.119–20), he exclaims
to Margaret, as if to shore up the legitimacy of his
claim by naming the queen as the outsider—female
and foreign and barbaric—responsible for all the
bloodshed to come. In the ensuing battle at St. Albans,
the Yorkists win the day. And Warwick, flush with victory, closes the play by sounding notes of heroic greatness, brimming with promise for a glorious future:

> Saint Albans battle won by famous York
> Shall be eternized in all age to come.—
> Sound drum and trumpets, and to London all;
> And more such days as these to us befall!
>
> (5.3.31–34)

But the war has only just begun, and as Gloucester
foretold before his death, "thousands more, that yet
suspect no peril, / Will not conclude their plotted
tragedy" (3.1.153–54). The only battlefield Cade's followers will ever see is the blood-soaked ground of England's civil war.

That *2 Henry VI* ends with a beginning full of possibility and dread is in part a sequel effect: Shakespeare
will, after all, continue the story of the Wars of the
Roses in *Henry VI, Part 3*. But the play's open-
endedness also suggests something about staging his-

tory—about the difficulty of confining a sprawling and contentious past within a tidy dramatic pattern, and about the inconclusiveness of historical narrative itself. On Shakespeare's stage, English history becomes an ongoing story, played before audiences asked to witness the trauma of a past that is part of their present.

———

1. Edward Hall, *The Union of the Two Noble and Illustre Famelies of Lancastre and Yorke* (1548), in Geoffrey Bullough, ed., *Narrative and Dramatic Sources of Shakespeare* (London: Routledge and Kegan Paul, 1960), 3:103.

2. Thomas Nashe, *Pierce Penilesse his Supplication to the Divell* (1592), in E. K. Chambers, *The Elizabethan Stage* (1923; reprint, Oxford: Clarendon Press, 1951), 4:238.

3. Historians usually associate this new form of political history with the influence of the Italian historians Machiavelli and Guicciardini; see F. J. Levy, *Tudor Historical Thought* (San Marino, Calif.: Huntington Library, 1967), pp. 237–85, and Phyllis Rackin, *Stages of History: Shakespeare's English Chronicles* (Ithaca: Cornell University Press, 1990), pp. 44–46.

4. The practice of enclosure—landlords appropriating common arable lands for pasture—was frequently blamed for rising poverty and social unrest in sixteenth-century England. See the discussions of enclosure and *2 Henry VI* in James R. Siemon, "Landlord Not King: Agrarian Change and Interarticulation," and William C. Carroll, " 'The Nursery of Beggary': Enclosure, Vagrancy, and Sedition in the Tudor-Stuart Period," both in *Enclosure Acts: Sexuality, Property, and Culture in Early Modern England*, ed. Richard Burt and John Michael Archer (Ithaca: Cornell University Press, 1994), pp. 17–33, 34–47.

5. Even as dramatists such as Shakespeare and Marlowe freely adopted a machiavellian tradition of political history, they also registered fears about its negative consequences through the popular figure of the ruthlessly ambitious stage-Machiavel, represented here by Richard, duke of York.

6. For a fuller discussion of this complex scene, see the editors' longer note for 2.3.96 SD, *They fight, and Peter strikes him down*, page 256.

Further Reading

Henry VI, Part 2

Abbreviations: *The Contention = The First Part of the Contention betwixt the Two Famous Houses of York and Lancaster; H5 = Henry V; 1H6 = Henry VI, Part 1; 2H6 = Henry VI, Part 2; 3H6 = Henry VI, Part 3; John = King John; R2 = Richard II; R3 = Richard III; RSC = Royal Shakespeare Company; Union = The Union of the Two Noble and Illustre Famelies of Lancastre and Yorke*

Bernthal, Craig A. "Treason in the Family: The Trial of Thumpe v. Horner." *Shakespeare Quarterly* 42 (1991): 44–54.

Bernthal analyzes the Thump versus Horner story in 1.3 and 2.3 in light of Tudor doctrines of order and obedience essential to political and family structures of the period. Each year, thousands of boys came to London to become apprentices, thereby entering into "new micropolitical units: the families of their masters," to whom, for all intents and purposes, they swore a loyalty oath. A contextual understanding of the patriarchal nature of the master-apprentice relationship reveals that the Thump v. Horner episode "tugs the audience in opposite directions: toward satisfaction about the victory of a loyal subject over a treasonous one, and toward dis-ease that such a victory is achieved by a servant against his master." On the surface, the episode replays the David vs. Goliath story, Thump's "ideological function" being to prove Henry VI's divinely sanctioned kingship. On a deeper level, however, the apprentice's victory dramatizes "Tudor England's prevailing social nightmare—betrayal to the authorities by friends, servants, family." By demonstrating loyalty to the crown, Thump's exposure of his master clearly contains subversive activity but at the expense of loyalty to the patriarchal family, the "fundamental political building block of the ideal commonwealth."

Berry, Edward I. "*2 Henry VI:* Justice and Law." In *Patterns of Decay: Shakespeare's Early Histories*, pp. 29–52. Charlottesville: University Press of Virginia, 1975.

Whereas *1H6* explores the death of chivalry and ceremony in medieval England, *2H6* centers on the death of the rule of law. Appropriately, the play begins with the interrupted reading of a legal agreement, a marriage contract; the subsequent dramatic action involves such legal terms and procedures as the right of petition exercised by the commoners before Suffolk and Queen Margaret; a trial by combat; the trial and punishment of Eleanor, the Duchess of Gloucester; an "ad hoc adjudication" of the St. Albans "miracle"; preparations for Gloucester's trial as Lord Protector; and an insurrection designed to overthrow all law. Like Talbot, who embodies the virtue of chivalry in *Part 1*, Humphrey of Gloucester personifies the law in *Part 2*; both men die as martyrs for a principle abandoned by the rest of society. Two contrasting views of the law contribute to a growing sense of social and political dissolution: Henry's belief that law is, above all else, "the law of God, executed directly and unambiguously by the king in earthly judgments" and York's belief in the rights of natural superiority over those of hierarchy and primogeniture. After Cade's rebellion, which symbolically extends the anarchy York implicitly sanctions, the play ends with lawlessness "achiev[ing] its apothe-

osis in civil war." As part of the first tetralogy, *2H6*
depicts the second stage in a process of decay that
begins with the death of Henry V and continues
through the breakdown of the family in *3H6* and of the
self in *R3*.

Blanpied, John W. *"Henry VI, Part 2:* 'Undoing all as all
had never been.' " In *Time and the Artist in Shakespeare's English Histories,* pp. 42–63. Newark: University of Delaware Press; Toronto: Associated University
Presses, 1983. (The chapter incorporates "The *Henry VI*
Plays: In Pursuit of the Ground," *Susquehanna University Studies* 10 [1978]: 197–209.)
    Viewed from a metatheatrical perspective, *2H6*
"enacts a cultural collapse," which Blanpied analyzes
by focusing on three characters: the mirror figures of
the "self-absenting" Henry and the "self-aggrandizing
York," and the tragic figure in the middle, Gloucester,
whose rigidity in bodying forth the law is "both his
strength and weakness." As the first scene flows from
"Henry's static ceremony, through Gloucester's reckless
passion, and into York's compacted monologue," its
structure "adumbrates the course of the play itself by
demonstrating how power will be transferred from
King to Protector to Usurper." While this three-way
relationship provides an "elegant structure" that
appears to subdue the "weight and diffusion" of the
text's various characters, episodes, speaking styles, and
on- and offstage rhythms, the result is one of "emo-
tional incoherence." Gloucester's line "Undoing all, as
all had never been" (1.1.108) holds the key to the "dis-
integrative energies" that affect characterization and
overall design. Henry increasingly manifests a self-
conscious desire to be absent; Gloucester's character
emerges as being the product of Henry's "own self-
evasion"; and York's various improvisations anticipate

their own dissolution in his belief in an all-consuming role as "England's lawful king." In Act 4, as Cade's rebellion gets under way and the anarchic surrogate becomes a monster that his creator cannot control, the design itself begins to dissolve. Finally, in the tableaux-like scenes of Act 5, the violence proceeds without audience involvement, the main characters "dwindle . . . to puppetry," and new characters with no interior life suddenly appear (e.g., Richard and Young Clifford). The author contends that Shakespeare allows the play to disintegrate "in hopes of finding out the sources of disintegration"; the downside of this choice is an abandonment of the artist's role "of making chaos humanly intelligible." In *2H6*, Shakespeare "looked for sources of corruptibility in human experience and found himself looking at the corruptibility of his medium."

Cartelli, Thomas. "Jack Cade in the Garden: Class Consciousness and Class Conflict in *Henry VI, Part 2*." In *Enclosure Acts: Sexuality, Property, and Culture in Early Modern England*, edited by Richard Burt and John Michael Archer, pp. 48–67. Ithaca: Cornell University Press, 1994.

Cartelli's essay addresses the issue of agricultural enclosure in early modern England by examining Cade's invasion of Alexander Iden's garden, a scene that "memorably stages claims for and against property." Although both men sound the pastoral note as the scene begins, Cade's "utilitarian" version of pastoral contrasts with Iden's idyllic construction of his garden state: Cade believes that "the lord of the soil" has walked forth for the sole purpose of "seiz[ing] me for a stray, for entering his fee-simple without leave" (4.10.25–27); Iden, on the other hand, thinks of his walk in the garden as a demonstration of a peaceful life "neatly balanced between private pleasure and social obligation." Cade's "legalistic and oppositional estimate" of his meeting with Iden derives from "a thoroughly class-conscious and class-stratified position": namely, that Iden's garden is "enclosed private property, not in any sense . . . a public or common domain." As the scene turns violent, Cade's "obstreperousness" reveals the extent to which Iden's notion of the garden—a place where rich and poor can meet on common ground—is "a deeply privileged ideological construction." By contesting the garden's "ideological hold . . . over all concerned parties, Cade effectively unlocks its actual status as a space intersected by mutually exclusive and competing class interests." The author finds a "politically motivated class consciousness" central to the play's discourse and contends that Jack Cade constitutes "the most realized example" in Shakespeare of a character "who is able to transform his political subjection into something amounting to our modern sense of class-based resistance."

Chartier, Roger. "Jack Cade, the Skin of a Dead Lamb, and the Hatred for Writing." *Shakespeare Studies* 34 (2006): 77–89.

Chartier examines Cade's vitriolic hatred of all things written in the context of early modern thinking on the merits of oral versus written testimony. By the time the play was written, although *"viva vox,"* the living voice, was granted superiority over parchment in matters relating to evidentiary testimony, Europe's legal, judicial, and administrative procedures were moving more systematically toward a preference for written documents "as instruments of proof and authentication." In constructing Cade's anti-writing discourse, Shakespeare conflated the 1450 rebellion (which manifested no hostility for the written culture) and the 1381 Peas-

ants' Revolt (which involved the destruction of legal
records and instruments). The conflation of the two
events imparts to the Cade scenes "the status of an
'*exemplum*,'" but with a "profound distortion" of what
the rebels of 1381 were protesting; for unlike Cade and
his men, the historical rebels had as their targets poll
tax receipts, legal records, and the Inns of Court, not
books, libraries, and intellectual culture. In Cade's
"impossible restoration of a time liberated from the
oppressive power of writing," we should, perhaps, see
"the lasting nostalgia for orality and the anxieties
created by the growing power of writing" in the
early modern period. Despite his rigid opposition
between the spoken word and the printed word, Cade's
anti-writing campaign "paradoxically helps us to
refuse the simplifications . . . that have deeded to us a
historical narrative according to which rationality and
modernity are exclusively identified with the written
culture."

Harris, Laurie Lanzen, and Mark W. Scott, eds. "*Henry
VI, Parts 1, 2, and 3.*" In *Shakespearean Criticism:
Excerpts from the Criticism of William Shakespeare's
Plays and Poetry from the First Published Appraisals to
Current Evaluations,* 3:11–164. Detroit: Gale Research,
1986.
   This volume presents significant passages from published criticism on the three parts of *H6*. The set of passages is introduced by a brief discussion of the "date,"
"text," and "sources," followed by a longer discussion
of the "critical history" of the plays. Each entry, beginning with Robert Greene's *Groatsworth of Wit* (1592)
and ending with Marilyn French's *Shakespeare's Division of Experience* (1981), is prefaced with a brief historical overview that places the excerpted document in
the context of responses to the play. Of the almost sixty

entries, early commentary derives from Thomas Nashe (1592), John Crowne (1681), Gerard Langbaine (1691), and from such eighteenth-century editors as Nicholas Rowe, Lewis Theobald, Edward Capell, Samuel Johnson, and Edmond Malone; nineteenth-century critics are represented by such figures as William Hazlitt, Samuel Taylor Coleridge, Hermann Ulrici, and Georg Gottfried Gervinus; entries from the twentieth century include excerpts from the writings of Carolyn Spurgeon, E. M. W. Tillyard, Hereward Price, Wolfgang Clemen, Muriel C. Bradbrook, Harold Goddard, David Bevington, Irving Ribner, Robert Ornstein, Michael Manheim, John Cox, and Larry Champion. A briefly annotated bibliography of fifty-five additional items concludes the section. A subsequent volume, edited by Michele Lee (2002), updates the criticism through the 1990s under such headings as Character Study, *Henry VI* as Comedy, Playing with History, and Unity and Design (vol. 63, pp. 113–218).

Helgerson, Richard. "Staging Exclusion." In *Forms of Nationhood: The Elizabethan Writing of England*, pp. 193–246. Chicago: University of Chicago Press, 1992.

In his study of how a single generation of Elizabethan writers spanning the fields of poetry, law, cartography, travel writing, drama, and ecclesiastical policy laid the foundation for England's development from a dynastic kingdom to the modern nation-state, Helgerson discusses Shakespeare's history plays as the dramatist's major contribution to this "generational project" of "writing England." The focus of the chapter is *The Contention*, which Helgerson refers to as the text "we now know as [*2H6*]." What fascinates him is the inclusiveness of 1.1, in which no one onstage is under the rank of an earl and yet much of the talk is about doing well by "the people," who are made "fundamen-

tal to the nation's identity and to the legitimacy of its
governing order" (see, e.g., 1.1.165, 190, 200, 206, 207,
212–14). Although the play was written by a commoner, performed by commoners, and played before
an audience of mostly commoners, the italicizing of
the popular presence in the opening scene does not
conform to Shakespeare's general practice in the history genre, where he often seems to identify England
"exclusively with its kings and nobles." While the first
two-thirds of *The Contention* are open and univocal in
their political ideology, the Cade rebellion in the last
third "pushes [the] inclusionist ideal toward its own
exclusionist extreme," the treatment of the rebels
exposing popular rule "as inimical to the very existence
of the institution by which it and other plays like it
were produced." Abandoning the position with which
it began, *The Contention* violently pits peasants and
craftsmen against nobles. For Helgerson, the play's
inclusion-to-exclusion dynamic mirrors what was
happening to the theater in the transitional 1590s,
when the "institutional setting" of Shakespeare's history plays, patronized by the Crown and nobility but
dependent for its income on a popular audience, "was
riven by internal animosities that set . . . university-
educated poets against the professional players for
whom they wrote." The exclusive tendencies of the former would eventually prevail in the shift from a players' theater to an authors' theater. In their "fixation on
monarchic power," Shakespeare's history plays "con-
tributed at once to the consolidation of central power,
to the cultural division of class from class, and to the
emergence of the playwright—Shakespeare himself—
as both gentleman and poet." As Shakespeare continued to write, the less privileged still had a place in his
audience, but they lost their place in the dramatist's
representation of England.

Hodgdon, Barbara. "Enclosing Contention: *1, 2,* and *3 Henry VI.*" In *The End Crowns All: Closure and Contradiction in Shakespeare's History*, pp. 44–99. Princeton: Princeton University Press, 1991.

Combining performance criticism (mostly of RSC productions) with study of the play texts, Hodgdon explores "closural strategies" in the three parts of *H6*. In the commentary specifically devoted to *Part 2* (pp. 59–68), she finds the contrasting title pages of the 1594 Quarto text (*The Contention*) and the 1623 Folio text (*2H6*) to be useful guides to understanding the play's structure and closure. With no mention of the King or Queen Margaret, the lengthy title of the Quarto "maps out . . . its multiple centers of narrative privilege": Duke Humphrey, Suffolk, Winchester, Cade, and York. The much shorter Folio title "predicts another play, one that centers on the King and his surrogate father-Protector." The Quarto's title indicates a "two-part narrative strategy" that involves a division of the kingdom resulting in the deaths of Gloucester and Winchester and then a reopening of the action with two events that close the play: Cade's insurrection and York's efforts "to reconstitute the monarchy, with himself as King." The Folio's title is equally helpful in the way it signals what might be called *2H6*'s "internal close, where power is transferred from Protector to King." The first half of the play deals with the female misrule of Gloucester's and Henry's ambitious wives; the second, with "another form of festival inversion: Cade's transgressive pseudosocialist commonwealth." Although both texts look forward to Henry's future Parliament and to another confrontation that will secure the throne, the Quarto is less hesitant than the "ambiguous 'Lancastrian'" Folio in relocating "true" right in York. Hodgdon claims that "the existence of two versions of a play that duplicates, even reduplicates, kingship constitutes one of the rarest coincidences in the strange, eventful history of Shakespeare's multiple-text plays." Later in the chapter (pp. 76–99), the author discusses the play's stage life as performed in John Barton and Peter Hall's *The Wars of the Roses* (RSC, 1963), Terry Hands's "(relatively) uncut and unadapted" revival of the complete *H6* trilogy (RSC, 1977), Michael Bogdanov's *The Wars of the Roses* (English Shakespeare Company, 1988), and Adrian Noble's *The Plantagenets* (RSC, 1988).

Hutson, Lorna. "Noises Off: Participatory Justice in *2 Henry VI*." In *The Law in Shakespeare,* edited by Karen Cunningham and Constance Jordan, pp. 143–66. London: Palgrave/Macmillan, 2007.

In her reading of *2H6*, Hutson refutes the tradition of identifying early modern legal processes with decisions reached by official figures of the court. She argues instead for an emerging sense of "participatory justice," which depended on "the collection of evidence rendered to the court by the testimony of witnesses who, expecting to be interrogated, needed to have 'forensic or detective habits of mind.'" Central to the essay is Warwick's description of Duke Humphrey's corpse (3.2.164–85), a form of coroner's inquest in response to the outrage of the people. Prior to the speech, which belongs "to the judicial culture of the pretrial examination of the later sixteenth century," the intrigues and legal/judicial corruption of the first two acts reveal the law as "nothing but aristocratic power cloaked in procedure." That image changes with the important stage direction "Noise within" (3.2.125), a powerful signal of the offstage presence of the commons. In keeping with the English criminal justice system, it is the people who first call for an investigation of Duke Humphrey's death, "and in responding to that call, Warwick enfolds us, the audience, into his response to the commons." While his simile of an "angry hive of bees" (3.2.129–31) implicitly raises the threat of a mob's unconstrained violence, it also recalls the traditional image of the *res publica* as a beehive, common in sixteenth-century political treatises, and thus identifies the noise of the people with "the commonwealth," i.e., with the public interest. In contrast to the popular rebellion that erupts in the next act, "the appeal to the intelligent judgement and moral passion of the commons implied in Warwick's forensic inquiry offers a powerfully utopian image of participatory justice as a form of the commons' political agency."

Lee, Patricia-Ann. "Reflections of Power: Margaret of Anjou and the Dark Side of Queenship." *Renaissance Quarterly* 39 (1986): 183–217.

Lee compares Shakespeare's depiction of Margaret of Anjou in *2* and *3H6* and *R3* with depictions of the historical Margaret found in letters and other documentary records. The queen who appears in the plays as pitiless and cruel but also determined and vigorous shares much with her historical counterpart, but the theatrical image was "overlaid" with years of cumulative bias and myth that had already made Margaret "the symbol of a particular kind of female ruler and a pattern of negative feminine power." Shakespeare's "archetypal villainess"—the product of both his own artistic creativity and a tradition established by generations of propagandists and chroniclers—serves as a commentary on feminine rule. Noting how the playwright was interested in Margaret as both a queen and a woman, Lee observes the character's strength and ambition from the beginning of *2H6*, while also pointing out her "signs of weakness for she lacks the true qualities of royalty": see, for example, her jealousy of Eleanor, her adultery, and her all-consuming desire for revenge after the death of Suffolk. As the play draws to an end, Margaret grows more malign and evil in her promotion of contention over tranquillity; finally, she perverts the patriarchal order by usurping Henry's place as both husband and sovereign. To have depicted such a negative view of queenship while a queen occupied the throne of England would seem to have been a risky endeavor on Shakespeare's part, but because Elizabeth I had successfully "turn[ed] her femininity to positive purposes" in a careful construction of androgynous power, thereby reversing the dark images associated with female rule, Shakespeare's depiction of Queen Margaret and her illegitimate queenship posed no practical threat to either Elizabeth or the playwright.

Levine, Nina. *Women's Matters: Politics, Gender, and Nation in Shakespeare's Early History Plays*. Newark: University of Delaware Press; London: Associated University Presses, 1998. (Chapter 2 reprints with revisions Levine's essay "The Case of Eleanor Cobham: Authorizing History in *2 Henry VI*," *Shakespeare Studies* 22 [1994]: 104–21.)

While Shakespeare's early histories (*1, 2,* and *3H6, R3,* and *John*) rewrite the Tudor chronicle record so as to acknowledge the importance of women in ensuring patrilineal succession, Levine contends that they also "generate a critique of patrilineal inheritance and legitimacy" that speaks to the Elizabethan present in which the plays are "situated." The author is especially interested in how the *H6* trilogy uses political contexts—"both on- and offstage"—to frame and qualify negative stereotypes of women. In chapter 2, "Dangerous Practices: Making History in *2 Henry VI*" (pp. 47–67), Levine focuses on Eleanor Cobham to argue that contrary to the stereotypical "virago-witch-traitor," Shakespeare's Eleanor is "double-voiced": she is both the aggressor in thinking treasonous thoughts and consorting with necromancers and the victim of political entrapment. To see her only in the negative terms of Buckingham's assessment (2.1.178–89) is to miss Shakespeare's version of her crime, which attends to "the complex politics underwriting" Eleanor's activities and punishment. Levine attributes Shakespeare's probative rather than polemical characterization to John Foxe's account of the episode in the 1570 edition of *Acts and Monuments,* a book that served as both source and context for Shakespeare's duchess. Whereas Yorkist writers consistently vilified Eleanor and Tudor chroniclers such as Hall and Holinshed presented contradictory "facts" from which the reader could choose, Foxe defended her, conjecturing that she may have been set up by those out to advance their own agendas against the king. To support the claim that Shakespeare provides a theatrical version of Foxe's interrogation of the chronicle accounts, Levine notes (1) the use of framing soliloquies by York (1.1.223–71) and Hume (1.2.90–110) that portray Eleanor as an unwitting pawn, and (2) the casting of Eleanor as a passive observer in the actual conjuring scene (1.4). Furthermore, *2H6*'s depiction of Eleanor "contests the authority of the patriarchal narrative": instead of preserving the state, the duchess's " 'containment' [her trial and punishment] ironically . . . contributes to its ruin"—the "good Duke Humphrey" (1.1.170) is murdered; York advances his own absolutist agenda; and social rebellion ensues with Jack Cade. By creating a "double-voiced" Eleanor, Shakespeare "opens up . . . the political faultlines in this gendered story, inviting consideration of the conflicts and contradictions at work in representations of power, both past and present."

In a subsequent chapter, "Ruling Women and the

Politics of Gender in *2* and *3 Henry VI*" (pp. 68–96),
Levine brings Tudor chronicle accounts of Queen Margaret and sixteenth-century debates over female rule to
bear on her discussion of the role of Margaret in *Part 2*
(pp. 79–87). Unlike his chronicle sources, Shakespeare's depiction of the queen interrogates "gendered
attacks on women rulers and calls instead for a political ethos based on the nation's welfare." As Levine
argues, Shakespeare encourages censure of Margaret
not because of her gender but because she, "like York
and Cade, abuses the common people and the nation's
laws." By the end of the play, Shakespeare further qualifies *2H6*'s depiction of female misrule by allowing at
least a temporary place for women in politics. Fighting
to keep the crown in the Lancastrian hands of her husband and son (5.2.73–84), Margaret "emerges as a
courageous and pragmatic leader," her boldness as-
suming a heroic quality as her politics moves toward
the center in contrast to York's "tyrannical absolutism."
Throughout the dramatic action, the spectacle of her
misrule may invoke anxieties about ruling women, but
concerns for the commonwealth—a rationale deployed
in early defenses of Elizabeth's monarchy—"supersede
. . . gender as the principal criterion for assessing her
rule."

Patterson, Annabel. "The Peasant's Toe: Popular Cul-
ture and Popular Pressure." In *Shakespeare and the
Popular Voice*, pp. 32–51. Cambridge, Mass.: Basil
Blackwell, 1989.
   In her study of Shakespeare's social assumptions and
treatment of popular resistance, Patterson contends
that a fresh interpretation of *2H6* would start not with
Jack Cade but with the "formal act of ventriloquism"
performed by Salisbury, who, after the murder of "good
Duke Humphrey" (1.1.170), repeatedly uses the phrase

"they say" to inform the king of the people's conviction about Suffolk's treachery against them (3.2.251–78). In the course of his speech—one of crucial importance for Shakespeare's conception of the popular voice— Salisbury emerges as the people's spokesman and their true advocate (as Duke Humphrey had been before him). Patterson finds in the people's success against their enemy Suffolk "conditional approval" of popular protest—"conditional, that is, on rightful motives, a basic loyalty to the crown, and a proper spokesman." As for the notorious Jack Cade, he "fails every test for" such a spokesman. Because York's scheme to use Cade as a surrogate precedes the Salisbury intervention—the order is reversed in the historical sources—Shake- speare's Cade enters the dramatic action (4.2) as an "impostor aristocrat and a traitor to his class," every- thing he says "already suspect." In Cade's attack on lit- eracy (4.7.31–46), followed by Lord Saye's "salaried version of liberal humanism" (4.7.71–76), Patterson finds an example of "double ventriloquism": "the voice of popular protest speaking through [an insincere Cade] speaking through Shakespeare's playtext." As further evidence of Shakespeare's efforts to dramatize different styles of populism, the author points to the scene involving John Holland and Bevis on Blackheath (4.2.10–21); by introducing the criterion of labor as a test of social values, the two minor characters, "free of . . . cynicism . . . and natural in their echoes of the tropes of popular protest," demonstrate "beyond a shadow of a doubt that the real popular consciousness, as distinct from the impostor, is capable of penetrating hegemony's aphorisms." In contrast to Helgerson (see above) and Wilson (see below), Patterson concludes that there is nothing in *2H6* "that can justify its use as the court of last appeal in a claim for Shakespeare's conservatism."

Pearlman, E. "The Duke and the Beggar in Shakespeare's *2 Henry VI.*" *Criticism* 41 (1999): 309–21.

  Pearlman observes that the "innovative" scene in
which a beggar's "miracle" is exposed as a sham (2.1)
warrants more scholarly interest than it has received.
With its color, bustle, and humor, the St. Albans
episode performs several functions: (1) it adds welcome tonal variety to a plot dominated by factious
wrangling; (2) it reinforces themes relating to issues of
perception and (as one of several dramatized conflicts
between rich and poor) social class; and (3) it clarifies
and deepens the character of Duke Humphrey. Even
more significant, however, may be the scene's theologi-
cal implications for the period's religious conflicts.
Finding the story not in the chronicles of Edward Hall
or Raphael Holinshed but in John Foxe's polemical
Acts and Monuments, Shakespeare would have recognized its relevance to contemporary debates on miracles (associated with the Catholic Church) that pitted
the old faith against the new faith of the Church of England, which regarded miracles as "smack[ing] of pre-
Reformation ignorance." In his praise of the duke for
trying "to reforme that which was amisse," Foxe uses
the non-neutral "reforme" as a clue "that at the heart of
the episode is an implicit conflict between the old and
the reformed religion." But as Pearlman demonstrates,
to read the encounter in the play as simply a case of
"Protestant debunking of Catholic magic" is to miss its
potential for evoking a more complicated response
from its Elizabethan audience. In turning to Foxe for
the story, Shakespeare would have come upon a tanta-
lizingly brief mention of Foxe's own sources: Thomas
More and William Tyndale, two warring polemicists in
the first decade of the English Reformation with dia-
metrically opposed interpretations of the sham miracle. Whether or not Shakespeare traced the genesis of

Foxe's tale thoroughly, he certainly would have known that the story was subject to different readings and, consequently, of topical value. Shakespeare, of course, may simply have "appropriated the story of the duke and beggar for sheer delight in its craft. And if so colorful a conversation happened to carry doctrinal implications that raised hackles on both sides of the aisle, why then, so much the better."

Pendleton, Thomas A., ed. *Henry VI: Critical Essays*. Shakespeare Criticism. New York: Routledge, 2001.
    The volume's fourteen original essays include two that focus solely on *2H6:* Maurice Hunt's "Climbing for Place in Shakespeare's *2 Henry VI*" (pp. 157–76) and M. Rick Smith's "*Henry VI, Part 2:* Commodifying and Recommodifying the Past in Late-Medieval and Early-Modern England" (pp. 177–204). Hunt discusses the motif of social climbing in the play as it relates to political and social disorder and suggests that it "may amount to Shakespeare's response to Marlowe's latent intermittent admiration for the 'overreacher.'" Focusing on Humphrey of Gloucester and Cade, Smith examines Shakespeare's theatrical treatment of commodified historical narratives in the context of sixteenth-century cultural commercialization. Several essays deal in part with *2H6:* Steven Urkowitz's "Texts with Two Faces: Noticing Theatrical Revisions in *Henry VI, Parts 2* and *3*" (pp. 27–37), Harry Keyishian's "The Progress of Revenge in the first Henriad" (pp. 67–77), Naomi C. Liebler and Lisa Scancella Shea's "Shakespeare's Queen Margaret: Unruly or Unruled?" (pp. 79–96), Nina da Vinci Nichols's "The Paper Trail to the Throne" (pp. 97–112), Frances K. Barasch's "Folk Magic in *HVI, Parts 1* and *2:* Two Scenes of Embedding" (pp. 113–25), Yoshio Arai's essay on the *H6* trilogy in Japan (pp. 57–66), and Irene Dash's "*Henry VI*

and the Art of Illustration" (pp. 253–71). The volume also contains several essays on performance: Thomas A. Pendleton's "Talking with York: A Conversation with Steven Skybell" (Duke of York in Karin Coonrod's production) (pp. 219–34), H. R. Coursen's "Theme and Design in Recent Productions of *Henry VI*" (with the emphasis on Michael Kahn's and Karin Coonrod's revivals in 1996) (pp. 205–18), and Patricia Lennox's "*Henry VI:* A Television History in Four Parts" (Peter Dews's *An Age of Kings* in 1960, Peter Hall and John Barton's *Wars of the Roses* in 1965, Jane Howell's BBC revival in 1983, and Michael Bogdanov and Michael Pennington's *Wars of the Roses* in 1988) (pp. 235–52). Pendleton's introduction provides an overview of the scholarship, especially as it relates to issues of text, authorship, date, sequence, relationship of the plays as parts of a tetralogy, and critical assessment. Much attention is paid to the providentialist views of Tillyard (*Shakespeare's History Plays*, 1944), who has served "both as stimulant and irritant" and thus "has had an enormous effect" on the criticism of the *H6* trilogy. The past fifty years have seen scholarly interest move beyond questions of text and authorship; as a result, the three parts of *H6* are now discussed and appreciated more than at any time since they were first performed.

Rackin, Phyllis. "Historical Kings/Theatrical Clowns." In *Stages of History: Shakespeare's English Chronicles*, pp. 201–47. Ithaca: Cornell University Press, 1990.

Rackin devotes the first half of chapter 5 to *2H6* (pp. 207–22), focusing specifically on the representation of Jack Cade's rebellion. Noting that Renaissance historiography was both an aristocratic and masculine enterprise, she examines the "discursive position" commoners shared with women in the plays. "Silenced and marginalized" by the historiographic record, both groups in Shakespeare present "a constant challenge to the mystifications" of patriarchal history. For all the similarities, however, one major difference emerges in their respective stagings. Played by male actors, speaking lines by a male playwright, Shakespeare's female characters appear as "instruments of male ventriloquism." The commoners, on the other hand, played by actors occupying the same social position, and delivering lines written by a commoner, "spoke with their own voices and appeared in their own bodies." Because of this material connection between role and actor, scenes like those involving Cade and his followers constituted a potential moment of danger for the patriarchal establishment: as the rebellion's "licensed disorder of fictional theatrical representation . . . invade[d] the actual world of the audience," the actors threatened to produce in real time what they were portraying in fictional time. Observing how similar scenes of rebellion in *Sir Thomas More* were censored, Rackin conjectures that *2H6*'s uprising passed the censor's test because it seems "designed to justify oppression": "Dissident sentiments are first evoked, then discredited and demonized as sources of anxiety, and finally defused in comic ridicule and brutal comic violence." Even though contained, the subversive energies of the popular voice in *2H6* are not completely effaced, Rackin contends. When Cade dies at the hands of Iden, the rebel's last words point not to patriarchal order or the chivalric code of martial valor as the cause of his defeat but to the urgent materiality of his physical hunger.

Riggs, David. "The Hero in History: A Reading of *Henry VI*." In *Shakespeare's Heroical Histories: Henry VI and*

Its Literary Tradition, pp. 93–139. London: Oxford University Press, 1971.

Riggs's analysis of the three parts of *H6* within the context of exemplary history and heroic drama (as defined by Marlowe's *Tamburlaine*) leads him to conclude that the trilogy is crucial to Shakespeare's developing conception of the history play as a dialectic between heroic ideals and ethical and political realities. In his anti-Tillyardian reading, the *H6* plays become "an extended meditation on the decline of heroic idealism between the Hundred Years War and the Yorkist accession." What makes *2H6* (discussed on pp. 113–27) so innovative as a history play—and for many the best of the *H6* trilogy—is not only more localized settings (the battlefields of France in *Part 1* give way to the "public halls and inmost recesses of the English court") but also an "elaboration of social details" and a variety of action. The play's portrayal of a weak king, "flanked by a loyal counselor and a set of courtly 'caterpillars'" and faced with open revolt from disaffected nobles, "marks the line of development that leads from" the exotic world of *Tamburlaine* and *Selimus* to such plays as *Woodstock*, *Edward II*, and *R2*—dramas of "ambition and disruption that anatomize the ambivalent status of the Elizabethan peerage." With the murder of the judicious Gloucester (3.2), the play's dynamic changes as Suffolk and York, "drastically reduced in stature" in the first half of the play, go on to enjoy in the final acts "a renewed vitality": the former as "an idealized and gracious amorist," the latter "as a visible embodiment of heroic authority." By urging York's claim to the throne on the basis of his natural right rather than his ancestry (5.1.5–9, 97–106), and by setting Cade's revolt "within a continuous parody of the conventional formulas for heroic self-assertion," Shakespeare reformulates the idiom and topics of *Tamburlaine* to create a new type of history play.

Saccio, Peter. "Henry VI and Edward IV: The Rival Kings." In *Shakespeare's English Kings: History, Chronicle, and Drama*, pp. 115–55. 2nd ed. Oxford: Oxford University Press, 2000.

Having devoted an entire chapter to *1H6*, Saccio turns to *Parts 2* and *3* in chapter 6. The author discusses *2H6* under the headings "The Disorders of the 1440s" and "The Fortunes of the Duke of York," reserving the final section, "Edward IV, 1461–1471," for *3H6*. Unlike the radical rearrangement of chronology found in *Part 1*, the second and third parts of the trilogy extensively exaggerate the historical record, especially with respect to the peasants' rebellion (risings of the commons were exceptional) and the Wars of the Roses—really nothing more than "a skirmish in 1455 (first St. Albans), six battles in 1459–1461, and three . . . in 1469–1471." To read *Parts 2* and *3* is to see the period as one of ceaseless turbulence, with widespread devastation in the land, a vision of mid-fifteenth-century England "born largely of [Tudor] propaganda," which Shakespeare "converts . . . into eloquence." Among Shakespeare's specific departures from his historical sources in *2H6*, which covers the years 1445 to 1455, are the following: the rivalry between Eleanor of Cobham and Queen Margaret (good from a dramatic perspective but historically inaccurate, since Eleanor's downfall occurred four years before Margaret arrived in England), the emphasis on Gloucester's opponents in contriving to bring Eleanor down, the image of "good Duke Humphrey" (the historical figure was just as headstrong as his fellow magnates "and more pugnacious than most"), the active role of Cardinal Beaufort in hatching malign schemes (by the early 1440s, the Cardinal was no longer actively involved in government matters), the planned murder of Gloucester (who probably died of natural causes), the love affair between Suffolk and Margaret (a Shakespearean invention "based upon a mere hint in the Tudor chronicles"), the treatment of Cade's following as a "rabblement" (the men were actually a "reasonably well-organized group of artisans and gentry who made the standard requests of most middle- and upper-class medieval rebels"), and the "sheer invention" of the future Richard III (only two years old in 1455) as a young man actively engaged in the first battle of St. Albans. Although Shakespeare tightens the narrative sequence of events, the only major unhistorical element in the first four acts involves "an overhasty anticipation of [York's] career in the next decade." Shakespeare's compression of events leading up to the first battle of St. Albans, with which *Part 2* concludes, results in the omission of several of York's military/political reversals, his first protectorate, and King Henry's insanity from August 1453 until December 1454.

Wilson, Richard. " 'A Mingled Yarn': Shakespeare and the Cloth Workers." *Literature and History* 12 (1986): 164–80. (Reprinted in Richard Wilson, *Will Power: Essays on Shakespearean Authority*, pp. 22–44 [Detroit: Wayne State University Press, 1993]; also reprinted in *Shakespeare's History Plays* [Longman Critical Readers], edited by R. J. C. Watt, pp. 40–60 [London: Longman-Pearson Education, 2002].)

Wilson disputes the modern assessment of Shakespeare's mob episodes as demonstrating universal imperatives of law and order. On the contrary, there is nothing in the Shakespeare canon that is "more entangled with the exigencies of [the playwright's] own time and place" than his crowd scenes, which belong "to the period of the emergence of the city mob as a force to be reckoned with in English politics." In Shakespeare's treatment of the Cade uprising, a "blueprint" for the playwright's subsequent crowd scenes, Wilson finds an instance of the "brazen manipulation of documentary records practised to buttress the regime." Although Shakespeare found the actual 1450 rebellion in Edward Hall's 1548 *Union* (a chronicle glorification of Tudor rule), he chose to darken the historical Cade even further. Hall's Cade—a man who prohibited his followers from engaging in murder, robbery, or rape, and whose advisers were schoolmasters—is "metamorphosed" in *2H6* into a "cruel, barbaric lout, whose slogan is 'kill and knock down.'" By casting Cade as the enemy of literacy in general and of the law in particular, Shakespeare used this early play to show his scorn for popular/oral culture and to identify himself with an urban elite, who saw authority as belonging solely to the literate. Instead of viewing Cade as a universal embodiment of anarchy, Wilson relates the defamation of the character to a specific confrontation between prison officials and feltmakers who had gathered in 1592 to stage a play outside Marshalsea Prison. At a time when the London clothing workers were fighting a "rear-guard action against long-term structural changes in their industry," the author finds it no accident that Shakespeare (who, documents show, had a financial stake in these capitalist developments) switched the occupation of Cade's rioters from medieval peasants to Renaissance artisans, with Cade a shearman and many of his lieutenants weavers. Shakespeare's treatment of Cade and his followers reveals the playwright "not as the universal genius, but as a locus of contingent intentions and desires." Neither the playwright nor the commercial theater for which he wrote was sympathetic to popular protest. In fact, the Cade scenes illustrate Shakespeare's "revulsion" at the voice of the people.

Shakespeare's Language

Abbott, E. A. *A Shakespearian Grammar.* New York: Haskell House, 1972.

This compact reference book, first published in 1870, helps with many difficulties in Shakespeare's language. It systematically accounts for a host of differences between Shakespeare's usage and sentence structure and our own.

Blake, Norman. *Shakespeare's Language: An Introduction.* New York: St. Martin's Press, 1983.

This general introduction to Elizabethan English discusses various aspects of the language of Shakespeare and his contemporaries, offering possible meanings for hundreds of ambiguous constructions.

Dobson, E. J. *English Pronunciation, 1500–1700.* 2 vols. Oxford: Clarendon Press, 1968.

This long and technical work includes chapters on spelling (and its reformation), phonetics, stressed vowels, and consonants in early modern English.

Hope, Jonathan. *Shakespeare's Grammar.* London: Arden Shakespeare, 2003.

Commissioned as a replacement for Abbott's *Shakespearian Grammar,* Hope's book is organized in terms of the two basic parts of speech, the noun and the verb. After extensive analysis of the noun phrase and the verb phrase come briefer discussions of subjects and agents, objects, complements, and adverbials.

Houston, John. *Shakespearean Sentences: A Study in Style and Syntax*. Baton Rouge: Louisiana State University Press, 1988.

Houston studies Shakespeare's stylistic choices, considering matters such as sentence length and the relative positions of subject, verb, and direct object. Examining plays throughout the canon in a roughly chronological, developmental order, he analyzes how sentence structure is used in setting tone, in characterization, and for other dramatic purposes.

Onions, C. T. *A Shakespeare Glossary*. Oxford: Clarendon Press, 1986.

This revised edition updates Onions's standard, selective glossary of words and phrases in Shakespeare's plays that are now obsolete, archaic, or obscure.

Robinson, Randal. *Unlocking Shakespeare's Language: Help for the Teacher and Student*. Urbana, Ill.: National Council of Teachers of English and the ERIC Clearinghouse on Reading and Communication Skills, 1989.

Specifically designed for the high school and undergraduate college teacher and student, Robinson's book addresses the problems that most often hinder present-day readers of Shakespeare. Through work with his own students, Robinson found that many readers today are particularly puzzled by such stylistic devices as subject-verb inversion, interrupted structures, and compression. He shows how our own colloquial language contains comparable structures, and thus helps students recognize such structures when they find them in Shakespeare's plays. This book supplies worksheets—with examples from major plays—to illuminate and remedy such problems as unusual sequences of words and the separation of related parts of sentences.

Williams, Gordon. *A Dictionary of Sexual Language and Imagery in Shakespearean and Stuart Literature.* 3 vols. London: Athlone Press, 1994.

Williams provides a comprehensive list of the words to which Shakespeare, his contemporaries, and later Stuart writers gave sexual meanings. He supports his identification of these meanings by extensive quotations.

Shakespeare's Life

Baldwin, T. W. *William Shakspere's Petty School.* Urbana: University of Illinois Press, 1943.

Baldwin here investigates the theory and practice of the petty school, the first level of education in Elizabethan England. He focuses on that educational system primarily as it is reflected in Shakespeare's art.

Baldwin, T. W. *William Shakspere's Small Latine and Lesse Greeke.* 2 vols. Urbana: University of Illinois Press, 1944.

Baldwin attacks the view that Shakespeare was an uneducated genius—a view that had been dominant among Shakespeareans since the eighteenth century. Instead, Baldwin shows, the educational system of Shakespeare's time would have given the playwright a strong background in the classics, and there is much in the plays that shows how Shakespeare benefited from such an education.

Beier, A. L., and Roger Finlay, eds. *London 1500–1700: The Making of the Metropolis.* New York: Longman, 1986.

Focusing on the economic and social history of early modern London, these collected essays probe aspects of metropolitan life, including "Population and Disease," "Commerce and Manufacture," and "Society and Change."

Bentley, G. E. *Shakespeare's Life: A Biographical Handbook*. New Haven: Yale University Press, 1961.
   This "just-the-facts" account presents the surviving documents of Shakespeare's life against an Elizabethan background.

Chambers, E. K. *William Shakespeare: A Study of Facts and Problems*. 2 vols. Oxford: Clarendon Press, 1930.
   Analyzing in great detail the scant historical data, Chambers's complex, scholarly study considers the nature of the texts in which Shakespeare's work is preserved.

Cressy, David. *Education in Tudor and Stuart England*. London: Edward Arnold, 1975.
   This volume collects sixteenth-, seventeenth-, and early-eighteenth-century documents detailing aspects of formal education in England, such as the curriculum, the control and organization of education, and the education of women.

Dutton, Richard. *William Shakespeare: A Literary Life*. New York: St. Martin's Press, 1989.
   Not a biography in the traditional sense, Dutton's very readable work nevertheless "follows the contours of Shakespeare's life" as he examines Shakespeare's career as playwright and poet, with consideration of his patrons, theatrical associations, and audience.

Honan, Park. *Shakespeare: A Life*. New York: Oxford University Press, 1998.
   Honan's accessible biography focuses on the various

contexts of Shakespeare's life—physical, social, political, and cultural—to place the dramatist within a lucidly described world. The biography includes detailed examinations of, for example, Stratford schooling, theatrical politics of 1590s London, and the careers of Shakespeare's associates. The author draws on a wealth of established knowledge and on interesting new research into local records and documents; he also engages in speculation about, for example, the possibilities that Shakespeare was a tutor in a Catholic household in the north of England in the 1580s and that he played particular roles in his own plays, areas that reflect new, but unproven and debatable, data—though Honan is usually careful to note where a particular narrative "has not been capable of proof or disproof."

Schoenbaum, S. *William Shakespeare: A Compact Documentary Life.* New York: Oxford University Press, 1977.
   This standard biography economically presents the essential documents from Shakespeare's time in an accessible narrative account of the playwright's life.

Shakespeare's Theater

Bentley, G. E. *The Profession of Player in Shakespeare's Time, 1590–1642.* Princeton: Princeton University Press, 1984.
   Bentley readably sets forth a wealth of evidence about performance in Shakespeare's time, with special attention to the relations between player and company, and the business of casting, managing, and touring.

Berry, Herbert. *Shakespeare's Playhouses.* New York: AMS Press, 1987.

Berry's six essays collected here discuss (with illustrations) varying aspects of the four playhouses in which Shakespeare had a financial stake: the Theatre in Shoreditch, the Blackfriars, and the first and second Globe.

Cook, Ann Jennalie. *The Privileged Playgoers of Shakespeare's London.* Princeton: Princeton University Press, 1981.
Cook's work argues, on the basis of sociological, economic, and documentary evidence, that Shakespeare's audience—and the audience for English Renaissance drama generally—consisted mainly of the "privileged."

Greg, W. W. *Dramatic Documents from the Elizabethan Playhouses.* 2 vols. Oxford: Clarendon Press, 1931.
Greg itemizes and briefly describes many of the play manuscripts that survive from the period 1590 to around 1660, including, among other things, players' parts. His second volume offers facsimiles of selected manuscripts.

Gurr, Andrew. *Playgoing in Shakespeare's London.* 2nd ed. Cambridge: Cambridge University Press, 1996.
Gurr charts how the theatrical enterprise developed from its modest beginnings in the late 1560s to become a thriving institution in the 1600s. He argues that there were important changes over the period 1567–1644 in the playhouses, the audience, and the plays.

Harbage, Alfred. *Shakespeare's Audience.* New York: Columbia University Press, 1941.
Harbage investigates the fragmentary surviving evidence to interpret the size, composition, and behavior of Shakespeare's audience.

Hattaway, Michael. *Elizabethan Popular Theatre: Plays in Performance*. London: Routledge and Kegan Paul, 1982.

Beginning with a study of the popular drama of the late Elizabethan age—a description of the stages, performance conditions, and acting of the period—this volume concludes with an analysis of five well-known plays of the 1590s, one of them (*Titus Andronicus*) by Shakespeare.

Shapiro, Michael. *Children of the Revels: The Boy Companies of Shakespeare's Time and Their Plays*. New York: Columbia University Press, 1977.

Shapiro chronicles the history of the amateur and quasi-professional child companies that flourished in London at the end of Elizabeth's reign and the beginning of James's.

The Publication of Shakespeare's Plays

Blayney, Peter W. M. *The First Folio of Shakespeare*. Hanover, Md.: Folger, 1991.

Blayney's accessible account of the printing and later life of the First Folio—an amply illustrated catalog to a 1991 Folger Shakespeare Library exhibition—analyzes the mechanical production of the First Folio, describing how the Folio was made, by whom and for whom, how much it cost, and its ups and downs (or, rather, downs and ups) since its printing in 1623.

Hinman, Charlton. *The Norton Facsimile: The First Folio of Shakespeare*. 2nd ed. New York: W. W. Norton, 1996.

This facsimile presents a photographic reproduction of an "ideal" copy of the First Folio of Shakespeare;

Hinman attempts to represent each page in its most fully corrected state. The second edition includes an important new introduction by Peter W. M. Blayney.

Hinman, Charlton. *The Printing and Proof-Reading of the First Folio of Shakespeare*. 2 vols. Oxford: Clarendon Press, 1963.

In the most arduous study of a single book ever undertaken, Hinman attempts to reconstruct how the Shakespeare First Folio of 1623 was set into type and run off the press, sheet by sheet. He also provides almost all the known variations in readings from copy to copy.

Key to
Famous Lines and Phrases

Could I come near your beauty with my nails,
I'd set my ten commandments in your face.
                                [*Duchess*—1.3.145–46]

When such strings jar, what hope of harmony?
                                [*King Henry*—2.1.64]

Thus sometimes hath the brightest day a cloud,
And after summer evermore succeeds
Barren winter, with his wrathful nipping cold;
So cares and joys abound, as seasons fleet.
                                [*Gloucester*—2.4.1–4]

Smooth runs the water where the brook is deep[.]
                                [*Suffolk*—3.1.53]

Thrice is he armed that hath his quarrel just,
And he but naked, though locked up in steel,
Whose conscience with injustice is corrupted.
                                [*King Henry*—3.2.241—43]

I thank them for their tender loving care[.]
                                [*King Henry*—3.2.290]

The gaudy, blabbing, and remorseful day
Is crept into the bosom of the sea[.]
                                [*Lieutenant*—4.1.1–2]

        [I]t was never merry world in England since
gentlemen came up.   [*Holland*—4.2.8–9]

317

I will make it felony to drink small beer.
[*Cade*—4.2.66–67]

The first thing we do, let's kill all the lawyers.
[*Dick*—4.2.75]

It will be proved
to thy face that thou hast men about thee that usually
talk of a noun and a verb and such abominable words
as no Christian ear can endure to hear.
[*Cade*—4.7.37–40]

[I]gnorance is the curse of God,
Knowledge the wing wherewith we fly to heaven[.]
[*Saye*—4.7.73–74]

I'll make thee eat iron like an ostrich[.]
[*Cade*—4.10.29]

[A]s dead as a doornail[.]   [*Cade*—4.10.41–42]

THE FOLGER
SHAKESPEARE LIBRARY

The world's leading center for Shakespeare studies presents
acclaimed editions of Shakespeare's plays.

For more information on Folger Shakespeare Library Editions, including
Shakespeare Set Free teaching guides, visit www.simonsays.com.

WASHINGTON
SQUARE PRESS
A Division of Simon & Schuster
A CBS COMPANY